HIGH DEFINITION LIVING

Bringing Clarity to Your Life's Mission

ED YOUNG

HOWARD
PUBLISHING CO.

Our purpose at Howard Publishing is to:

• *Increase faith* in the hearts of growing Christians
• *Inspire holiness* in the lives of believers
• *Instill hope* in the hearts of struggling people everywhere
Because He's coming again!

High Definition Living © 2003 by Ed Young
All rights reserved. Printed in the United States of America

Published by Howard Publishing Co., Inc.
3117 North 7th Street, West Monroe, Louisiana 71291-2227

03 04 05 06 07 08 09 10 11 12   10 9 8 7 6 5 4 3 2

Edited by Sue Ann Jones
Interior design by John Luke

Library of Congress Cataloging-in-Publication Data

Young, Ed, 1961-
    High definition living : bringing clarity to your life / Ed Young.
        p. cm.
    ISBN 978-1-4165-7044-8
    1. Christian life. I. Title: At head of title: HDL. II. Title.

BV4501.3.Y68 2003
248.4–dc21

                                                                        2003040622

Scripture quotations not otherwise marked are taken from the HOLY BIBLE, NEW
INTERNATIONAL VERSION. Copyright © 1973, 1978, 1984 by the International
Bible Society. Used by permission of Zondervan Bible Publishers. Scripture quotations
taken from The Holy Bible, New King James Version, Copyright © 1994 by Thomas
Nelson, Inc. Scripture taken from the NEW AMERICAN STANDARD BIBLE®,
Copyright © 1960, 1962, 1963, 1968, 1971, 1972, 1973, 1975, 1977, 1995 by The
Lockman Foundation. Used by permission. Scriptures marked KJV are taken from *The
Holy Bible, New Century Version,* copyright © 1987, 1988, 1991 by Word Publishing,
Dallas, Texas 75234. Scripture quotations taken from The New Testament in Modern
English from J.B. Phillips © Copyright 1958, 1972, 1995. All rights reserved.

contents

contents

acknowledgments

I must thank Cliff McNeely for helping me transform my message material into the written pages you see before you. He has been an invaluable partner, now on five of my books. On this particular work, the due date for the manuscript was just a couple of weeks before the due date of his first child. And yet, somehow he managed to keep his composure and meet the first deadline before the second one arrived. Once again, Cliff, well done!

I also want to thank the dedicated staff at Howard Publishing, John Howard and Denny and Philis Boultinghouse in particular, for allowing me to partner with them in building up the body of Christ through projects like this. Thanks especially to the editor, Sue Ann Jones, for her efficient and excellent work on a very tight deadline.

Last but by no means least, I want to acknowledge the incredible people at Fellowship Church. I refer many times

acknowledgments

throughout this book to the members and staff at Fellowship. And I do that because this place has been a major catalyst over the past twelve years toward my understanding of the principles of high-definition living found in this book. I have learned so much about godly leadership here because I see it lived out by both the laity and staff alike, week after week. The many stories I tell about this church are a reflection of my great respect and love for its people. I could not have written this book without the inspiration of the dedicated Christ followers who honor me greatly by calling me their pastor.

part one

Mission Possible

Leadership doesn't depend on *where* you are—at home, office, school, or church—but on *who* you are. The Bible provides many great role models for learning how to be leaders, and one of the best examples is Nehemiah. In his Old Testament book of memoirs, we learn the secrets for how to recognize our leadership potential, impart our vision to others, learn the importance of delegation, deal with opposition, lead with integrity, and understand the power of persistence.

High-definition living sounds like a modern lifestyle, but the truth is, its key components can be found in the ancient story of Nehemiah and the way he fulfilled his mission from God.

high-definition principles

Discovering the Words You've Been Waiting For

- The high-definition life has a clear sense of purpose and reflects Christ's calling.

- The high-definition life has a higher price tag than the conventional life.

chapter 1

god's mission for you

Discovering the Words You've Been Waiting For

You're sitting in church listening to a sermon. Or perhaps you're reading a best-selling book on Christian living. Maybe you're listening to a recorded message by a well-known inspirational speaker and author. And then suddenly there it is—a statement you've been waiting for—a statement that could change the trajectory of your life. This is the statement: *God has a mission for you.*

God has a plan, a purpose, a special agenda for you. This is an exciting concept—one that is packed with power and possibility. You are on the edge of your seat in the church auditorium. Or you are fighting the temptation to skip to the last page of the book or to fast-forward the tape as you wait with breathless anticipation to find out what that mission is. At long last you will find out what you have been placed on this earth to do. Minute after minute passes. Page after page turns. Any moment now you will have the definitive answer to this crucial question of your existence.

But the answer never comes.

You come to the end of the sermon or the last paragraph of the book, and you begin to feel defeated and a little disillusioned. One question begins to loom large in your mind: *If God has a mission for my life, why won't anyone tell me what it is?*

That is a legitimate question, one that deserves a legitimate answer. And I am going to answer that question right now. That's right. You don't have to wait until the end of the book for the punch line. I'm going to give it to you right now. Are you ready? Are you sure? This is it. Don't wimp out on me now. The very next sentence will give you God's agenda for your life.

God's mission, if you choose to accept it, is…leadership.

I can read your thoughts right now. You're thinking, *That's it? That's your big revelation, Ed, of what God wants for my life? Are you kidding me? There are about a thousand definitions of leadership out there. Can you get just a little more specific?* Well, I'm glad you asked, because we are going to take a hard, up-close look at what it means to be a godly leader as we dial in to the life of one of the greatest leaders of all time. This whole idea of godly leadership will come into sharper focus as we learn from a master leader in God's economy. And when we understand and submit to God's overall mission of leadership for each of us, we will be able to identify and ready to pursue those unique opportunities that God places in each of our paths—opportunities that enrich our lives, sharpen our focus, and bring greater clarity to our Christian walk.

Leadership: Making a Difference for God

People love to read about leadership. From the *One Minute Manager* by Kenneth Blanchard to *Good to Great* by Jim Collins, from *The Leadership Secrets of Colin Powell* by Oren Harari to *Leadership* by Rudolph Guiliani, from *The Harvard Business Review* to *Fortune* magazine, new books and articles rehashing well-worn ideas on this perennial subject are continually hitting newsstands, bookstores, and cyber-shopping sites. Many of these secular books are great reads with excellent leadership principles for businesses and other organizations. I've read many of them myself.

In addition to these titles, we have within the Christian marketplace our own list of popular leadership books: *The 21 Irrefutable Laws of Leadership* by John C. Maxwell, *Courageous Leadership* by Bill Hybels, *Spiritual Leadership* by Richard and Henry T. Blackaby, and *Jesus on Leadership* by C. Gene Wilkes, to name a few. These are great books that present various principles and ideas from Scripture on what Christian leadership should look like. And they all have their place within the broad and multidimensional field of leadership.

Because there is such a plethora of leadership advice out

part 1

part 1

there, I think it's important, right from the start, to distinguish the kind of leadership I'll be addressing in this book. My focus is not limited to church leaders, business executives, political leaders, and others in various positions of professional leadership and management. While the ideas presented here certainly apply to these formal positions of leadership, my desire is to bring the role of Christian leadership down to a more personal and fundamental level. The leadership I'll be helping you develop applies to the role you play in your daily life—in your home, in your family, and in your marriage, as well as in your job outside the home, if you have one. The leadership I'm talking about is leadership that makes a difference for God, because that is what real, godly leadership is all about.

The High-Definition Difference

Perhaps the best way to explain this kind of leadership is to take a side trip into an electronics store. In the world of home appliances, something called high-definition television, or HDTV, is the newest rage. Recently I wanted to use an analogy to HDTV in a message I was preparing, so I took a camera crew to a local electronics store to find out the difference between high-definition television and conventional television. We found a very knowledgeable salesperson who was kind enough to explain the advantages and benefits of HDTV and show us what sets it apart from the rest of the pack.

The technical description he gave us, as best as I can convey, is that HDTV screens have many more lines of resolution than conventional television screens. These hundreds of lines of resolution, made possible by the digital technology, enhance the quality of the picture far beyond what was previously possible. The cutting-edge digital technology of both the HDTV and the high-definition broadcast signal gives a whole new dimension to the television-watching experience.

The salesman told us that, basically, HDTV has "superclarity." Whether you are looking at it from a distance or up close, the picture is perfectly clear. There are no fuzzy lines, no distortions, and no shadows that can appear in the pictures of regular sets. High-definition television serves up a richer, bolder, more vibrant picture than any kind of TV image you've ever seen before.

I must confess that I was amazed. The picture quality of HDTV compared with a conventional television was like the difference between seeing a photograph of someone and then seeing the person—in person! It was incredible. I almost bought one on the spot. Unfortunately, the price tag was a little too steep for me. One HDTV had a price tag of $9,999. Ouch!

While television isn't always the best thing for us to spend our time on, the example of this new technology makes an apt metaphor when I'm explaining the leadership principles we'll study together in this book. In these pages I'm going to show

part 1

you how following these leadership principles can transform your life from "conventional" to "high-definition." You're going to find that high-definition living is a life of superclarity and vibrant depth.

Surely all of us would like to experience that kind of life. That's why this is not just a book for church leaders, executives, or business managers. This book is for *everyone* who wants to make a difference for God. High-definition living helps us make that difference by giving us a richer awareness of God's presence in our lives. HD living brings clarity to the lessons the Bible teaches. And it helps us recognize the opportunities for leadership God puts in front of us—everywhere, every day.

As Christians in the world today, whether we are talking about marriage or dating or parenting—or whether we work in the mailroom or preside over a Fortune 500 company—in anything that occupies our time and energy, we should lead lives of high-definition clarity. This means we have a clear sense of purpose and a life that reflects Christ's calling on our lives, both at a distance and up close. Living a high-definition life as a follower of Christ means being a leader.

HDP *The high-definition life has a clear sense of purpose and reflects Christ's calling.*

When others look at you and me they should see a radical difference and want to follow us to the Savior. They should

8

look at us and say, "Wow! Seeing how you live your life and how you inspire others to better living is like looking at life in a whole new way. I thought I knew what life was supposed to look like, but I realize now that I've been looking at a conventional life all these years, not an HD life."

The Price of the HD Life

But just like buying one of the new televisions, obtaining an HD life is costly. It carries a much higher price tag than the conventional life. Once you see the difference the clear calling of Christian leadership can make in your life, you won't want to go back to the old life with its fuzzy lines and distortions and shadows. But I want to warn you right up front: It's not going to be easy. There's a price to be paid if we want to live the abundant life Christ came to give. But the rewards are well worth the price.

HDP *The high-definition life has a higher price tag than the conventional life.*

When I saw those high-definition TVs at that electronics store, I had a choice whether or not to fork out the cash to buy one and take it home. But the high-definition calling on the life of every believer is *not* a choice. Christ calls us out of the world and says, "Take up your cross and follow me." He calls out the impassioned plea, "Be fishers of men. Lead for me in a dark and desperate world."

part 1

9

part 1

Are you ready to take the plunge into the high-definition life to which Christ is calling you? Are you ready to accept the mission God has planned for your life? Are you ready to take on the mantle of Christian leadership in your business, your church, your home, your school, your club, and in every other circle of influence God has given you? If so, this book is for you. In the pages ahead, I'll be your salesman to explain all the benefits and advantages of this rich and vibrant life of godly leadership, and I'll offer principles and guidelines that will help you upgrade your life from conventional to HD. Trust me. You'll be amazed at the difference.

high-definition principles

Recognizing Your Leadership Potential

- High-definition leaders make a salt-and-light impact wherever they are.
- Leadership is not about how many people follow you—it's about being on God's side.
- Our ultimate mission is to inspire others and glorify God.
- In God's economy Mission Impossible becomes Mission Possible.
- Leaders ask the right questions of the right people.
- Wise leaders respond to problems by "sitting down."
- Fasting brings focus and clarity to your prayers.
- People of impact humbly acknowledge the greatness of God.
- Leaders accept the blame; losers pass the buck.
- Godly leaders gain confidence to accomplish impossible tasks by praying the promises of Scripture.
- Leaders are committed, available, and willing to be part of God's answers.

chapter 2

high-definition essentials

Recognizing Your Leadership Potential

Christ made a high-definition statement in Matthew 5:13–16 that clarifies our objective as believers and leaders. He said:

> You are the salt of the earth; but if the salt loses its flavor, how shall it be seasoned? It is then good for nothing but to be thrown out and trampled underfoot by men. You are the light of the world. A city that is set on a hill cannot be hidden. Nor do they light a lamp and put it under a basket, but on a lampstand, and it gives light to all who are in the house. Let your light so shine before men, that they may see your good works and glorify your Father in heaven. (NKJV)

Salt and light are not benign elements; they are high-definition essentials. They change, season, redefine, expose, and bring a new perspective to whatever they come in contact with. That is our mission as believers, to make a salt-and-light impact *part 1*

wherever we are. And we do this not so people will taste *us* and see that we are good, but so that they will taste *God* and see that he is good (see Ps. 34:8). We are to season life and expose the darkness for the glory of God.

HDP *High-definition leaders make a salt-and-light impact wherever they are.*

The very nature of our spiritual calling is leadership. We *follow* God, but we are to be *leaders* of men and women, calling them out of the darkness and into light, out of the mundane and into the meaningful. Biblical leadership has very little to do with what we *do*—with our vocation or station in this life— but everything to do with *who we are,* our position in Christ.

True biblical leadership also has nothing to do with how many people are following you. In fact, you might be leading in a particular area and have absolutely no one following you! OK, I hear you asking, "How can I be a leader if no one is following me?" Sometimes standing up for God means standing alone. Others may be impressed by the stand you take, but they may not follow you right away. Over time, though, the truth always wins out, and others will eventually see it in you and be compelled to follow.

Biblical leadership is not about leading throngs of people; it is about making an impact for God no matter what the personal cost. If thousands follow or a few follow or no one follows, as long as you are on the side of truth and the side of God, you are a leader. Remember, an individual plus God is always a majority.

HDP *Leadership is not about how many people follow you—it's about being on God's side.*

Consider the ministry of Jesus Christ while he was on the earth. Jesus had relatively few committed disciples, yet the impact of his message has changed the course of world history. In Acts 5:38–39, as a group of Jewish leaders were deliberating about whether to put Peter and the other apostles to death for their radical faith, a Pharisee named Gamaliel spoke up for this meager band of Christ-followers: "Leave these men alone! Let them go! For if their purpose or activity is of human origin, it will fail. But if it is from God, you will not be able to stop these men; you will only find yourselves fighting against God."

Gamaliel was a wise man who had great foresight, because regardless of its initial acceptance, the impact of the apostles' message has stood the test of time and truth.

Christ himself said that few would enter the narrow gate and find life everlasting but many would go through the broad gate that leads to destruction (see Matt. 7:13–14). He knew full well that his difficult message would initially only draw a handful of disciples who were willing to take up their crosses and follow him. So as you lead others to the abundant life that

15

Christ offers, don't be discouraged if few are being impacted by the message you share with your life and with your words. Being a leader for Christ means being willing to take a position that's tethered to truth and then tenaciously sticking to it, regardless of how unpopular it is. If you do not take the lead by walking down the right path, even when it is unpopular and no one is following, you will end up following someone else and potentially leading others down the wrong path.

The Tenacious Difference Maker

The biblical role model for leadership we are going to meet in the pages ahead was a tenacious difference maker whose story is memorialized in the greatest book ever penned on leadership. This man was very prominent in politics and business in the Middle East. He rose from obscurity to national recognition almost overnight. He knew a lot about leadership, and he put that knowledge into practice. His name was Nehemiah, and his story is told in the Old Testament book bearing his name.

- If you want to learn how to impart your vision to others, study Nehemiah.

- If you want to learn the importance of teamwork, study Nehemiah.

- If you want to learn how to deal with opposition, study Nehemiah.

- If you want to learn how to inspire with integrity, study Nehemiah.
- If you want to understand the power of persistence, study Nehemiah.

Throughout the first part of this book, we are going to turn to Nehemiah as a mentor who can help all of us, regardless of our positions in life, improve our leadership skills. And as we go along, I'll continue to highlight high-definition principles.

Now, you might still be thinking to yourself, *Self, I don't need to read this book, because I am not a leader. I am not a Nehemiah. I am not a Moses; I am not a David; I am not a Paul. I am not a leader.* That line of thinking is false, because if you are alive, you are a leader! Remember, leadership means impact, and each of us impacts people and events whether we are in the home, the office, the neighborhood, or at school. We all need to learn from Nehemiah so that we can clarify God's ultimate mission for our lives: to inspire others to live lives that please and glorify our Lord.

 Our ultimate mission is to inspire others and glorify God.

Setting the Stage: The Walls Fall

Before we dive into the Book of Nehemiah, it is important for us to get some history under our belts.

The year is 586 B.C. Enter King Nebuchadnezzar, the leader

of the Babylonian empire. King Nebuchadnezzar attacked Jerusalem and destroyed the temple, the house of Jewish worship. In the process of sacking the city, this very sadistic and legalistic tyrant did something really terrible: He destroyed the city's walls. Now, if you destroyed a city's walls back then, that was big, that was bad, and that was ugly.

We don't have city walls these days, so it's hard for us to relate to what a devastating and crippling event this was for the people of Jerusalem. We build fences around our houses, we live in gated communities, and we buy sophisticated alarm systems. But we do not build city walls. In biblical times, however, city walls provided protection for Jerusalem. They showed the other people living in the land that the Jewish God is a God of protection. The walls allowed them to worship in peace. And if enemies tried to attack Jerusalem, the walls could slow them down for three to six months.

But Nebuchadnezzar tore down the walls, and Jerusalem was left vulnerable and humiliated.

The walls are important to our study; they are one of the major themes in the Book of Nehemiah. King Nebuchadnezzar didn't stop with the destruction of the walls, though. After taking control of the city, he also took many of the Jews and deported them eight hundred miles through the desert back to Babylon. This is known in biblical history as the Babylonian captivity. The Jews lived in Babylon as slaves for several decades until the Medes and the Persians, under King Cyrus, attacked Babylon and conquered it, killing its current king, Belshazzer. King Cyrus of Persia took the helm in Babylon in 539 B.C.

King Cyrus had a sympathetic heart toward the Jews. He said, "Jews, I'll tell you what I'm going to do. I'll let you go back eight hundred miles to Jerusalem, and, if you want to, you can construct your house of worship. Also, if you want to, you can rebuild the wall."

So a lot of Jews went back, led by a man named Zerubbable and later by a man named Ezra, a contemporary of Nehemiah. The temple was rebuilt, but with only a shadow of its former glory. No one was able to rebuild the wall, because it was such a mammoth task. So while the Jews restored worship in Jerusalem, at the same time they were still open and vulnerable to opposing forces that might come in and tear them apart again.

In 464 B.C. a new king moved into the palatial oval office of Persia, which today is known as Iraq. His name was King Artaxerxes. He was now the man of the hour in Persia, and he said, "There will *never* be a wall around Jerusalem again." It seemed as though the Jews had missed their window of opportunity to rebuild the city's wall.

This is where Nehemiah comes into the picture.

The Book of Nehemiah is actually Nehemiah's memoirs. And one of the first entries in this book of memoirs tells us about Nehemiah's occupation. You might think he was on the

CEO level, since he is serving as a model of biblical leadership for us. But the job description Nehemiah records in chapter 1, verse 11, at first seems to be at the opposite end of the corporate spectrum: "I was a cupbearer to the king."

A what-bearer?

A cupbearer.

You mean, Nehemiah, Mr. Leader, was a table waiter, a camel-burger-flipping person?

No, not at all. In fact, the cupbearer was the second most important position in the empire. Nehemiah was a Hebrew, a non-Persian, yet he was second in command to King Artaxerxes.

He was the wine and food taster, assassinations being quite common back then. If a cupbearer tasted some wine and dropped over dead, the king would say, "Well, I guess that was a bad year." And, because they didn't have CNN back then, it was also Nehemiah's job to give late-breaking news to the king. He was the king's most faithful and trusted adviser, and aside from the ever-present threat of food poisoning, Nehemiah had it made. He had all the perks, all the benefits of being the cupbearer: the corner office, the cellular chariot phone, use of the company's team of camels. Major money. I can picture Nehemiah kicking back in his corner office overlooking the beautiful sights of Susa, the Washington, D.C., of ancient Persia, the place of power plays, power suits, and power lunches.

It was in the midst of this luxurious lifestyle that Nehemiah began to hear the *Mission Impossible* theme song playing in the background. Maybe, just maybe, as he heard the music, and I am paraphrasing a little bit, God stepped in and said, "Nehemiah, this is your mission should you choose to accept it: Travel eight hundred miles to Jerusalem and rebuild the wall around my city. And by the way, Nehemiah, you are going to face some major opposition, some major criticism. Also, Nehemiah, you will have to walk into King Artaxerxes's office, the man who can chop your head off if he is in a bad mood, and ask for some major time off while retaining all your salary and benefits. You will have to ask for the resources to go back to Jerusalem, along with the security forces and the travel documents."

It was then that God probably changed the theme of the assignment. I suspect he said something like this: "Nehemiah, I know you are a cupbearer, but I am going to change you from a cupbearer into a contractor. I will give you the ability to do it. This idea has been Mission Impossible for ninety years, but in my economy, it's now Mission Possible. And Nehemiah, you're the agent in charge."

HDP *In God's economy Mission Impossible becomes Mission Possible.*

Then maybe God added, "Nehemiah, if you choose not to accept this mission, one day Jerusalem could self-destruct in five seconds."

The Requirements to Lead Mission Possible

Why did God choose Nehemiah for Mission Possible? He chose him because Nehemiah met four basic requirements of godly leadership. And these are precisely the requirements we need to meet today if we are going to improve our leadership skills and accomplish the mission of making a real impact for the glory of God.

Whether you are a leader in the home or a leader in middle management, whether you are an hourly employee or the CEO of a major company, whether you are a lay or staff leader in the church, if you are going to be a true difference maker, you had better meet these four basic requirements of leadership: *Ask the right questions, respond the right way, pray the right prayers, and do the right thing.*

1. Ask the Right Questions

Let's look at the first requirement this great leader Nehemiah met. It's spelled out in Nehemiah 1:1–2, and it's the first basic requirement of leadership: "In the month of Kislev… while I was in the citadel of Susa, Hanani, one of my brothers, came from Judah with some other men, and I questioned them about the Jewish remnant that survived the exile, and also about Jerusalem."

Did you get that? Leaders ask the right questions. And notice also that Nehemiah asked the right person, his brother, who would shoot straight with him. He asked the right questions to the right person, the one who had the right information. Because he did that, he could do the right thing God wanted him to do.

Leaders ask the hard questions, the penetrating questions, the serious questions. And they ask the right people. Nehemiah asked his brother these questions. He didn't just ask someone who was a yes person. He didn't ask, "Hey, how's it going in Jerusalem?" and hear, "Oh, great, Nehemiah, everything is perfect. Morale is great." Instead, he asked someone who would tell him the truth.

I have two younger brothers. The youngest, Cliff, is the lead singer in the popular contemporary Christian musical group Caedmon's Call. My middle brother, Ben, has a syndicated talk show for singles about issues such as dating, living alone, and building relationships. He lives in Houston and leads one of the largest singles ministries in the country.

Because we are all in Christian ministry, my brothers and I often talk about different messages and ideas. If I ask Ben and Cliff what they think about using the Mission Possible theme regarding Artaxerxes and Nehemiah, they might tell me they think it sounds great. But I've also asked their opinions about other ideas and had them reply that they think I'm making crazy suggestions that couldn't possibly work. I listen to their opinions and consider what they say. I know they are shooting straight with me.

Conversely, Ben might ask me what I thought about a specific guest he had on his Sunday night talk show. And I might answer that the person was clueless and boring. Or Cliff might ask me about a certain song he has written, and I'll tell him, honestly, whether or not I like it. Brothers and sisters tell each other the truth, don't they?

So Nehemiah asked his brother Hanani some pointed questions about Jerusalem, and Hanani replied in no uncertain terms that the people were in trouble.

Whom do you need to ask some hard questions right now? Is it the person you have been in a long relationship with, perhaps a spouse, a child, a coworker, a trusted friend? Maybe you would ask that person questions like, how is your life going spiritually? What is the next character step you're going to work on? What is the main thing you struggle with? You may also need to ask someone you're close to some hard questions about your own life. For example, you might ask, "In what ways do you think I could improve as a spouse, a parent, a leader, or a friend?" or "What one area of spiritual weakness do you think I could improve upon?"

Ask someone with whom you have a natural affinity with the hard questions, and you will take the first step toward emerging and developing as a leader. Leaders ask the right questions of the right people.

 Leaders ask the right questions of the right people.

2. Respond the Right Way

Leaders ask the right questions, then they respond the right way. Before we look at how Nehemiah responded, let's look first at what he was told about the conditions in Jerusalem. We go back to Nehemiah 1:3: "They said to me, 'Those who survived the exile and are back in the province are in great trouble and disgrace. The wall of Jerusalem is broken down, and its gates have been burned with fire.'"

Let me just push the pause button here. As Nehemiah was hearing this negative report, he could have reacted very differently than he did. Since he had a cushy job and had it made with retirement plans and benefits, he didn't have to concern himself with the Jews in Jerusalem. He wasn't even born in Jerusalem. He was born in Persia and was more Persian than Jewish, with the exception that he believed in God. He didn't need to get involved with those other Jews.

He could have said, as many of us have said when we have been presented with a problem, "Who messed up? You mean those Jews have been back in Jerusalem *ninety years*, and the wall still hasn't been rebuilt? What's the deal? How inept! How

part 1

stupid! How ludicrous! How crazy! Send me their names. I'll get them fired."

But Nehemiah didn't do that. He didn't ignore the problem, and he didn't play the blame game. Let's take a look at what he *did* do. Actually, it's rather surprising. It doesn't sound like something a bold leader would do. In fact, you might say his response was just downright odd. Nehemiah wrote, "When I heard these things, I sat down" (1:4).

That's right. God's man, one of the greatest leaders to ever walk the face of the earth, *sat down*. This simple two-word phrase represents one of the first things we are to do as leaders when we are presented with a problem or a predicament: Sit down.

HDP *Wise leaders respond to problems by "sitting down."*

Nehemiah didn't just sit down, though. The text says that he "sat down and wept." He was identifying with his brothers and sisters in Jerusalem. Great leaders like Nehemiah are sensitive. They sit where others sit, they walk where others walk, and they feel what others feel. Are you identifying with people in your life? your company? your Bible study? Are you identifying with other people you rub shoulders with weekly? When you are willing to listen for and honestly hear the right answers, you also must be ready to identify and empathize with those who are in your circle of influence.

3. Pray the Right Prayers

After asking the right questions and responding the right way, the next basic requirement of leadership is praying the right prayers. Nehemiah's life is a handbook on prayer. He prayed short prayers, long prayers, and medium-length prayers. Leadership and prayer go hand in hand, and Nehemiah was a man of prayer.

You see, leaders do more than just pray, but they never do *anything* without praying first. Nehemiah sat down and wept, and then he prayed. His memoirs tell us, "For some days I mourned and fasted and prayed" (1:4).

Before we get into the content of Nehemiah's prayers, I want you to notice the process he went through. First, he mourned. Don't misunderstand this as just having a good cry or wearing a black armband as a superficial show of grieving. By mourning Nehemiah was again identifying with the Israelites. He was deeply grieved about what was happening to his brothers and sisters in Jerusalem, and he began to enter into their world. In Galatians 6:2 Paul gave us a similar admonition as brothers and sisters in Christ by telling us, "Bear one another's burdens, and thus fulfill the law of Christ" (NASB). The idea here is to carry the burden of another—to literally take it off that person's shoulders and carry it yourself.

part 1

1

part

How does bearing one another's burdens fulfill the law of Christ? We know, based on Jesus' teachings, that the Law and the Prophets can be summed up in two fundamental commands: Love God first, and love your neighbor as yourself. To mourn, to bear someone else's burden, to help carry it for him or her, is an unselfish act of love for that person. To mourn with others, to deeply feel what they feel by entering into their world, is to demonstrate your love for them. And as we will soon discover, Nehemiah felt the burdens of the Jews in Jerusalem so greatly that his mourning turned to action. He did not just emotionally grieve; he resolved to help carry their burdens and bring an end to their suffering.

Next, by fasting, Nehemiah did more than just miss a lot of meals. This spiritual discipline helped him improve his relationship with God. It also helped him pray with more focus and clarity so he could better hear what God would have him do.

DP *Fasting brings focus and clarity to your prayers.*

Again, this was not a performance that Nehemiah put on for the benefit of others; he didn't do it so they would pity him as he mourned. Fasting, as Richard Foster reminds us in his book *The Celebration of Discipline,* is an act of worship before God, an act that should center on him alone.

For Nehemiah, fasting was a precursor to honestly and

humbly communicating with the God of the universe. It helped remove any distractions that would keep him from hearing a word from the Lord. Foster describes well the spiritual benefit of this discipline:

> More than any other discipline, fasting reveals the things that control us. This is a wonderful benefit to the true disciple who longs to be transformed into the image of Jesus Christ. We cover up what is inside us with food and other good things, but in fasting these things surface. If pride controls us, it will be revealed almost immediately.

It was with this attitude that Nehemiah fasted. I believe he felt in his spirit that God had an important word for him, and he knew he needed to get right before God in order to hear that word, to receive his marching orders. Nehemiah felt compelled to act because in love he had entered into the suffering of his people. But before he acted to help them, he prepared by fasting, by humbling himself, and by getting his heart and mind ready for whatever God had in store for him. And then he prayed.

The Bible says—and don't miss this—Nehemiah prayed for days. When I have a problem in my life, I will often say, "God, I am really going to pray about this." This is often the scenario that plays out:

- Sunday: "Dear God, please deal with this problem."

- Monday: "Dear God, please help me with this problem."

- Tuesday: "Dear God, help me with this problem."

And by the time Wednesday and Thursday come, I'm thinking, *OK, he hasn't answered. I guess I'll stop praying.*

When Nehemiah said he prayed "for some days," those days actually added up to four months! All this time, while he was praying, while he was getting in touch with God, while he was mourning, fasting, and praying, he was also prioritizing and carefully considering the problem that lay before him.

In order to pray the right prayers as difference makers, we need to not only understand Nehemiah's persistence in prayer but also examine the content of his prayers. God answered Nehemiah's prayers, and if we can learn how to pray the prayers Nehemiah prayed, God will answer our prayers too. With that goal in mind, I want to point out four important principles that flow from the kinds of prayers Nehemiah prayed. These four components are what I call the four Cs of a true difference-maker's prayer: acknowledging the *character* of God, *confessing* sins, showing *confidence* in God's promises, and staying *committed* to being part of the answer.

1. *Acknowledge the Character of God.* First, notice how Nehemiah concentrated on the *character* of God. This is how all great prayers begin. You don't have to use big words to do this. I have been in a lot of religious circles during my forty years,

and after hearing some people pray, I have been so impressed with their amazing vocabulary that I wanted to give them a round of applause. But while that kind of eloquence, diction, and perspicuity (See, that impressed you, didn't it? *Perspicuity* means to be easily understood or lucid.) may impress others, it doesn't impress God a bit. God wants authenticity. God wants vulnerability. God wants people to talk to him the same way they talk to others. Don't freak out about praying to the Creator of the universe; just talk to God the Father. That is what Nehemiah did.

Nehemiah prayed, "O LORD, God of heaven, the great and awesome God..." (1:5). With his first breaths of prayer, he acknowledged God's super character qualities and praised him for who he is: God, you are unbelievable. You are awesome.

HDP *People of impact humbly acknowledge the greatness of God.*

2. *Confess Your Sins.* The second C in the prayer of a difference maker is *confession*. All great prayer includes confession of sin, admitting the truth about your condition. Look in the middle of Nehemiah 1:6: "I confess the sins we Israelites, including myself and my father's house, have committed against you." Leaders stand back in the pocket and take the hit, but losers run out of bounds.

I saw a television commercial not long ago that I thought was a perfect illustration of this principle. I honestly can't

part 1

remember the company that was being advertised, but it had something to do with being a leader in the financial world, financial planning, investing, and that sort of thing. The commercial begins with several young neighborhood boys hitting the baseball around on a summer afternoon. One of them steps up to bat, takes a swing, and *smack!* He gets a solid hit—right in the direction of one of the neighbors' houses. Sure enough, the ball goes right through the front window of this house.

HDP *Leaders accept the blame; losers pass the buck.*

Immediately the panic-stricken boys begin to run away. No one wants to get caught holding the bat and taking the blame. No one, that is, except one boy. As the rest of his friends and teammates take off down the street, this one young man picks himself up, sucks in his gut, gingerly steps up onto the front landing of this house, and rings the doorbell. The concluding message of the commercial is that leaders don't take the easy way; they take the right way.

Are you willing to admit the truth of your sinful condition before a holy God? Or are you running down the street hoping not to get caught? When you pray, do you confess sin, specific sin? Some people pray, "Oh, God, change my husband; he's not treating me right. He is ungodly. Change him, Lord. Strike him with lightning, Lord, and bring him to his senses."

While that may (or may not!) be a legitimate prayer, prayers like that ignore personal sin and selfishness. Worry about yourself first. Yes, pray for others that they will change. But confess your own sins before turning your prayer to the spiritual needs of others. Nehemiah confessed his own sins and also the sins, corporately, of Israel. He was real before God. Like Nehemiah, leaders accept the blame and confess their sins to God.

3. *Show Confidence in God's Promises.* The third C in a difference-maker's prayer is *confidence.* Nehemiah showed confidence in God's promises. In Nehemiah 1:8 he seems to be asking God to remember something he had promised. Of course God is omniscient and doesn't forget anything. So has Nehemiah lost it? No. The Bible says again and again that we are to recite to God the promises of God when we pray. There are more than seven thousand promises in the Bible. We don't recite them for God's benefit. He knows what he has promised. We recite them for our benefit so we can remember what he said and remember that he will do what he said he would do.

Nehemiah recited the promise that God had given Moses regarding Israel: "If you are unfaithful, I will scatter you among the nations, but if you return to me and obey my commands, then even if your exiled people are at the farthest horizon, I will gather them from there and bring them to the place I have chosen as a dwelling for my Name" (1:8–9). Nehemiah was

part 1

part 1

praying back to God what God already knew, and in doing so he was allowing God to build in him the confidence he needed to trust God more.

HDP *Godly leaders gain confidence to accomplish impossible tasks by praying the promises of Scripture.*

It's important here to understand that the promise to Moses that Nehemiah recited was contingent on obedience. Notice the words "obey my commands." You see, if we are living in sin, we can pray the promises of God all day and all night, and our prayers won't get very far. Sin dealt with radically is sin dealt with effectively, and when it is dealt with radically and effectively, then we can pray. Then we are pure vessels. Then we can talk to God and get it right.

If you have a problem with your earthly parent and have not dealt with it, your relationship may not be broken but your fellowship is. It is the same way with God. For example, if you are single and you're sexually involved with someone before marriage, you can pray all day every day, but your prayers are not going to get very far because you are living in sin. But when you say you will keep yourself pure until marriage and turn from that sin, then you can begin to pray effectively. That is when God's promises are moved into performance.

You have to deal with sin. You can't just say, "God, here I am. I want you to bless me, but I'm really not going to change. I'll continue to lie to my business partner. I'll continue my lustful-thought life. I'll continue to stab this person in the back relationally. But please, God, keep your promises in my life. Bless me like you said you would." It's not going to happen without repentance and obedience.

We've already discussed the need to confess our sin in prayer. But as we begin to make requests of God and lay claim to his promises, we must also take the next step—repentance and obedience. You may be thinking, *How does confession differ from repentance and obedience?* Confession is admitting guilt and asking God's forgiveness—a very important and life-giving step. Repentance is committing to God that you are ready to turn from that sin and go the other direction—his direction. Pledging obedience to him is submitting to his lordship in your life.

If you want to have confidence in the promises of God, you must both confess your sins *and* seek his will with an obedient and submissive heart. Many of God's promises to us are contingent upon this fundamental attitude of the Christian life. Confidence comes from living rightly, and living rightly comes from doing what God says. As you seek the confidence of living under the promises of God, be on the lookout for the "if" clause in those promises. More often than not, God says, in essence, "If you obey me, I will bless you."

4. *Stay Committed to Being Part of the Answer.* The difference

maker's fourth C is *commitment*. Nehemiah was committed to being a part of God's answer to his prayer.

HDP *Leaders are committed, available, and willing to be part of God's answers.*

Nehemiah told God he was available. And God looks for availability much more than he looks for ability. Nehemiah was not the man you or I would choose to lead this great work. He was a cupbearer. He had soft hands. He didn't know anything about working in the broiling hot sun of Jerusalem. Yet God wanted him to be his man, because he knew Nehemiah had the heart of a great leader. He was committed, available, and willing to be part of the answer.

4. Do the Right Thing

Leaders ask the right questions, respond the right way, pray the right prayers, and, finally, leaders do the right thing. Whatever you are praying for right now, I can guarantee you that, in most situations, *you* are most likely the answer to your problem. You have mourned and fasted and prayed; now get up and start doing something!

Start becoming proactive, as Nehemiah did. Realize that God wants to use you in a significant way to become the answer to your own request. Nehemiah knew that. He was ready. He concluded his prayer in Nehemiah 1:11 by saying, "Give your servant success today."

Let me ask you a question: Do you ever pray for success? You should. So should I. We should pray that God will make us successful if—and here is the contingency—if what we are doing is openly for the glory of God. We might pray, "God, make me successful, I mean supersuccessful." But if we can't ask God to bless what we are doing, then we'd better not do it. Nehemiah said, "Give your servant success today by granting him favor in the presence of this man."

"This man" was Artaxerxes, and Nehemiah was justifiably freaking out and frightened to go before him. Here is what I think happened: I suspect Nehemiah was praying, fasting, and mourning, praying, fasting, and mourning—contemplating the problem over and over again. Then one day a little light came on that was inspired by the Holy Spirit of God. God began to communicate to him, "Nehemiah, you are a major part of this prayer request. *You*, Nehemiah, are a major piece in the answer to this puzzle. I'll be with you, but you have to get up and get going. This is your Mission Possible."

This Is Your Mission

Think about God's mission for your life. No matter how impossible it may seem, it is possible. Christ follower, God is

part

1

saying to you in no uncertain terms, "This is your mission: You are to be a leader, a person who stands up for God in the home, at the office, in the neighborhood, and in every slice of life." Maybe God is also saying that if you refuse to accept this mission, then one day out of nowhere your life could self-destruct in five seconds. Accept God's Mission Possible and recognize the leadership potential in your life. Continually seek out ways to impact people and events for the glory of God. You can begin by incorporating the essentials of high-definition living into your life and following Nehemiah's guidelines for leadership requirements:

- Ask the right questions.
- Respond the right way.
- Pray the right prayers.
- Do the right thing.

high-definition principles

Imparting Your Vision to Others

■ When leaders pray, they often experience a delay.

▶ Leaders plan because we are created in God's image, and God is a planner.

● When you make time for think time, your think time will make time.

■ Leaders master the task of the ask.

▶ Leaders keep it low until everything's ready to go.

● Leaders transfer the vision from me to we.

■ Leaders know when to transform talk into action.

▶ Leaders understand that there is no opportunity without opposition.

● Focused leaders know when to say no.

chapter
3

master caster

Imparting Your Vision to Others

One of the most crucial elements of fishing is casting. Whether you are bait casting, spin casting, or fly casting, the presentation of the lure, minnow, or fly to the fish is extremely important. You have to help the fish see that thing on the end of your line as the most appealing, tantalizing morsel that fish has ever seen. Otherwise, the fish won't bite. So if you want to be a great fisherman, you had better become a master caster.

Likewise, if you want to be a great leader, you've got to become a master caster. As you follow God's mission of biblical leadership, he will give you opportunities to present specific plans and purposes to your family, to the person you're dating, to those you work with, or to others whose lives interact with yours. To be ready, you've got to know how to present those ideas in such a way that they are the most appealing, tantalizing concepts those people have ever seen.

But just how do you become this kind of master caster? You begin by learning to communicate. And Nehemiah's just the man to teach you. He knew how to cast and communicate his leadership vision to others.

Becoming a Master Caster

God wants us to develop our leadership gifts to their maximum potential so we can communicate in every outlet of our lives the great love he demonstrated in the death and resurrection of his Son, Jesus Christ. Everyone who is hooked up with Jesus has an important, life-giving message to communicate to others. In this chapter we will learn, from Nehemiah's example, some principles on doing just that.

We have already learned that Nehemiah was an important man in the Persian empire, but still, he was a Jew, a captive. So he was probably shocked one day when God said to him, in essence, "Nehemiah, I want you to rebuild the wall around Jerusalem. I want you to lead this effort. I want you to stand up and do what no one else has been willing to do."

If Nehemiah were like you and me, he probably said, "God, wait a minute. I am a cupbearer, not a contractor. I am not a great leader who can accomplish such a great task. Give me a break, God."

But God said, "Nehemiah, this is my vision for you."

God had cast the vision in Nehemiah's heart and life, and now it was time for Nehemiah to cast the vision to none other than King Artaxerxes.

Have you ever had to cast a proposal or present an idea to an individual when you knew he or she would not like the plan you were proposing? Have you had to convince someone—maybe at work or in a dating relationship or at home or maybe around the neighborhood—when you knew he or she would not accept your idea very well? It was probably a frightening or at least an unsettling experience. Maybe you dreaded having to approach that person when you knew the response was likely to be negative.

If so, that gives you a little feel for the predicament Nehemiah was in. Remember, back in biblical times, if the king didn't particularly like your request, he had the power of life and death. The stakes were high. Today, we've all probably used the expression someone "bit my head off" when a cranky person hasn't liked something we've said. Nehemiah found himself in this exact scenario—literally! Now it's easier to understand why he waited four months to approach the king with his request! But he wasn't just stewing and fretting during that time. Instead, he was preparing to cast his vision on the king. And by his example we can learn the five steps in becoming a master caster. In those anxious days and weeks

part 1

before he went to the king with his request, Nehemiah prayed it over and thought it through, then he kept it low, gave it away, built it up, and tuned out the criticism.

Pray It Over

It probably doesn't surprise you that the first thing Nehemiah did was pray over the problem. The first aspect of imparting a vision to others, the first step toward becoming a master caster, is to pray it over. Throughout Nehemiah's story, he prays and he prays and he prays. But there in the beginning, as he was preparing to act, he prayed and he waited.

Praying and waiting go hand in hand. When God is delaying, he is building and maturing us. He is telling us, "Be patient. I will answer this according to my timetable, according to my plan for you."

MDP *When leaders pray, they often experience a delay.*

God's plan for Nehemiah was to wait and to pray for four months. One day when Nehemiah was just carrying out the normal, everyday task of giving King Artaxerxes some wine, the opportunity presented itself and Nehemiah was ready. Leaders persist in prayer, and they wait for the right opportunity to act; during this stage, the strongest position for leaders is on their knees in prayer.

It's tough to wait, isn't it? In our microwave culture, we

want things *now*. Over a decade ago, my wife and I began praying for the church that we would someday pastor. We didn't know about Fellowship Church. We only knew God had put a strong desire in our hearts to pastor. And after months and months of praying, I remember asking Lisa if she believed God was listening. I had the desire, but nothing was happening. I would talk to a church here and a church there, but we seemed to be hitting dead ends. One day, though, I met a group of six visionary leaders who were beginning a church in Irving, Texas. And in that meeting, my prayers seemed to be answered. We came up from Houston to the Dallas area to become part of Fellowship Church, and my time here has been the greatest ride of faith I have ever experienced. But I have to tell you, it was fourteen months of praying and waiting, praying and waiting, praying and waiting. Leaders must persist in prayer and then be ready for God's timing.

Nehemiah was facing a challenge, and he was nervous about it. So he prayed. I love what he said in Nehemiah 2:2: "I was very much afraid." Don't you love that vulnerability, that honesty? If you are going to be the best leader possible, you have to be open to others. Nehemiah was open. He was vulnerable. He admitted he was very much afraid. But he did what he had to do; he went to the king.

Artaxerxes asked him, "What is it you want?" (2:4). What an opportunity! The king was asking Nehemiah what he wanted.

45

And what did Nehemiah do in response? He "prayed to the God of heaven."

In Nehemiah 2:4 he prays a powerful microwave prayer. You know the type: Time. Cook. Five seconds. Beep. Send to God. In essence, Nehemiah was saying, "God, help. God, give me the words. God, this is my defining moment. God, this is it. King Artaxerxes has opened a window. I have to share with him the vision you have given to me." It was crunch time.

Nehemiah had prayed prolonged, persistent prayers for four months. And there, in the midst of casting his vision to the king, he was *still* praying.

Think It Through

Notice, also, that Nehemiah thought through his mission. Faced with a challenge, leaders pray it over, then they think it through. In other words, Nehemiah planned. He wasn't just praying for four months. He was praying, and he was planning.

God Is a Planner

Why did Nehemiah plan? Why should we plan? Haven't we heard time and again that we are to live by faith? That is certainly true, but we should also plan. Why?

IDP *Leaders plan because we are created in God's image, and God is a planner.*

First Corinthians 14:33 reveals that "God is not a God of disorder." We should plan because God suggests it. First Corinthians 14:40 tells us, "Everything should be done in a fitting and orderly way." The Bible says we should also plan because it gives us the best use of our time.

Make Time for Think Time

Awhile ago I had the privilege of spending the day with John Maxwell, a man who's invited all over the world to speak on leadership. John told me, "Ed, I make time just to think."

I challenge you to do the same thing.

Do you ever just draw away and think? Think time sounds deceptively easy. But Howard Hendricks said it best: "Serious thinking is the most demanding and rewarding thing I know." I have definitely found that to be true in my own ministry.

I have a team of three or four people who spend time with me on a weekly basis to creatively brainstorm and think through every aspect of our weekend services. We spend hours sometimes just thinking about effective and compelling titles. We take time to think and plan, because it is the best use of our time. We are communicating the nature and character of God when we share his Word, so we want to spend time working on that message.

You might think that this kind of brainstorming is effortless, that it's basically just a friendly rap session. But it's not.

part 1

Creative thinking in order to impart serious truth is one of the hardest and most taxing things we can do. Sometimes it's not a particularly fun thing to do. It is difficult to think seriously and yet creatively to come up with something that can be understood by listeners whether they are in the first grade or the twelfth grade or graduate school. On any given message that I deliver, I may spend five or more hours just developing the sermon outline, then condensing it, rethinking it, and going through the appropriate scriptures. And that is just the beginning of the process, before I get into the actual meat of writing the message itself.

To be honest, this kind of thinking is not always my favorite thing to do. I'm an action-oriented person. I want things done now, and I don't always want to fit thinking and planning into my schedule. But I have discovered the hard way that leaders make time for think time because think time makes time.

MDP *When you make time for think time, your think time will make time.*

Thinking and planning also create incredible opportunities. For Nehemiah it created the opportunity to present his vision to King Artaxerxes. And because he had planned, he was ready to seize that opportunity when it arose. In Nehemiah 2:5 he said, "And I answered the king." He didn't say, "King, I'll get back to you," or "King, I'll fax you later," or "King, we need to do lunch next month." He answered the king. And the next three things he talks about in the verses that follow are evidence that he planned.

First, he set a deadline; he put a time line in front of King Artaxerxes. He told the king he wanted to rebuild the wall, and when the king asked him how long that would take, Nehemiah gave him a well-thought-out answer. Every vision, every goal must have a deadline. If it doesn't, it is not a goal or a vision that is worth anything.

Next, Nehemiah requested letters to be written to the governors of the Trans-Euphrates. Nehemiah, having thought through the process, knew that when he traveled from Persia to Jerusalem he would have to cross province after province after province. He needed passports and visas and letters from King Artaxerxes.

I have often heard people say, "I'm just living by faith, just by faith." What if Nehemiah had said that to the king? "Your majesty, I don't have any specifics. I'm just living by faith. So how about it? Do I have your blessing?" I think the king might have nodded to his executioner to start sharpening the blade and getting the chopping block ready. Yes, Nehemiah prayed. Yes, he had faith in God. Yes, he asked God to show him what to do. But he also planned so that when it was God's timing to begin his mission he (and not his head) would be ready to roll. God has given us an intellect, and he wants us to use it. That's why think time is so important.

1

part

Let's briefly play out the scenario of what might have happened if Nehemiah had just operated by faith without planning or making provision for his journey: He leaves Persia, and in the first province he hits, he gets rebuffed by the border patrol. They want to see his passport and his visa. Since he hasn't planned for this contingency, he has to return to the king to request what he should have already secured. It takes awhile to get the papers, but he's finally back on the road.

When he gets just outside of Jerusalem, he hits the royal forest. Asaph is the foreman in charge of the forest, and Nehemiah tells him, "Asaph, by faith I am going to Jerusalem. Would you give me about four million dollars' worth of timber to rebuild the wall and construct my residence?"

Asaph probably asks Nehemiah if he is crazy. He wants documentation.

Faith is not a synonym for *disorder.* We live by faith. But we also plan out our mission as best we can. We think it through. We do our homework. We do the background studies, then we rely on God to give us success.

Nehemiah thought things through. He set a time line for the king, and he got the king to write letters to the governors and to Asaph. Here is Nehemiah, a cupbearer, and he already knows there is a royal forest outside the city of Jerusalem as well as the name of the man who runs the show there. He had thought over his mission, and he was ready.

Master the Task of the Ask

As you absorb this lesson, I hope you don't miss another important point: Nehemiah asked for help. He requested things.

If you are afraid to ask for help, if you are afraid to do some team building, you will never become the Nehemiah-type leader God wants you to be.

HDP *Leaders master the task of the ask.*

You may want to argue, "But, Ed, you don't understand. No one can do it like I do. No one can make the calls at work like I do. No one can do the finances like I do them. No one can present the project like I do." That attitude is a formula for failure. You have to ask for help. You have to ask for things. Nehemiah asked for help and look what happened: God opened up the floodgates of heaven. King Artaxerxes said, "Sure, Nehemiah, you can have four or five years off. I'll still pay you a salary. I'll even give you the timber to build the wall. And I'll give you a secret-service escort to go from Persia to Jerusalem."

Thinking things through prepares us for opportunities; planning helps us grow and develop. Thinking and planning

stretch us. And asking for help can net big rewards. Nehemiah 2:8–9 says, "And because the gracious hand of my God was upon me, the king granted my requests. So I went to the governors of Trans-Euphrates and gave them the king's letters. The king had also sent army officers and cavalry with me."

Can't you picture Nehemiah going to Jerusalem on the back of a camel thinking how amazing it was the way everything had happened? *Twelve months ago it was just a dream. God had just picked up a rod and reel and cast a vision into my life, and I thought about it and wondered who would lead the effort. Then God said that I was the man. And now I am riding with the king's escort to Jerusalem with his cash, with his resources, to rebuild something he said would never be rebuilt. What a great God, what an awesome God I serve!*

Keep It Low

Now, when Nehemiah got to Jerusalem, do you think he loudly announced he had arrived to rebuild the wall that hadn't been rebuilt in ninety years? No. He did something sort of strange. In his memoirs he recorded, "I went to Jerusalem, and after staying there three days I set out during the night with a few men" (2:11–12). People were probably wondering why he was there and what he was up to. But he didn't say a word. "By night I went out through the Valley Gate toward the Jackal Well and the Dung Gate, examining the walls of Jerusalem, which had been broken down, and its gates, which had been destroyed by fire" (2:13).

Nehemiah was still doing his homework. He was still investigating. He was still thinking about who would be in charge of what part of the wall, where the material would come from, how big, how tall, and how wide the wall should be. But he wasn't making a big deal out of his investigation. He wasn't calling attention to himself or his plans.

Nehemiah's words reveal the lonely side of leadership. "The officials did not know where I had gone or what I was doing" (2:16). The officials surely wondered. After all, Nehemiah was a top executive who had come to Jerusalem under the king's authority. But Nehemiah wasn't ready yet to announce his intentions.

HDP *Leaders keep it low until everything's ready to go.*

You have to protect that vision from premature death. After all, it is much easier to kill an idea than to launch one.

Do you want to grow spiritually? I believe you do. That is why you are reading this book, and that is why I am writing it, to help you mature in your spiritual walk. Do you want to develop your relationships? Do you want to reach your maximum potential at work? Do you want to get in shape, lose a couple of pounds, and increase your aerobic capacity? Have you thought through your vision? Have you made plans for it?

Have you set a time line? Have you looked at the possible pit-
falls and problems you might face? Nehemiah would tell you
to pray it over and think it through. And then he would tell
you to give it away.

Give It Away

The vision of rebuilding Jerusalem's wall came from God
into the life and heart of Nehemiah. He prayed it over and
thought it through, kept it low, and then, when everything was
ready, Nehemiah transferred the plan to a team concept.

Look at Nehemiah 2:17–18: "Then I said to them, 'You see
the trouble we are in: Jerusalem lies in ruins, and its gates have
been burned with fire. Come, let us rebuild the wall of
Jerusalem, and we will no longer be in disgrace.'" He was
finally imparting to others the vision God had given him. The I
turned to we as he began to cast his vision outward. "I also told
them about the gracious hand of my God upon me and what
the king had said to me" (2:18).

LDP *Leaders transfer the vision from me to we.*

Nehemiah was pointing to God. He did not speak of messing up, of failing, of facing impossible conditions. He knew
that what seemed impossible for them was possible with God.
Leaders face their fears. They go for it, and they always have

success in mind. Always. And successful leaders are able to impart the vision God has given them to others.

Build It Up

As a leader with a vision, you pray it over. You think it through. You keep it low. You give it away. And next, you build it up. Nehemiah had given his vision to the people, and now they replied to him, "Let us start" (2:18). Nehemiah was motivating them, and they were ready to begin.

■DP *Leaders know when to transform talk into action.*

There is a major difference between leadership and leader*slip*. Both start off great. You go to a national conference on leadership. You listen to a tape from the hottest motivational speaker on the circuit. You read his or her book. You articulate a certain mission statement, a certain goal, agenda, or plan. You're going to start this company, do something special with your life, build this relationship, get involved with a specific area of ministry. You look good, you smell good, you sound good, but if you don't take that next step—if you don't actually build up your vision—people look at your life and say, "Where are the results? Where's the life change? What's the take-home value?"

Leaderslip people never quite have it, because they keep the ship in the slip, and it just bumps against the dock day after

part 1

day after day. It makes a lot of noise. It says, "I'm going to do it. I'm going to change. I'll be different." But when it comes to real results, the ship never leaves the dock.

In contrast, people who have leadership also go to the conferences. They rub shoulders with visionary people. Then they fire up those engines, and they leave the slip. Many times they will break the ropes as they leave the dock; they're that eager to go. They set sail. They get out there on the open water, and they ride the waves. They face the bad weather head-on. They sail determinedly and run quickly because they are involved in leadership, not leaderslip.

Nehemiah built up his vision with people who also had the gift of leadership. "They replied, 'Let us start rebuilding.' So they began this good work" (2:18).

Tune It Out

Master casters who want to implement a vision pray it over, think it through, keep it low, give it away, and build it up.

There are a couple of ways to live life without opposition. If you want to live life without any criticism, do nothing and say nothing. But if you are going to try to accomplish anything extraordinary in this life, beware of the vision vandals. Every time God gives a person or family or church a vision, the vision vandals soon arrive on the scene. They take out their vision extinguishers, and they try to just squelch the idea.

HDP *Leaders understand that there is no opportunity without opposition.*

You will find Nehemiah's vision vandals in Nehemiah 2:19: "But when Sanballat the Horonite, Tobiah the Ammonite official and Geshem the Arab heard about it, they mocked and ridiculed us." Nehemiah probably wanted to say to these scoffers, "I can't believe you are criticizing me. What has gotten into you? Don't you realize God sent me here? I am God's man. This is God's thing." But he didn't say that. Instead, he said simply and confidently, "The God of heaven will give us success. We his servants will start rebuilding" (2:20).

Every time you receive criticism and opposition, consider the source. Critique the opposition and consider the spirit of the criticism. If it is vindictive, if it is meanspirited, then turn and go the other way. But if it is given in the spirit of love and tenderness and grace, take it in. Some of it will be right, and some of it will be wrong. And all of it will hurt.

I have heard some people say criticism doesn't bother them. I have heard CEOs and presidents, prime ministers and pastors say it doesn't bother them, but I just laugh. Criticism always hurts, but it doesn't have to tear you apart or destroy your vision.

part 1

We receive very little criticism at Fellowship Church, but the criticism we have received hurts. I have learned something, though, throughout my years in ministry leadership. Pioneers take the arrows. There is no opportunity without opposition. You have to love everybody, but you need to move with the movers. Nehemiah cast his vision to the people who were on God's team. He didn't worry about the criticizers. He said he loved them, and they were free to join him, because the wall was going to be built regardless of the opposition. He went for it. He rebuilt the wall in a record time of fifty-two days, because he tuned out the vision vandals.

Know When to Say No

Nehemiah had a focus. He could have involved himself in a certain political agenda, in an action group, or in a neighborhood project. And though those were probably good things, wonderful things, fine things, he had to decline. He had to say, "No. There is one thing I'm here for. God told me to rebuild the walls around Jerusalem, and that's what I'm going to do."

IDP *Focused leaders know when to say no.*

You have to say no regularly, sometimes hourly, to be the kind of leader that God wants you to be.

Successful people in God's economy are focused people.

They don't try to do 334 things. They just do one thing. The evil one loves to push his way into your life and mine with these good things. He says, "Ed, get involved in this good thing. Ed, get involved in that good thing." And we are so involved in good things that we miss out on the main thing. We have to say no.

Are you saying no regularly? Or are you saying yes just so you won't hurt someone's feelings or because you feel the pressure to conform to someone else's agenda? It's a tough thing to do, but you have to be willing to say no more than you say yes. It's the only way you can accomplish the unique task God has given you.

How's Your Cast?

How is your vision casting going? Are you making progress toward becoming a Nehemiah-style master caster? Sharing your vision with others may seem like a daunting task when you first consider it. But if you learn and practice the steps—pray it over, think it through, keep it low, then give it away, build it up, and tune out the criticism—you'll soon be leading others in enjoying the high-definition life God has planned for you. Remember, this isn't something you buy at a store or learn from a book—even *this* book! It comes from God. And it's already within you. When God gives you his vision, he will equip you to become a master caster.

HDP

high-definition principles

Learning the Importance of Delegating

■ Leaders organize around natural groupings.

▶ Leaders know the value of teamwork.

● Leaders work with those who want to work.

■ Leaders make detailed assignments.

▶ Leaders establish a clear line of authority.

● Leaders recognize and compliment others.

chapter
4

the lone danger

Learning the Importance of Delegating

I want to expose a major flaw in some well-known individuals. You might know these folks as superheroes: Batman, the Green Hornet, Superman, Wonder Woman, and Spider-Man. Here is the flaw: Each of these superheroes thinks he or she is the only one who can carry out the task at hand. But each one is wrong. Even the Lone Ranger fell into the trap of the lone danger when he tried to go solo without his faithful companion, Tonto. Think back for a second to the comic books, television shows, and movies you grew up with that featured these icons. All the superheroes could have achieved greater status in the crime-fighting world had they only learned the secret and the power of delegation.

Take Batman, for example. Now, we all know and love this caped crusader. He had a lot of talented people right at his fingertips. He had Robin. He had Commissioner Gordon, Chief O'Hara, Alfred, and even Aunt Margaret, plus the entire

Gotham City Police Force. If you study his crime-fighting history, though, he rarely used those individuals to their fullest potential. Granted, he was the best crime-fighter in Gotham City, but he could have multiplied himself, his effort, and his vision, if only he had delegated responsibility to others around him. Trying to do it all alone is the lone danger.

Interestingly enough, delegation was not invented by some Harvard Business School grad, some modern-day leadership expert, or some CEO of a Fortune 500 company. Delegation was thought up and invented by our transcendent and loving God. All you have to do is read the second chapter of Genesis, the first book of the Bible, and you find God entrusting the responsibility of caring for the Garden of Eden to a husband-and-wife team known as Adam and Eve. Later in the Old Testament, God delegated responsibility to people like Moses, Deborah, and David. In the New Testament we find the Son of God, Jesus Christ, delegating his ministry to the twelve disciples. And then, right before he ascended into the heavens, Jesus delegated the spreading of the gospel to people like you and me.

Obviously, delegation matters a lot to God. Again and again in Scripture he shows us how it was done by Jesus and by other biblical leaders, one of whom was Nehemiah. Nehemiah's example will teach us several important lessons regarding the dynamics of delegation. God delegated the rebuilding of

Jerusalem's wall to this great man, and Nehemiah had to delegate some of the responsibility in order to accomplish that mission.

Do you have problems with delegation? Do you have a difficult time giving responsibility to others in your life? If you ever want to try to organize a family, a business, or a project, study the third chapter of Nehemiah. You'll find the principles of delegation at work as Nehemiah rebuilds this wall. In this chapter I'll show you those principles.

Simplification

If I want to do something big, if I want to build my vision in a company or an organization, I have to simplify the company or the organization's structure and then organize its people around natural groupings.

HDP *Leaders organize around natural groupings.*

What if Nehemiah had said this when he hit the city limits of Jerusalem, "I'm going to do it by myself, because no one else can do it like I do. I will make every brick. I will mix the mortar. I will work in the hot, broiling sun. I will repair section after section after section"? The wall wouldn't get built, that's what would happen! But, of course, Nehemiah didn't say that. Instead, he delegated. And he began this delegating by organizing the people who were willing to work on the wall into groups based on natural commonalities.

part 1

Nehemiah was a leadership genius who had the ability to reduce the complex to the simple; he understood that the strongest organizations have the simplest structures. Nehemiah didn't arrive in Jerusalem and decide to form some huge think tank complete with committees, trustees, and subsidiary companies. He didn't need to do that to accomplish his mission. Instead, he simplified the work force by organizing the workers around natural groupings.

We've discovered some great names in this study, and in Nehemiah 3:1 we find another one: Eliashib. Nehemiah's memoirs record that "Eliashib the high priest and his fellow priests went to work and rebuilt the Sheep Gate." Now, the priests would be a natural grouping. The pastors hung out together, and it was natural for them to repair the Sheep Gate, the gate near the temple through which the sacrificial animals were herded into the city so they could be used in ceremonial worship. Imagine Nehemiah looking at the project and thinking, *Where would the priests really want to work? What would they get fired up about repairing?* To Nehemiah, the answer was obvious: They could repair the Sheep Gate.

Then in Nehemiah 3:10 we see another grouping: "Jedaiah...made repairs opposite his house." Families were commissioned to help repair the portion of the wall nearest their homes. So we see that first the priests and then the families became natural groupings.

Let me ask you something: If your city council decided to build a wall around the city in which you live and you had a chance to build the portion of the wall in front of your house, would you do a good job? You better believe it! You would say, "If this is going to be in front of my house, it's going to be the best wall possible. It will be quality work." Nehemiah saved time by delegating workers in this way. It wouldn't be necessary for them to jump on the bus or drive here, there, and yonder. Work in front of your house, he told the families. And they did. I especially love the family mentioned in Nehemiah 3:12: "Shallum...repaired the next section with the help of his daughters." Women were rarely mentioned during these days, so Nehemiah probably included this little phrase to show how smart Shallum was. He had his beautiful daughters working out there on the wall, so you just know the single men who were working next to Shallum helped and assisted him in the rebuilding efforts.

When I read about Nehemiah using simplification to delegate responsibilities, I think back to the pastoral search committee that interviewed me before I took the position as the first pastor of Fellowship Church. One of the members of that committee asked me a very profound question: "Ed, you are coming from a church that has three hundred staff members and moving to a mission church that has no staff members. What are you going to do about that?"

I thought for a second, and then the Lord just gave me these words: "I'll tell you what I am going to do," I said to the committee members. "You will be my staff. We can't pay you, but you'll be my staff." And that's what happened. The people on this committee became the first staff of our church. Some were interested in the financial realm, and they handled the finances. Some were interested in the administrative realm, and they handled that part of the church's business. Some were interested in Bible study and teaching, and they handled that.

Delegation is a biblical concept. It is a concept God wants us to use. And frankly, one of the reasons God has blessed and anointed Fellowship Church is because we are a church that delegates. Anytime we have an opportunity, we try to delegate, to train someone, and then give that ministry away.

Participation

The second high-definition principle of delegation is participation. In other words, godly leaders use a teamwork approach—they strive for cohesiveness, togetherness.

Sometime back I was with my brother on his boat negotiating the tricky waters of the Trinity River in Texas. I am a big wildlife kind of a guy, and I saw something on the river that day that I had never seen before. I was amazed to see a family of feral pigs come sprinting down the bank. Those pigs dived into the muddy, swift currents of the Trinity and began swimming across the river. I could not believe what was unfolding before my eyes. The riverbank they were approaching was practically vertical. I thought there was no way those pigs were going to make it up the bank. I was certain they would drown. But they were wild pigs with big tusks, so we kept our distance. The smaller pigs couldn't climb the bank, but finally, I saw the sows and boars plant their hooves into the bank, and as they clung to the shore, the little ones climbed onto their backs and jumped to safety. Incredibly, they all made it out. Even feral pigs know the importance of teamwork!

HDP *Leaders know the value of teamwork.*

As we study Nehemiah's methods of delegating in Nehemiah 3, something interesting happens. Or maybe I should say something interesting doesn't happen. You will not read Nehemiah's name in this particular chapter. Don't look for it. It's not there. You won't see it, because at that point Nehemiah had stepped out of the picture. Nehemiah had received a vision from God, and he had cast it to the people. He gave them ownership of the mission and allowed them to complete their tasks as they were gifted. He helped those who wanted to work get started. Then he stepped back and let them do their jobs.

I want you to notice a phrase that's repeated beginning in Nehemiah 3:17: "Next to him, the repairs were made by the

part 1

Levites under Rehum son of Bani." Verses 17–22 all contain the phrase "next to him." It's mentioned twenty-two times in chapter 3. When God mentions something once, you'd better pay attention; twice, you had better really listen; but twenty-two times, you need to get out the highlighter and take notes. This phrase, "next to him," indicated the participatory nature of the work that was taking place there in Jerusalem.

I know so many leaders whose time is eaten up because they spend hour after hour trying to corral, coerce, and convince nonworkers to participate. Work with those who want to work. The teaching is reinforced in Ecclesiastes 4:9–10: "Two are better than one, because they have a good return for their work: If one falls down, his friend can help him up. But pity the man who falls and has no one to help him up!"

In every group, church, organization, and school, you have people who want to work, who want to sacrifice, who want to give. And you have others who want to sit back. You have the workers and the shirkers. Don't waste your time on the shirkers. Work with those who want to work.

HDP *Leaders work with those who want to work.*

I go back again to the early days of Fellowship Church. We used to have projects and big events where a good-sized group from the church was in attendance, but not everyone was there.

I would get all worried and stressed-out because of who wasn't there, wondering, *Why aren't those other families here? Where are the other single adults?* Then, a few years ago, God showed me that I should work with those who want to work. I still love everybody involved with our church, but I've experienced first-hand the reality that 20 percent of the people do 80 percent of the work, and 20 percent of the people give 80 percent of the money.

Take a look at who wasn't working in Nehemiah 3:5: "The next section was repaired by the men of Tekoa, but their nobles would not put their shoulders to the work under their supervisors." (I can't help but wonder, *If these nobles had known that they would be mentioned in the Word of God that would be read by millions of Jews and Christians throughout the ages, would they have worked?*)

The nobles wouldn't work, and what did Nehemiah do in response? He did not fret, "Oh, no! Why aren't these men working? Is it me? Is the work disorganized? Do they disagree with the plan to rebuild the wall? Is it the temperature outside? Oh, no! What is wrong?" Instead, Nehemiah just ignored them. He paid no attention to the nonworking nobles.

Think about your own work. Think about your vision. Are you so worried about who is not there that you are missing the people who are there? Love everybody, but work with the workers. Some are going to participate, and some are not.

part 1

Specification

Nehemiah didn't hit J-Town and say, "OK, guys, we are going to build a wall. Just start where you want to start. You can use wood, you can use brick, you can use masonry, or you can use sand—whatever you want." If he had done that, the wall would have been ugly and unsafe. Instead, Nehemiah specified detailed assignments.

HDP *Leaders make detailed assignments.*

We see this in Nehemiah 3:2, which begins, "The men of Jericho built the adjoining section, and Zaccur...built next to them." The word *section* is used thirteen times in Nehemiah 3. Nehemiah organized this project to build the wall counter-clockwise, section by section. In verses 4–9 we read, "Meremoth...repaired the next section....The next section was repaired by the men of Tekoa....Uzziel...repaired the next section....Rephaiah...repaired the next section." The list of sections specified for the workers continues through the chapter.

Specification in the Home

The principles of delegation we learn from Nehemiah's wall-building project in ancient Jerusalem can be applied to our leadership roles in the church, in business, and in all aspects of our lives. But do you know where we can really delegate? This might scare you. It is in the family. Especially when it comes to parents delegating responsibility to their children, giving their children specific jobs that are their responsibility.

How in the world are our kids going to learn how to delegate if we don't first delegate responsibility to them? Learning what it means to be responsible starts at an early age. Even when children are only twelve months old, parents can gently begin to delegate responsibility to them—for example, showing them how to put their toys away or to put their dirty clothes in the hamper. As children get older, parents can delegate more responsibilities, again specifying exactly what is expected of each child. I talk to too many teenagers who say, "Well, I don't know what my father wants. He tells me this one day and that the next. It's chaotic."

The Ritz Bits Method of Specification

Think about your coworkers, your friends, and the members of any organization you may lead. Think about a project you are working on. Think about the Little League team. Do the people around you have specific, clear-cut job descriptions? Do they know what is expected of them? They do if you have been clear in describing the jobs they're responsible for and given them specific, detailed assignments. How do you give these kinds of assignments without overwhelming people? Well, you can use what I call the Ed Young Ritz Bits method of specification.

part 1

Have you ever eaten Ritz Bits? They're delicious. Just ask our twins, Laurie and Landra; they love Ritz Bits. One day I came home for lunch and they had carpeted our home with Ritz Bits. But that's another story. What I want to show you is that when it comes to learning how to give someone specific, detailed instructions, Ritz Bits, of all things, offer a great example. You see, Nabisco, the company that makes Ritz Bits, was both smart and sly. Those corporate cracker-makers knew that if we ate one or two Ritz Bits we would think we weren't eating very much. So we would eat a few little Ritz Bits—and then a few more and a few more until, before we knew it, we would have eaten the whole box!

That is the same way you can present detailed assignments effectively: Break down the job to be done into Ritz Bits–sized sections. Break down the mission into bite-sized chunks and then give clear assignments about what is expected. Giving out work in easy-to-swallow increments keeps your children, your team members, your coworkers, and your committee members from becoming overwhelmed and disillusioned with the enormity of the overall task. Give them step-by-step instructions they can complete one segment at a time. Following your instructions, they complete one small part of the mission, then they move on to the next little part and the next little part, and before they know it, they've completed the project.

Administration

Nehemiah 3:17–18 records, "Repairs were made by the Levites under Rehum....Next to him, the repairs were made by their countrymen under Binnui." Notice the word *under*. It indicates there were tiers of leadership: Under Nehemiah there were administrators, and under the administrators there were subordinates.

HDP *Leaders establish a clear line of authority.*

Again, Nehemiah didn't say, "Look at me: I'm the man. This is my vision." Instead, he shared his vision; he owned it with the people. Delegation is not an excuse for relaxation but a reason for multiplication. As an administrator, you don't say, "Well, I can just sit back and chill for the rest of my life while everyone else does the work." No, no, no!

When Fellowship Church hit 275 people in attendance regularly, it outgrew me. One person can effectively oversee about 250 people. Any more than that, and you need help. So what do you do in your business, in your church, in your school, in your project when it grows beyond your own abilities? You delegate. You assign tasks in bite-sized chunks. You establish a clear line of authority.

Nehemiah went around the wall counterclockwise seeing people, learning from people, understanding their names, and

73

listening to what was bothering them. He noticed those people who were doing a good job and those who needed a pep talk. Administrators have to check up on people, because people often do not do what you *expect* but what you *inspect*.

Everything in the universe has a chain of command. We are under the authority of God and God's Word. Growing up, we are children under the authority of our parents. We have authority in churches, authority in schools, authority in hospitals, authority in the court system. Wherever you turn, there is a chain of command. God has put people over you and over me for certain reasons. We have to honor those people and love them. And when we find ourselves in positions of authority we have to say, "I am going to be the best administrator possible, so I am going to establish a clear line of authority."

Affirmation

Nehemiah mentioned seventy-four people in his account. Why? He gave them credit for doing a great job. In chapter 3 alone, we see these names: Eliashib, Zaccur, Meremoth, Meshullam, Zadok, Joiada, Melatiah, Jadon, Uzziel, Hananiah, and the sons of Hassenaah. Because Nehemiah affirmed their efforts, all these people are still remembered today for the part they played in this mammoth project.

 Leaders recognize and compliment others.

There's a wonderful story about affirmation in Luke 17. As Jesus was walking into a city, ten lepers came up to him and asked for healing. Jesus told them to turn around and show themselves to the priests. They did, and they were healed. Not one blemish remained on their skin. Thrilled with their restored health, the healed lepers scampered away—except for one who made a quick U-turn, ran back to Jesus, fell down before him, and showed the Lord affirmation, recognition, and love. He thanked Jesus for healing him.

Jesus asked, "Where are the other nine?"

The others probably felt feelings of gratitude, love, and recognition, too, but they didn't express them.

Who in your life is doing a great job? Your spouse? Your son? Your daughter? Who in your business is doing a great job? Who on your team is doing a great job? Have you told them? Do you have feelings of gratitude but never verbalize them? Don't think up excuses. Don't say things like, "I didn't have that kind of stuff growing up. My parents never told me I was doing a good job. I wouldn't know what to say." Just say it! Or maybe you think you can't compliment someone because the person might get a big head. Such issues didn't worry Nehemiah, and they shouldn't worry you. You see, most people who are on ego trips today were never affirmed as children. That's why they are trying so hard now to hear the applause. Or maybe you think that everything has to be just right—the timing, the place, etc.—before you can pay someone a compliment. Or maybe you think that a word of thanks or affirmation from you won't make any difference. That is simply not true.

The people in my church have been so encouraging to me as their pastor over the years. Their letters always seem to come at just the right time, just when I've needed a kind word to encourage me and lift my spirits. Because I know how important these affirmations can be, I encourage you to follow Nehemiah's example and take the time to encourage, applaud, affirm, recognize, and compliment others, because it really does make a huge difference.

The results of recognition and affirmation are tangible. Just look at the man named Baruch in Nehemiah 3:20: "Baruch... zealously repaired another section." You know what the word *zealously* means? It is the only adverb used in Nehemiah 3. It means "to be full of God." I guarantee you, Baruch felt full of God because Nehemiah was cheering him on. There is nothing like recognition and affirmation.

Avoid the Trap of the Lone Danger

God has cast a vision of leadership in each of our lives, and one of the ways we serve as godly leaders is by delegating, by sharing our mission. To do this we organize our helpers around natural groupings. We focus on those who want to work. We specify detailed assignments and establish a clear line of authority. And as the work proceeds, we recognize and compliment the workers.

Are you trying to do everything yourself? Take a cue from Nehemiah: Delegate, delegate, delegate. If you do that, you will never fall into the trap of the lone danger.

part 1

HDP

high-definition principles

Dealing with Opposition and Criticism

- Use criticism as a catalyst to run faster and work harder.

- Analyze the opposition's methods to learn how to deal with them.

- Be aware that the opposition substitutes ridicule for reason.

- When handling resistance, leaders remember that hurt people hurt people.

- Leaders handle rumors like gum. They chew on them for awhile, but they never swallow them.

- Leaders fight the battle on their knees.

- Leaders do the divine thing, but they also do the practical thing.

- Biblical leaders know that Christianity is a group thing.

- Remember the Lord who is great and awesome.

- Leaders always outwork the opposition.

chapter 5

dancing with wolves

Dealing with Opposition and Criticism

The team you manage at the office has been working on a landmark proposal for your company for the last couple of weeks. Everyone in your organization says this is the best idea the company has ever had, and they are already patting you on the back. Now it's the day of the big presentation before your boss and the management team. As you pitch your idea to the group, you feel great about what you're saying. You feel like you're really connecting with the people. When you're finished you stand there wanting to give yourself a high-five. You really think you've hit a home run. Then your boss looks at you and, in a very condescending tone, says, "That was it? That was the creative idea we've been waiting to hear? That was what all the commotion was about?"

And you watch as, before your very eyes, your proposal is thrown into the trash. While this is occurring, the managers sitting around the board table snicker and roll their eyes.

How do you respond to that?

Or let's say you've spent an entire afternoon preparing a special meal for your husband to show him how much you love him. The table is set with the good china, the candles are lit, and soft music is playing in the background. Your husband bolts through the front door, glances at the table, grabs the remote, and clicks on the television set. As he settles into his favorite easy chair, he looks up at you and says, "Honey, I had a huge lunch, and I really want to watch the seventh game of the NBA finals."

How do you respond? How do you deal with that one?

Or maybe you've just received a promotion, which means that you will have to move to California. There's a big raise involved plus new benefits and even a company apartment overlooking the Pacific. You can't wait to tell your family and your friends about the promotion. But when you tell them they say, "California? You won't like California. The weather is nice, but the people are kind of strange and superficial. You'll be back in a month; I guarantee it."

How do you respond to that?

Facing criticism and opposition is like dancing with wolves. It can be a frightening, discouraging, disheartening thing—or it can be a catalyst pushing you to run faster and work harder.

MDP *Use criticism as a catalyst to run faster and work harder.*

What happens when you find yourself facing criticism and opposition from a mate, a coworker, a friend, a neighbor, an ex-spouse, or from someone you don't even know? What do you do about it? The stinging barb of criticism hurts, doesn't it? Opposition and criticism have the potential to depress us, disable us, and debilitate us.

Once again, Nehemiah is our biblical role model who will teach us this next step toward high-definition living. He's going to show us how to handle criticism and opposition as we heed God's call to leadership.

In Jerusalem Nehemiah took some serious flack as he planned this project, as he built the project, and even when the project was completed. Let's dive in and observe how this great man handled all of the junk thrown his way.

To study how Nehemiah handled opposition and criticism, we need to look at the lesson in two parts. First we will look at the opposition's mission, then we will change gears and look at the leader's commission.

The Opposition's Mission

The first thing we need to do when we're confronted by opposition is to understand where the other person is coming from, to get a glimpse of what is motivating him or her to respond with criticism. Often we can analyze the opposition's mission by studying the methods being used and learning how

81

part 1

to deal with them. Three of the most common are ridicule, resistance, and rumors.

■DP *Analyze the opposition's methods to learn how to deal with them.*

Ridicule

The first method of the opposition's mission is old, something used all the time today: ridicule. In the first verse of chapter 4 in his memoirs, Nehemiah wrote, "When Sanballat heard that we were rebuilding the wall, he became angry and was greatly incensed. He ridiculed the Jews." The heart of a critic always resists change; those who are the most inflexible are, for the most part, the most critical. That is true on every athletic team. It is true in every company. It is true in every church. It is true in every family. Those who don't want to change, those who don't want to think outside the box, are usually the most critical.

You would think that Sanballat would have sat back and applauded the Jews. He should have said that what they were doing was phenomenal, a small band of people rebuilding the walls around a whole city. Since the walls had been in shambles for ninety years, you would think that he would compliment them on their mission. Instead, he ridiculed the Jews. And not only that. Nehemiah 4:2 tells us he ridiculed them "in the presence of his associates and the army of Samaria."

Critics love to put people down in front of others, don't

they? When they ridicule someone, when they mess with that person, when they take cheap shots at him or her, they do it when other people are around to jump on the bandwagon and fire their own darts of criticism. If someone takes the lead and criticizes you or me, we can expect other people to be waiting in the wings to add their criticism. Sanballat led the attack of criticism by ridiculing the Jews, and right behind him, if you read a little bit farther, you have Tobiah applauding Sanballat and echoing his criticism.

The opposition substitutes ridicule for reason, laughter for logic, and viciousness for vision. Sanballat continued his jab by asking sarcastically, "Will they finish in a day?" (4:2). His words provide the first pointer in how to major in ridicule: exaggerate.

HDP *Be aware that the opposition substitutes ridicule for reason.*

Nehemiah had never said they would finish the project in a day. But, of course, Sanballat didn't care about that. He was on a ridicule roll, and he kept right on going. Next he said, "Can they bring the stones back to life from those heaps of rubble—burned as they are?" Sanballat obviously knew how to do this criticism thing.

Then it was Tobiah's turn: "Tobiah the Ammonite, who was at his side, said, 'What they are building—if even a fox climbed up on it, he would break down their wall of stones!'" (4:3). This is trash talking at its best, or worst. But Tobiah made a blunder here.

part 1

83

He called it "their wall." And, of course, it wasn't *their* wall at all. It was God's wall. Nehemiah was the superintendent, but the wall was God's, and the opposition was criticizing God's work.

There have been times in my life when I have criticized something only to figure out a couple of months later that I had been criticizing God's work, God's vision, God's agenda. That is exactly what Sanballat and Tobiah were doing in Jerusalem. With ridicule, they were attacking God's work.

Ridicule is effective because it attacks our self-worth. It tears apart our self-esteem. Godly leaders have to know how to deal with ridicule if they are going to be effective.

The opposition loves to maintain the mundane. Leaders, on the other hand, always attempt to stay SLIM. Here's how it plays out:

S —They consider the *source.*

L —They *listen* and *learn* from every bit of criticism.

I —They *ignore* it in most circumstances and situations.

M—They always discern the *motive* behind the attack.

Resistance

Another mission of the opposition was to start a resistance rally. First they used ridicule, and next they rallied the troops to resist the workers' efforts. Have you ever noticed that critics run in packs, kind of like wolves? Nehemiah 4:8 says, "They all plotted together to come and fight against Jerusalem and stir up trouble against it." And you had better believe that they were organized. In the north, Sanballat and the Samaritans were ready. In the south, the Arabs were ready. In the east, Tobiah and his forces were ready. In the west, Ashdod was ready. They had surrounded Jerusalem, and they were ready to fight. They organized a big, negative, moan-zone, flack-smacking, criticism-crying resistance rally.

Have you ever met people who, after a while, you discern have only one mission: to take opposition to anything and to stand against everything? There are categories of people who traffic in resistance. The first one is the assassin. This is the man or woman who shoots insults at you from unexpected places: maybe the grassy knoll, maybe a neighboring home. They get you in the cross hairs, and *wham!* They fire the shot, and you wonder where it came from. Do you know any assassins?

Another category of people who traffic in discouragement is laundromat people, the ones looking for dirty laundry. Their speech is punctuated by statements like, "Oh, really? He said that?" "She did that?" And once they find the dirty laundry, they hang it out for everyone to see: "You're not gonna believe this one!" "Have you heard what so-and-so did?" "Let me tell you what I heard."

Next are the hackers, the people who traffic in discouragement by always trying to crack the code, saying things like, "I wonder what makes him tick." "I wonder what's behind her behavior." They specialize in collecting negative information. Do you know any hackers? If you do…run!

Another category of people who hang out in critical packs is the fire extinguishers. These are the folks—men, women, teenagers, and children—who extinguish any creative idea, any change, any suggestion that might move them out of their comfort zone. Whenever growth is involved, they extinguish it.

The resistance rally in Jerusalem was composed of all these negative types of people; they plotted together to come to Jerusalem and stir up trouble against the wall-rebuilding project. Nehemiah's detractors, Sanballet and his friends, were conspiring to keep the wall from being completed because they were enemies of Israel and of Israel's God. The Samaritans, represented by Sanballet, and the other opposition forces—the Arabs, the Ammonites, and the Ashdodites—all shared borders with Israel. The historic relationship between Israel and the Samaritans, the Arabs, and others who share their borders has been one of constant contention. (We see that even today.) In this instance there were obviously feelings of anger among the opposition. Nehemiah 4:7 tells us, "They were very angry" as the gaps in the wall began to close. The bitterness, resentment, and anger of these different groups stemmed from Israel's claim to the Promised Land.

These were the same enemies who had been defeated and

displaced by the Jews in the past, from the time of Joshua to the expansion of Israel's territory under the reigns of David and Solomon. The cumulative effect of generations of hurt was being expressed against Nehemiah and the Jews in Jerusalem in the sixth century B.C. Now, I'm not saying that Israel did not have a right to that land or a right to rebuild the city of Jerusalem. This was clearly God's plan for his chosen people. But that does not negate the hundreds of years of conflict and pain the enemies of Israel experienced. As Nehemiah rebuilt the wall, they were lashing out because of the hurt they had experienced, and they are still lashing out today.

HDP *When handling resistance, leaders remember that hurt people hurt people.*

Most of the time the people who are after you, the people who are criticizing you, the people who are opposing you, are hurt people. When you get behind their masks, when you check their pasts, when you see what is happening in their relationships, you usually find that they have been hurt or damaged somewhere along the way. And as a result of that— maybe even without knowing it—they are looking for anyone or anything to lash out at. Hurt people hurt people.

Rumors

The third method used in the opposition's mission is spreading rumors. Nehemiah 4:11 says, "Our enemies said, 'Before they know it or see us, we will be right there among them and will kill them and put an end to the work.'" Here is a great way to spread rumors: Fuel people's fears. You see, these people surrounding the Jews couldn't take them on. They didn't have the firepower to fight the Jews; they didn't have the muscle. They didn't have the intestinal fortitude to do it. So they fueled the Jews' fears instead. And the Jews began to buy into those fears, saying to each other fear-fueled statements such as, "They're going to kill us. They might be behind the wall. They might be in the trees. Watch out." Their actual response is found in Nehemiah 4:12: "Then the Jews who lived near them came and told us ten times over, 'Wherever you turn, they will attack us.'"

Notice two characteristics of these rumors. First, they are spread by those individuals who live closest to the enemy. Second, they are exaggerated the more they are repeated.

If you swallow them, they will stay in your stomach for seven years and really mess you up.

When rumors are swirling around you, take some time to chew on them. Figure out where they originated, and if they have any basis in truth, deal with them appropriately. Then let them go.

■**DP** *Leaders handle rumors like gum. They chew on them for awhile, but they never swallow them.*

Most rumors are just that, rumors. They are unfounded and

usually serve only as distracters to take your time and energy away from more important things.

A Leader's Commission

In the midst of the opposition's mission, we find Nehemiah and the Jews modeling a leader's commission. By their response to the opposition, we can learn additional lessons in how to deal with opposition and criticism. As the forces mounted during the Jews' wall-building mission, Nehemiah led them in doing the divine thing, the practical thing, and the group thing, in remembering God's greatness, and, finally, in outworking the opposition.

Do the Divine Thing

In response to opposition, the leader does the divine thing: He or she prays. Leaders rely on God in good times and in bad, and especially when the opposition is growing. And Nehemiah certainly did that. Again and again, Nehemiah turned to God in prayer as the wall-rebuilding project proceeded. And that's what he did as the opposition mounted. But the prayer he prayed at this point is a little weird.

Throughout the Bible we find prayers like this: "Lord, forgive us our sins." "Lord, take away our transgressions." "Lord, forgive me and forgive my family." But look at what the man of God prayed in Nehemiah 4:4: "Hear us, O our God, for we are

89

despised. Turn their insults back on their own heads. Give them over as plunder in a land of captivity."

Nehemiah wasn't name-calling; he wasn't trying to solve the problem himself. He was calling on the Lord to take care of the opposition for him. While Sanballat was saying, "Oh, those dirty Jews," Nehemiah wasn't saying, "Oh, those despicable Samaritans and those horrible Arabs." He was simply asking God to turn the opposition's insults back on their own heads. The human side of Nehemiah, the human side of you or me, when we heard the insult, would want to find Sanballat, Tobiah, and the rest of the forces and punch their lights out, call them names, and curse right back at them. But Nehemiah didn't do that. Instead, he called on God.

MDP *Leaders fight the battle on their knees.*

Remember when David was getting ready to rumble with Goliath, the behemoth? What did David say? Did David get in a shouting match with Goliath? No. David said, in essence, "God, this is your battle. I am giving myself to you. You take charge. You'll give me victory." When Daniel was forced to pray to King Nebuchadnezzar, did he start crying or complaining? No. His first response was to go into his house and pray to the one true God.

I also want you to notice something else that's different in Nehemiah's prayer here. In chapters 1, 2, and 3, Nehemiah's prayers were first-person singular: "I prayed..." Nehemiah apparently prayed alone, calling on the Lord. But here in Nehemiah 4:9, he says, "We prayed to our God." Nehemiah prayed, and the Jews saw him praying. The next thing you know, they were praying too.

Do you want your leadership team to change at work? If you begin to pray, others will follow. If you want your family to change, let them see you praying; soon they will follow your lead.

Do the Practical Thing

We see Nehemiah doing the divine thing by praying. We also see him doing the practical thing. Nehemiah did something practical to defend himself and the people of Jerusalem. He prayed, and then he acted.

HDP *Leaders do the divine thing, but they also do the practical thing.*

As it was being constructed, the wall was weak in some areas. So Nehemiah "stationed some of the people behind the lowest points of the wall" (4:13). Whenever the enemy attacked a certain section of the wall, Nehemiah had someone blow a trumpet. When the trumpet sounded, everyone who heard it would run over to that section of the wall and reinforce it. Nehemiah was smart; he had things worked out. He put a plan in place so that the Jews were ready to take on the opposition.

If you are lying in your bed tonight and you pray, "Dear Lord, protect my family from burglars," that's a great prayer. The Bible says God will put a hedge of protection around your family; but God has also given you a brain. He wants you to lock the doors! Do the divine thing, but don't neglect the practical thing. Over and over again, the Bible teaches us to watch and pray. Watching is the practical thing. Praying is the divine thing.

We all have walls around our lives, and there are weak points in those walls—weak spots in your life and mine. Where are you weak personally? In the financial area? Are you tempted to do something shady to get ahead? Are you tempted to take some money under the table? How about in your thought life? Are you tempted in the area of lust, in sexual immorality? You need to reinforce the weak points in your wall with people who can help you.

Do you know the weak points of your company? You had better reinforce those weak points. Are you getting ready to make a presentation next week? Before the presentation think about the weak points in your proposal and reinforce them. Yes, pray hard, but then get ready for the opposition.

Nehemiah's memoirs continue his report of how he responded to the opposition's mission, stationing people behind the lowest points of the wall "at the exposed places, posting them by families, with their swords, spears and bows" (4:13). Here we see the principle of delegating and organizing according to natural groupings coming into play again. The security details around the wall were posted by families. They were defending the wall together in community. They were doing the practical thing.

Do the Group Thing

Let's take a minute to bring this lesson down to the nitty-gritty of our lives. We are engaged with an enemy, a spiritual enemy, of vast resources. If we are not connected into a local church, the body of Christ, and if we are not connected into a small group or a Bible study or Sunday school class, we are going to have a tough time when the enemy attacks. If this describes your situation right now, I have two words for you when opposition inevitably comes your way: Good luck. I doubt that you will be able to stand. You can't fight this battle alone.

Caribbean-island Christians are those who move to a spiritual island on their own. For awhile it's beautiful there. The sands are white, the water is clear; the palm trees sway peacefully in the breeze. They can do their own thing, with no one to bother them. One day, though, the force-five winds blow. One day the hurricane hits. One day the waves come crashing ashore. And those people are devastated by the storm. They have no one to reinforce their beliefs, no one to stand behind them and hold them up.

Nehemiah's leadership example reminds us that Christianity is a family thing. It's a group thing, a togetherness thing.

part 1

93

HDP *Biblical leaders know that Christianity is a group thing.*

Another biblical hero, Elijah, helps us learn that lesson as well. Elijah was a great prophet of God who tried to live a Caribbean-island life. He tried to do things on his own. Unfortunately, Elijah was being chased by Jezebel, one of the meanest women who ever lived. One day when he got tired of running, he sat down and said, "God, take my life. Please."

But God didn't take Elijah's life. Instead, God fed him and told him, "Elijah, get up. I have sent someone to help you." The helper's name was Elisha, and he ministered to Elijah.

And here's another biblical example that shows us God intends us to work with others. Remember how King Saul of Israel went on a rampage chasing David and trying to kill him because David had been handpicked by God to replace Saul as king? David was praying to God to be delivered from Saul's furor, but he was also running like mad. God saw David's predicament, and he put someone in David's life to help him through the hard times. A man named Jonathan, the son of King Saul, became David's best friend and confidant.

We aren't meant to be Caribbean-island Christians. Do you have someone you can share your life with, someone who can come alongside you in the midst of your personal battles? Do you have someone who loves you? Do you have someone you can be in real community with and really connect with? You have to have this kind of community to live the Christian life. You have to be an active part of some local body of believers, because as an active member of a faith community, you are not going to be as vulnerable to temptation or to those force-five winds that come your way. You'll be part of a group that backs you up and reinforces your faith.

Remember God's Greatness

As a leader, Nehemiah reassured the people. He told them, "Don't be afraid of them. Remember the Lord, who is great and awesome, and fight for your brothers, your sons and your daughters, your wives and your homes" (4:14).

HDP *Remember the Lord who is great and awesome.*

If you study the wars, many were fought with slogans that began with the word *remember.* The Texas war of independence: Remember the Alamo. The Spanish-American War: Remember the *Maine.* World War I: Remember the *Lusitania.* World War II: Remember Pearl Harbor.

When you think about those slogans, you realize they were about remembering defeats. The people would take that memory of when they had been hammered and use the defeat to motivate themselves to go after the enemy. But Nehemiah did just the opposite. He didn't say, "Remember the Babylonian captivity." Instead, he said, "Remember the Lord, who is great

95

and awesome. Remember all the good things Yahweh has done for you." He empowered the people by reminding them of the awesome God who stood behind them. He motivated the people by reminding them of all that God had done for them.

Make sure that around your office, your house, or your apartment—wherever you consistently spend your time—you have trophies of God's greatness to remind you of what he has done for you. When the difficult times come, let those reminders empower you and remind you that with God anything is possible.

In my office at church where I work and study, I have three or four pictures that mean something to me spiritually. When I feel down, depressed, or despondent, all I have to do is look up and see those pictures to remember how God changed the life of the family that is pictured or how he moved to heal a situation that seemed hopeless. I remember how God used me in various people's lives. I remember how he's been faithful in this church or that church, in this mission or in that mission. Maybe a particular poem or a special verse of Scripture helps you remember the Lord. Whatever it takes for you, surround yourself with reminders of God's greatness.

Outwork the Opposition

After reassuring the people, Nehemiah found that they still needed extra encouragement to remain loyal at the critical halfway point in this massive project. In Nehemiah 4:6 we read,

"So we rebuilt the wall till all of it reached half its height, for the people worked with all their heart." But by verse 10, another kind of opposition is beginning to set in: "Meanwhile, the people in Judah said, 'The strength of the laborers is giving out, and there is so much rubble that we cannot rebuild the wall.'"

When the Jews got halfway done with the wall, they began to concentrate on the rubble from the past instead of finishing the wall for the future. They began to concentrate on the old mortar and the old brick still to be cleared away, and they lost their focus on the task at hand. They became overwhelmed with the amount of work that still lay ahead of them. With the continuing threat of an enemy attack and their weakening resolve, many were ready to quit.

We face the same kind of opposition in our lives today. Think about when you buy a brand-new car. Initially you're excited about your big purchase and vow to take extra-special care of it so it will last a long time. Usually, though, when you get halfway through paying for it, it begins to lose its newness, and you want something different. The same thing often happens when you start a new exercise routine or a new diet. You're exercising and when you get thirty minutes into your one-hour workout, you feel exhausted and you want to quit. Or when you're three months into a six-month weight-loss program, you hit a plateau and you begin to hear the cookies and ice cream calling to you. Or you might be

part 1

hiking up the mountain, and when you get winded and fatigued at the halfway point, thinking how far you still have to go, you want to turn around and head back down the mountain.

That's how the Jews felt when the wall was half completed. They wanted to quit. But they didn't. Nehemiah 4:21 says, "We continued the work with half the men holding spears, from the first light of dawn till the stars came out." They persisted. They kept on working from dark till dark. In spite of the enemy's threat, in spite of the aching muscles and the nagging desire to quit that were opposing them at every turn, they pushed through the halfway point and finished the job. Even with half the work force standing guard with spears, the other half was able to complete the task. Talk about persistence and hard work! Nehemiah did not give up or give in, and his persistent spirit spread to everyone around him.

The word *work* is used five times in Nehemiah 4. You can talk about vision. You can talk about conferences. You can talk about money. You can talk about image. You can talk about all the auxiliary stuff, but the bottom line is work.

HDP *Leaders always outwork the opposition.*

I was amazed to read somewhere that the Walt Disney Corporation invites its competition to come in and study their facilities. You would think they might be afraid of their competitors stealing ideas from them, but apparently they're not. Do you know why? They know that no one is going to work like the Disney people. Others can steal ideas and visions all day long, but if those others are not willing to work as hard as they do, the other guys will get nowhere.

Are you working? Are you persisting? In what area of your life are you tempted to give up? In what area are you saying the challenge is too tough? Don't give up on that marriage. Don't give up on that relationship. Don't give up on that business dream. It's always easier to quit than to commit. It's easier to throw in the towel than to stay in the game. It's easier to bail out than blast through.

Opposing the Opposition

Leaders persevere in spite of the opposing forces that try to dissuade them at every turn. They continue on in the face of criticism. The opposition's mission will always be there; there will always be people out there who jump at the chance to knock down a creative idea or an innovative proposal. But if we fulfill the leader's commission and follow the high-definition principles, we are ready to go dancing with the wolves of opposition.

high-definition principles

Leading with Integrity

- The secret to handling a promotion is integrity—an undivided heart.

- The first stage in protecting unity is anger.

- Wise leaders don't take action on their first reaction.

- Leaders transform their anger into action.

- Leaders of integrity jealously guard against anything that threatens unity.

- Leaders use benefits, but they never abuse them.

- Leaders fight fragmentation by keeping a 3-D focus.

- Integrity means honoring God instead of yourself.

- Godly leaders leverage their wealth for the eternal purposes of God.

- Hospitable leaders offer where they live, what they have, and who they are.

- Leaders who handle responsibilities well on earth will be given a greater leadership role in heaven.

chapter 6

honorable mention

Leading with Integrity

Integrity can be defined as "the state of being complete, unified." When we have integrity, our honorable words match our honorable deeds. We are who we are, no matter where we are or who we're with.

Sadly, integrity is a vanishing commodity in our culture today. Our society is trying to take shortcuts to success and premature pathways to prosperity. We are watching our standards crumble before our very eyes. From Whitewater to Watergate, from day-care providers to professional athletes, from televangelists to telecommunications, from the stock market to the stockyards, it seems that everywhere we turn we run into scandal and problems. And in most cases, the problem can be traced back to the leaders' lack of credibility and integrity.

Now, if you have a job outside the home, I'm going to tell you something that will most likely please you: Over the next few years, you'll probably receive a promotion. Data and research indicate that a high percentage of people in the work force will receive a promotion within the next three to five years. Strangely, though, it is easier for most people to handle a demotion than a promotion. We have an easier time negotiating the difficult days than riding the crest of success. Thomas Carlisle put it best when he said, "Adversity is tough on a person, but for every one person who can handle prosperity, there are one hundred who can handle adversity."

Struggling our way to the top is often a much stronger character-building experience than actually getting to the top and trying to stay there. With a promotion there is the temptation to let the additional power, prestige, and prosperity become the driving forces in our lives. Our moral compass can begin to lose its bearings as we make decisions based not on what we know to be right but on what will help maintain our new position. During adversity we are often brought to our knees in humility. Sadly, pride and hubris can be the most appropriate descriptors of the person who has been promoted. The Bible does not say that humility goes before a fall. Proverbs 16:18 says, instead, "Pride goes before destruction, a haughty spirit before a fall." With a proud and, might I add, divided heart, many a leader has fallen. A proud heart is divided between worship of self and worship of God.

MDP *The secret to handling a promotion is integrity–an undivided heart.*

Integrity is descriptive of wholeness of being, not division. How do you keep your integrity intact when you have been given more money and more power, a better position, and more prestige? Our loving God wants all of us to be able to handle this elevation in responsibility. He really does. That is why he has given us a great leader like Nehemiah to follow. Nehemiah was one of the best difference makers who ever lived. That is why we are going to dissect a portion of his life as he mentors us on how to lead with integrity.

To set the stage for this chapter, let's jump ahead a little bit in our story about Nehemiah answering God's call to rebuild the wall around Jerusalem. Right in the middle of this project, Nehemiah got another call, this time from King Artaxerxes. The king promoted Nehemiah to be governor of Judea.

As he accepted this new position of authority, did Nehemiah take an ego trip? Did he let his promotion go to his head? Did he set up a little clique of leaders around him? No. Nehemiah led with integrity. And you can, too, by following the example of this great biblical leader. In this chapter you'll see three of the ways Nehemiah served with integrity. He refused to lose his people's unity. He refused to abuse his position. And he refused to confuse his priorities.

Refuse to Lose Your Unity

The first thing to understand when you're learning to lead

103

with integrity is that you have to refuse to lose your unity. You can't let anything splinter your organization or your family into bickering components.

I find it interesting to see that Nehemiah was right in the center of God's plan and purpose for his life, yet God still allowed him to go through a lot of conflict. Some of it was external conflict, such as the opposition and criticism from Sanballat and his cohorts. But Nehemiah also had to deal with internal conflict as the Jews began to fight among themselves.

Nehemiah 5:1 says, "Now the men and their wives raised a great outcry against their Jewish brothers." Now, guys, you know it is bad when the Bible singles out not only the men as raising an outcry but also their wives. You see, women have a sensitivity, an emotional radar, that men don't have. The men probably joined in the outcry after hearing their wives. But the women were probably saying things like, "Honey, can you believe what is happening? Can you believe that those wealthy Jews are taking advantage of us? My little son doesn't even have enough food to eat, and they are taxing us too much."

The Jews involved in the wall-rebuilding project were starting to bicker among themselves, and their bickering threatened their unity. Nehemiah, our role model as a leader with integrity, went through three stages as he worked to protect his people's unity: anger, reflection, and resolution.

Anger

What was happening? Why were the men and their wives so upset? Actually, they were upset about several things. They were having to deal with overpopulation. They were struggling through a food shortage. And they were being hit with high taxation. Sounds a lot like the front page of today's newspaper, doesn't it? But the real problem arose because the rich Jews were exploiting the poor Jews, and Nehemiah didn't like it one bit. The discord was threatening the unity in his project, and Nehemiah reacted the same way most of us would react. He got mad. Nehemiah wrote, "I was very angry" (5:6).

It might surprise you to learn that the first stage you must go through when the unity is threatened in your home, in your business, on your athletic team, in your corporation, in your church, is to get very angry.

HDP *The first stage in protecting unity is anger.*

One of my favorite television programs is *Sesame Street*. I was forced to watch the show all the time with my kids, and now I've grown to love it. A great song on *Sesame Street* is sung by Oscar the Grouch, the perpetually cranky guy who lives in the trash can. He sings, "When I'm climbing up a tree, and I fall and skin my knee, I get mad. Very angry. Very, very angry. Real mad. Very angry. Very, very angry."

The next time your unity is threatened, remember Nehemiah and remember Oscar the Grouch. The Bible says you'd better get angry if you're going to refuse to lose your unity.

Reflection

When your unity is threatened, get angry. But don't take action on your first reaction. If you do, you will inevitably say and do things you will later regret. Nehemiah got angry, but notice what he did next. In the second stage of protecting the unity of his people, he took time to reflect on the situation around him. In Nehemiah 5:7 he recorded, "I pondered them in my mind."

HDP *Wise leaders don't take action on their first reaction.*

In Hebrew the word *ponder* means "I consulted with myself." Nehemiah talked to himself, perhaps saying something like this: "I can't believe these wealthy Jews. I can't believe the people financing the rebuilding of the wall are taking advantage of the less fortunate. What am I going to do about this? How should I respond?"

What is the benefit of such reflection? How many times have you responded to a situation out of frustration without thinking through the best way to approach it? How often have you hurt someone or made a situation worse by lashing out in misdirected or nonproductive anger? Nehemiah was angry, but he was wise enough to know that venting his feelings right away, to whomever happened to be in his way at the time, was not the best course of action. He needed to think through his response and have an internal dialogue with himself so that positive resolution would be the result. In doing so, his anger had a purpose and a proper focus. He was resolute in his anger; therefore his anger led to the next stage—resolution.

Resolution

The third stage of protecting your family's or your organization's unity is the most difficult. It's tough to transition from stage two, the reflection stage, to stage three, the resolution stage. Godly leaders, though, take the initiative to resolve the problem so that unity is not compromised. They courageously confront problems and difficulties head-on. When there is a problem, especially in marriages, most people will get angry and reflect, reflect and get angry, get angry and reflect. They get locked into a vicious circle and dig themselves into a hole. Godly leaders, on the other hand, move on to the third stage that leads to resolution—action.

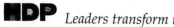 *Leaders transform their anger into action.*

Nehemiah moved through the stages of anger to reflection to resolution. He wrote, "So I called together a large meeting to deal with them" (5:7). Talk about having guts and courage!

Nehemiah confronted those heavy hitters, those power players, face to face.

Leadership is not a popularity contest. If you are trying to please everybody, you are doing something that God doesn't do. If you are trying to be a buddy to everyone, you are not really being a leader to anyone. Nehemiah taught us to concentrate on the project and forget what the bickerers think of us. Refuse to lose the unity.

Nehemiah called the people together and told them, "What you are doing is not right. Shouldn't you walk in the fear of our God to avoid the reproach of our Gentile enemies?" (5:9). In other words, Nehemiah was telling them their behavior was a bad testimony, a poor example. He was saying, in effect, "Hey, Jews, all the nonbelievers are looking at you. They know about our belief in God; they know we maintain that following him makes us different. Yet here we are, fighting among ourselves to such a degree that we are the laughingstock of the Arabs and the Samaritans. They are making fun of us."

Internal conflict was threatening to tear the Jews apart and destroy their work. But Nehemiah refused to let them lose their unity.

Every time God wants to build, Satan will always battle. You can count on it every single time. Try to build a marriage—Satan will battle. Try to build a family—Satan will battle. Try to build a company or a church—Satan will battle.

High-definition living starts with unity in your relationship with God. God took the initiative to maintain our unity with him by sending Jesus Christ to pay the price on the cross for all of our foul-ups and sins. And today God offers us continued unity with him as we know and follow Christ. Once we establish a relationship with Christ, we have unity with God.

After unity with God, the next most important relationship is unity with your spouse. God says that the relationship between husband and wife is a reflection of our relationship with him and that we should do everything possible to refuse to lose the unity with our spouse.

From your unity as a husband and wife flows your family unity, those parental relationships and sibling relationships. If you and your spouse are living in unity, harmony, and love, your family system will be rock solid. Next comes your relationship in the marketplace, your vocation in life. As you work and live and perform your God-given tasks, you are to do everything possible to refuse to lose unity with your coworkers.

HDP *Leaders of integrity jealously guard against anything that threatens unity.*

The leadership team with whom I'm privileged to work is very jealous for the unity of Fellowship Church. This is the most unified church I have ever seen in my life, bar none. But when we do hear about someone spreading rumors or causing division or some other problem threatening the church's unity, we deal with it rapidly, biblically, and lovingly. Titus 3:10 tells us, "Warn a divisive person once, and then warn him a second time. After that, have nothing to do with him." I'm glad to say we have only had to use this verse a few times in the history of our church.

Leaders who serve with integrity must have the courage to confront those who threaten the unity of their ministry, their marriage, their family, or their business. Do you want to keep your integrity intact? Refuse to lose your unity. Become a jealous defender against anything that threatens the unity of what you are involved in.

Refuse to Abuse Your Position

Nehemiah had been promoted, and he was in the big time now. He could have used that position to his personal advantage, but he refused to abuse his position.

Have you ever been watching something interesting on television only to have the picture suddenly disappear and an announcement commence saying the station was conducting a test of the Emergency Broadcasting System?

Think of that statement whenever you are promoted, whenever you receive a windfall, whenever your company goes public, whenever you become the president or the head coach or the senior pastor. Listen for the announcement interrupting the ego trip that threatens to fill your head: *This is a test.*

God always gives us a little bit more responsibility, a little bit more stuff, to see if we are going to be faithful. If we are faithful over little, the Bible says that God will let us be faithful over much. This promise works in more than the financial realm. God will send increases in many profound ways as he finds us ready to handle the added responsibilities.

In Nehemiah 5:14 we start to see how Nehemiah handled his test. He wrote, "When I was appointed to be their governor…neither I nor my brothers ate the food allotted to the governor." Nehemiah had a huge expense account. He could have charged thousands on his credit card for food and entertainment. He didn't, though. Why? He knew that if he racked up a huge expense account, he would have to increase the taxes on the people to pay for his indulgences. Talk about losing credibility with the Jews! That would do it! All the people who had been working with him day after day to rebuild the wall would have lost confidence in him. Nehemiah would have shattered his reputation and his impact as their leader.

HDP *Leaders use benefits, but they never abuse them.*

The greater the elevation you achieve, the greater the temptation you receive. What kind of temptation? It is the temptation to use our position to become more, to use our power to do more, and to use our privilege to have more.

Nehemiah refused to abuse his position by exploiting and extorting the people, as other governors had done. Here is what he said about the rulers prior to him in Nehemiah 5:15: "But the earlier governors—those preceding me—placed a heavy burden on the people and took forty shekels of silver from them in addition to food and wine." I'm sure the people around Nehemiah were urging him to do what the other governors had done so that he could make an extra buck here and an extra buck there. But he refused to abuse his position. The Bible also says Nehemiah did not acquire any land. This guy could have bought land when the prices were low and the market was depressed. Then he could have flipped the land and made millions of dollars. But Nehemiah said no.

Check out another example of this kind of abuse in Nehemiah 5:15: "Their assistants also lorded it over the people." The assistants of the ungodly governors had followed their bosses' examples. In the same way, your children will parent their children as you are parenting them. Your children will have values like your values. The people in your company will lead like you are leading. The people you manage will talk like you are talking. That is how the previous assistants had developed their supervisory style. They had taken their cues from the ungodly governors and decided to be autocratic and meanspirited, just like the governors. But Nehemiah would have none of it. He refused to abuse his position, and so should we. We know that God holds the ultimate position, power, and privilege. He could flick his fingers and knock the world a billion miles off its orbit if he wanted to. But he doesn't. God is perfectly balanced. And he says, "Reflect my character in the way you lead others. This is a test. I'm going to see if you are really faithful."

Refuse to Confuse Your Priorities

The third thing you have to do as a godly leader, if you want to keep your integrity intact, is to refuse to confuse your priorities. William H. Henson tells us that wild-animal trainers walk into a cage of lions carrying the most important instrument known in the wild kingdom: a stool. They take the stool and hold it by the seat. When the lion begins to roar, they thrust the legs of the stool in the face of this king of beasts. Animal trainers say that looking at and concentrating on the four legs of the stool literally paralyzes the lion because it fragments the beast's attention. It may want to pay attention to other things going on around it—the other lions, the trainer, the people in the audience—but it can't because its attention is repeatedly jerked back to that stool. Thus the lion is weak and mild and ineffective.

What a lesson for us. So many of us have conflicting priorities. We want to focus on too many things, and our attention gets jerked from one thing to another. As a result we become paralyzed and fragmented. Instead of doing first things first, we try to do the second through the tenth things first—and all at once. And this lack of real priority keeps us from being the kind of leaders and having the kind of integrity, or wholeness, that God wants.

God says, "Just focus on a couple of things, a couple of absolutes, and I will take care of the rest."

IDP *Leaders fight fragmentation by keeping a 3-D focus.*

So, you ask, how do I do that? How do I restore wholeness to my fragmented life? Nehemiah provides the lesson we're looking for. His example teaches us how to prioritize and how to keep integrity at the forefront of our lives.

Have you ever been to an IMAX theater, one of those places with the huge screens? The first IMAX movie I ever saw was a film about helicopters. Watching that movie, there were moments when I actually had the sensation of flying as the filmmakers gave us a bird's-eye view of the thrills and chills of flying through the sky inside a chopper. The uniqueness of the experience came from the film's use of perspective, the way it was made, and the vantage point from which the scenes were shot. Plus, there was one more reason why this IMAX presentation was extra thrilling: It had been filmed using 3-D technology. As a result of this extraordinary three-dimensional perspective, the scenes that unfolded were like nothing I'd ever seen.

As leaders, we also need to have a 3-D perspective, one that provides greater depth and added dimensions to our view of life. We will change as we gain this perspective, and we will see things as we've never seen them before. Nehemiah shows us how we become this kind of leader by deepening our reverence for God, developing our generosity and hospitality, and by disciplining ourselves for eternal rewards.

Deepen Your Reverence for God

The previous governors of Judah had been greedy, taxing the Jews heavily. And their assistants, following the governors' lead, had "lorded it over the people" (5:15). Everyone probably expected Nehemiah to govern the same way. But that wasn't Nehemiah's style. In his memoirs he wrote, "But out of reverence for God I did not act like that. Instead, I devoted myself to the work on this wall" (5:15–16).

Nehemiah operated "out of reverence for God." To be 3-D leaders, to have greater depth and additional dimension in leadership, we, too, have to have a deep reverence for God. Nehemiah knew it was God who had promoted him to his new position. He knew it was God who placed him as the cupbearer to King Artaxerxes for a special time in history so he could one day be sent to rebuild Jerusalem's wall and be promoted to governor of Judea. Nehemiah said, in effect, "God, it's all because of you—because of my worship and my reverence for you."

Nehemiah wasn't the first person to be promoted by God. It was God who promoted Joseph from the pit to the pinnacle of Egypt. It was God who promoted Daniel from a Babylonian boot camp to a big-time leadership role. It was God who promoted Amos, that hick fig-picker from the countryside, into the hallowed halls of Bethel. When you study the stories of Joseph, Daniel, and Amos, you see that they didn't say, "Oh, God, you are so lucky to have me. I am so eloquent. I am so handsome. I have it together. I bet you are so happy that I am on your side."

The fact is, the moment we start congratulating ourselves, the moment we begin to pat ourselves on the back, God will remove his hand from our lives.

HDP *Integrity means honoring God instead of yourself.*

"But this is my company." Oh, it is?

"But this is my idea." Oh, it is?

"This is my creativity." Oh, it is?

"This is my church." Oh, it is?

No, it's not. It's all God's! He gave you the mind; he gave you the drive; he gave you the thought and the perseverance to achieve what you have achieved. God hard-wired you so you could accomplish the mission he planned for you. To be a 3-D leader, deepen your reverence for the One who created you.

Develop Your Generosity and Hospitality

Nehemiah was a wealthy man. Nehemiah had cash, but cash didn't have Nehemiah. Nowhere does the Bible say that Christians can't be wealthy.

Make no mistake: There are numerous warnings in Scripture about the deceitfulness of wealth and the danger of the things of this world pulling us away from the kingdom of God (see Matt. 13:22 and Mark 8:35). The caution, though, is not against being wealthy. The caution is against misusing our possessions or allowing wealth to become our god. Many biblical characters— Abraham, Jacob, Job, David, Solomon, Nehemiah, and the list goes on—were wealthy with God's blessing. Some, like Solomon, misused their wealth. But others, Nehemiah included, leveraged their wealth for the eternal purposes of God, and we can learn many valuable lessons from their lives.

HDP *Godly leaders leverage their wealth for the eternal purposes of God.*

First Timothy 6:17–19 spells out for us God's expectations regarding the material blessings he has given us:

> Command those who are rich in this present world not to be arrogant nor to put their hope in wealth,

part 1

which is so uncertain, but to put their hope in God, who richly provides us with everything for our enjoyment. Command them to do good, to be rich in good deeds, and to be generous and willing to share. In this way they will lay up treasure for themselves as a firm foundation for the coming age, so that they may take hold of the life that is truly life.

To some, God opens the floodgates of heaven in a material way so that they can use those blessings to bless others. But the lesson is clear: Put your hope not in the possessions but in the One who provides them.

I know many Christians who are extremely wealthy. The issue for those Christians is, Do you have things, or do things have you? The Bible says we're to hold on to the things of this world very loosely so that when God wants to move them, rearrange them, or take them away, we don't wig out and exclaim, "My dream house is gone! My car is gone! My life is worthless!" Measure your worth in the contents of your heavenly account, not your bank account.

Our man Nehemiah was rich, but look what he did. You won't believe this. If you don't usually have big gatherings in your home or you are kind of scared to entertain people, your heart will probably flutter as you imagine the dinner party Nehemiah hosted: "A hundred and fifty Jews and officials ate at my table, as well as those who came to us from the surrounding nations" (5:17). But this dinner wasn't just a one-time thing. If you read further, you learn that this group ate at Nehemiah's house every single day! The Bible says the fires never went out in Nehemiah's kitchen. And take a wild stab at who picked up the tab. That's right. Nehemiah did. As a 3-D leader, Nehemiah developed his generosity and his hospitality.

I have known a lot of different kinds of people in my life. I grew up in the country, so I've known some good ol', down-home, country folk. Because of basketball, I've known a lot of inner-city people as well. I've been acquainted with many we'd consider middle-class, and I've rubbed shoulders with quite a few of the wealthy. Through my interaction with all these individuals, I've noticed that many who are wealthy do not give of themselves or their finances as generously as those who are middle class and lower income. I'm not sure why, but a lot of them don't. I suspect it is because they have lost sight of the fact that everything they have is God's. They think they are responsible for their own success. I laugh when I read in the newspaper that a movie star donated $175,000 to a local charity or that a professional athlete gave $400,000 to an AIDS benefit. That's giving? A multimillionaire athlete giving $400,000 is like me giving twenty bucks. A megastar Hollywood actor giving $175,000 is like me giving a dime. That's not giving!

Actually, God doesn't care about the amount we give. He looks at what is left over. We have to become people of generosity

part 1

if we are going to really get serious about this quality called integrity. This may seem harsh, but if you start thinking you've finally got it made, if you're thinking your comfortable lifestyle is secure, your finances are bulletproof, and you're completely self-sufficient, think again. Just like that, it can all be gone. I know of ten people in one city in Texas who were multimillion-aires and lost it all.

Consider the chilling parable of the wealthy farmer in Luke 12:13–21. The New International Version uses the heading "The Parable of the Rich Fool," because that's exactly what he was. He had so much grain, so much stuff, he didn't know what to do with it all. His brilliant idea was to tear down his barns and build bigger ones. Then he talked himself into believing that he would have it made for the rest of his life: "And I'll say to myself, 'You have plenty of good things laid up for many years. Take life easy; eat, drink and be merry'" (v. 19).

Look, though, at the next two verses. These verses send chills up my spine every time I read them, because they represent the tragic end of so many, many people in our society today: "But God said to him, 'You fool! This very night your life will be demanded from you. Then who will get what you have prepared for yourself?' This is how it will be with anyone who stores up things for himself but is not rich toward God" (vv. 20–21).

Instead of building bigger barns to store more grain, today

we open more accounts to accumulate more money, we invest in more stocks and bonds to beef up our portfolios, or we buy more cars, more houses, more boats, and on and on. But if our souls are required of us today, who will benefit from all this accumulation? It won't be us. Don't be a rich fool, storing up exorbitant amounts of treasure for some expected future life of ease. Be rich toward God, give generously to the needs of others, and enter eternity with a vast treasure stored up in heaven.

From generosity flows hospitality. The Bible commands hospitality in 1 Peter 4:9: "Offer hospitality to one another without grumbling." Hospitality is not optional. If we are generous people, freely sharing with others what God has given us, hospitality will be a natural and regular part of our lives.

Here is a brief definition of hospitality: It is offering where you live, what you have, and who you are to others. It is offering where you live: a trailer, an apartment, a tract home, a custom-built home, or a mansion. It is offering what you have: from soup to sushi. It is offering who you are: man or woman, rich or poor, high-school dropout or college professor.

HDP *Hospitable leaders offer where they live, what they have, and who they are.*

The Bible says you are to offer yourself to others. It's so easy relationally to get involved in tight little cliques, isn't it? It's comfortable that way. We come to church, and it's so easy to hang out with the same people, talk about the same things. It's great to have a core group of friends, but we need to engage in and explore new relationships as well.

The early church met in a large group. Some of their church services on the weekends had thousands of people in attendance. During the week, though, smaller groups moved from house to house to house for their meetings. The early Christians were people of hospitality, opening their homes to others on a regular basis. This is one of the keys to hospitality that is sadly missing today. We no longer open our homes to others as we should. We go out to eat together, we go to the mall together, we go to the movies together, we even go on trips together, but we neglect the most fundamental aspect of hospitality: sharing our homes.

Perhaps we are ashamed of where we live. Maybe our house isn't as nice as the friend's or the neighbor's. Or it could be that we feel that our home must be immaculately clean and decorated before we can invite anyone over. Why is the home so important to this whole aspect of hospitality? It's important because there is no other place where we are truly ourselves like we are in our own home. If you want people to truly know you and experience you, you must—I repeat, you *must*, no options—invite them into your home. And I will tell you that once you start practicing hospitality in this way, you will wish you had started much sooner.

Discipline Yourself for Eternal Rewards

Deepen your reverence for God. Develop your generosity and hospitality. And finally, discipline yourself for eternal rewards. Nehemiah wasn't worried about the here and now that much. Sure, he was wealthy and had a lot of possessions. But he gave much away. He wasn't thinking about the jewels or other valuables he possessed on earth. He was thinking about standing on the stage in heaven with God's gold medal around his neck.

Every few years when we watch the Olympics we see profile after profile of athletes who have sacrificed and disciplined themselves through years of preparation and training just so they could stand on that platform with the gold medal hanging around their neck and hear the "Star-Spangled Banner" or the national anthem of their respective country. We see the tears. We see the emotion. It's a riveting scene.

In the same way, 3-D leaders have to discipline themselves to do what has to be done to achieve their mission, but they have the promise of a much more valuable reward that keeps them focused and motivated. Instead of a few moments of glory of standing on a podium and wearing a gold medal around their neck, they discipline themselves to work by focusing on the promise of an eternal reward in heaven.

God says that the way we handle leadership, the way we lead with integrity, has a direct relationship to how we will be rewarded and the responsibility we will have in heaven. If we handle leadership well on earth, God will give us greater responsibility and a greater leadership role in heaven.

HDP *Leaders who handle responsibilities well on earth will be given a greater leadership role in heaven.*

Nehemiah is a great example of a wise, disciplined leader who served with integrity. And so is Moses. I like what Hebrews 11:26 says about Moses: "He was looking ahead to his reward." Moses turned his back on the things most of us are trying to get today, the three Ps of life—position, power, and privilege—to lead a bunch of Jews around the desert. He disciplined himself to look beyond the temporal rewards of this earth and instead he kept his eyes on the eternal reward.

Integrity Takes Grit

Think about the word *integrity* for a second. Look at its spelling—I-N-T-E-G-R-I-T-Y—and just focus on the letters. Does another word pop out at you? As I was praying and thinking about what it means to be a person of integrity, just like that, the word *grit* leapt out at me. You can't say integrity without saying grit. You can talk all day long about vision and leadership and this and that, but if you want to refuse to lose your unity, if you want to refuse to abuse your leadership, if you want to refuse to confuse your priorities, it takes grit. It takes commitment. It takes work. And it takes die-hard perseverance, the focus of our next chapter.

part 1

high-definition principles

Understanding the Power of Persistence

- Beware of temptations that come on the verge of breakthroughs.

- Leaders make way for the affirmative by responding in the negative.

- Leaders ground gossip to avoid getting fried.

- When you are struck by gossip, pray.

- Discerning leaders don't waste energy debating what God has already decided upon.

chapter
7

mission accomplished

Understanding the Power of Persistence

When my son, E. J., was four years old, our junior-high pastor at Fellowship Church gave him a tattoo at a youth concert. Not that E. J. needed another tattoo. He already had more tattoos than Dennis Rodman: superhero tattoos, action-figure tattoos, sports tattoos. Let me explain something to set the record straight. My wife, Lisa, is not putting the four kids into the Suburban and driving them down to an inner-city tattoo parlor for the real deal. We are talking about fake tattoos, temporary tattoos, the kind you peel off, wet, and stick to your skin. E. J. was crazy about tattoos back then. He called them tattunes.

When he was handed this prized possession at the youth concert, the first words out of E. J.'s mouth were, "Daddy, please put the tattune on now, now, now."

I said, "E. J., I can't do it right now. We're in a concert. I

part 1

promise you once we get home we will put the tattoo on before you go to bed."

"OK, OK, OK."

Thirty minutes later, "The tattune, Dad, the tattune."

"I can't do it now, but I will when we get home."

As we were driving home from the concert, E. J. had an attitude problem. He had a brief altercation with his nine-year-old sister, LeeBeth. Then he made the mistake of talking back to Lisa and me. At that point I interjected a statement that children hate to hear: "Son, because of your behavior, there will be no tattoo tonight."

Hysteria and theatrics followed.

Later, we were saying our bedtime prayers, and E. J. said, "God, please give me the tattune now." The next morning E. J. woke up at six when Lisa and I were still sleeping. He walked to my side of the bed, put his face about three inches from mine, and said, "Daddy, will you please put the tattune on now?"

E. J. did a few semivoluntary acts of service that morning—for example, sharing with the twins—and finally I broke down and gave him the tattoo. He wore it on his left forearm for several days.

My four-year-old son was modeling a characteristic that will be our topic in this chapter: persistence. You see, E. J. was focused; he was relentless. He had a mission, and his mission was to secure that tattune to his forearm.

Nehemiah's Lessons in Persistence

Nehemiah was also focused and relentless in his mission. He had been asked by God to do something that seemed impossible, and at times Nehemiah surely started thinking it was going to be impossible to rebuild the wall around Jerusalem. He met discouragement, he met defeat, and he met danger, yet Nehemiah persisted. We can learn a lot about persistence from this Old Testament man of God.

Think about two or three areas in your life where you need to persist. Could it be that you really need persistence right now in maintaining that marital covenant with your spouse? Or are you in the midst of a serious dating relationship and you need persistence in maintaining sexual purity until marriage? Are you in a business opportunity that requires an extra measure of persistence during uncertain financial times? Are you pursuing a special long-term project at work that is going to take some serious persistence to bring it to successful completion? Maybe you're taking graduate courses at night to help you pursue a new career path and you have to persist against sometimes feeling that you will never get that degree. Do you need the power of persistence in maintaining consistent

part 1

guidelines with your children? Where do you need to be persistent in your life right now?

Nehemiah shows us how to persist by dodging distractions, grounding gossip, and facing fears.

Dodging Distractions

Right up front Nehemiah shows us that if we are going to persist, we have to learn how to dodge distractions. By now the wall Nehemiah was building was almost complete. The workers were planning the ribbon-cutting ceremony, and everything was working beautifully. They were putting the finishing touches on the wall. We see the near completion in Nehemiah 6:1: "When word came to Sanballat, Tobiah, Geshem the Arab and the rest of our enemies that I had rebuilt the wall and not a gap was left in it—though up to that time I had not set the doors in the gates...." The wall was almost done, a defining moment in the life of Nehemiah. But look what happened. Just when everything seemed to be going smoothly again, Nehemiah began to go through a time of temptation, testing, and conflict, a time when his personal security and self-esteem were threatened.

Yes, we have to watch out for temptation when times are tough, but we also have to watch out during the good times, right before we reach the peak, right before we are at the pinnacle of our leadership role at the office, at school, in some relationship, or in the athletic domain. Think about it. When did

Bathsheba cross the gaze of David? When David was number one, when he had never known defeat in any area of his life, *that* is when he looked and lusted and fell.

HDP *Beware of temptations that come on the verge of break-throughs.*

Remember Jonah, the quintessential running man? God said, in effect, "Jonah, go to Nineveh. There are a lot of people who matter to me there and who don't know me. I want you to preach about me to them." Jonah said no, and as a result he had a close encounter with a great fish. But he finally and reluctantly went to Nineveh, and there God used him to bring forth a great spiritual awakening. Over 100,000 people repented and turned to God. Right after that, you would think Jonah would be elated. He'd surely reached the pinnacle of his preaching career. Instead, he entered the moan zone. He had a little pity party.

Before or after a defining moment, or oftentimes after a tremendous victory, Satan loves to get us off our game. He wants to tempt us and distract us. Think about Jesus' time of temptation. It came right after his spiritual high point of being baptized, with the three persons of the Trinity involved. Right after that, Jesus was led by the Spirit into the wilderness and tempted by Satan. For me, the most difficult part of the week is either Sunday evening or Monday. We could be riding the crest

of a wonderful weekend service in which God may have blessed Fellowship Church in a mighty, mighty way, but for some reason in the hours following that high I often feel down.

It helps to expect those distractions and temptations and understand where they're coming from. We have to learn to watch out for those times, just as Nehemiah did. Just as the wall was nearing completion, his distraction arrived in the form of a message: "Sanballat and Geshem sent me this message: 'Come, let us meet together in one of the villages on the plain of Ono'" (6:2). Nehemiah's enemies wanted to sidetrack him, to distract him, to get him involved in this meeting so he would miss doing what he should have been doing.

Do you know people who get trapped in a maze of meetings? They go from one luncheon to the next luncheon, from one breakfast to another, from seminars to conferences to conventions, and they just get lost in the maze of meetings. Many meetings are good, of course, but for the most part, in meetings you talk about what you should be doing. If we *did* what we already *know*, we would be a lot further ahead than we are by going to another meeting or another conference and talking about what we should be doing.

For instance, we all know what it takes to be in great physical shape and what it means to eat properly: no fried foods, very little red meat, lots of vegetables and fruits, work out aerobically four to five times a week for thirty to forty-five minutes, pump some iron, do some push-ups. It's not complicated. But instead of *doing* these things we opt to read another book about dieting or fitness. We buy another Abdominizer. We set up a time to talk to the trainer.

I kind of laugh when people say that spiritual maturity is some mysterious thing way out there, when they think they have to have a special anointing or a special blessing or a particular truth from the Hebrew or the Greek before they can be spiritually mature. Hey, spiritual maturity is simple: Spend time in God's Word, spend time in prayer, get involved in a local church, and begin to serve others in ministry.

It takes discipline to dodge the distractions Satan throws our way, to put into practice what we already know. If we are going to be effective leaders, we have to say no about a hundred times for every yes we agree to.

I challenge you to play a brand-new game every day, whether you are a homemaker, a student, or a businessman or businesswoman. It is called Dodge the Distraction. You dodge the distraction by saying no. Say no to the golf game every now and then. Say no to the hunting trip every once in awhile. Say no to coaching yet another Little League team. Say no to one more ballet recital. In the words of Nancy Reagan, "Just say no." Say no when there is a bigger yes behind the no. One more meeting, one more conference, one more social event, one more responsibility—they will all eat up our time if we don't watch out. If we can say no more often, the things we say yes to will be more rewarding and meaningful.

HDP *Leaders make way for the affirmative by responding in the negative.*

Nehemiah said no to the proposed meeting on the plain of Ono. He knew his enemies were "scheming to harm me" (6:2). How did he know that? To the undiscerning eye, this invitation seemed like a harmless little meeting, but Nehemiah said, in essence, "No, I see the deal; they're scheming to harm me."

Nehemiah was able to dodge distractions because he had something we all need: discernment. Discernment is the God-given ability to read between the lines, to see what is really going on. Discernment helps us cut through the glare of deception, to understand the implications of the situation. Nehemiah said, "They were scheming to harm me; so I sent messengers to them with this reply: 'I am carrying on a great project and cannot go down. Why should the work stop while I leave it and go down to you?' Four times they sent me the same message, and each time I gave them the same answer" (6:2–4). They e-mailed him, they faxed him, they left messages on his voice mail. (I bet Nehemiah's recorder sounded like this: "You've reached the home of Nehemiah. I am not here; I am carrying on a great project right now. If this is Sanballat, Tobiah, or

Geshem, sorry, but there is no chance I am talking with you. If it is someone else, please leave a message after the beep.") Each time they asked, Nehemiah gave them the same answer.

The people who have the best discernment are those who spend time learning about what God says in his Word. They are people who spend quality time on their knees in prayer. And they are also people who communicate and live in community with other brothers and sisters in Christ. Yes, you can have a natural gift of discernment, but if you want that gift to be multiplied exponentially, if you want to be able to dodge distractions—and many times the distractions seem good or harmless—begin to pray and see as God sees. As you begin to read Scripture, everything will change, and you will begin to see distractions for what they truly are.

Grounding Gossip

To be leaders with persistence, we don't just stop with dodging distractions. We also have to ground gossip.

The first five chapters of Nehemiah describe how the opposition went after the group of Jews rebuilding the wall. Next the enemies turned their attention to the leader of the wall builders. They began to get personal with our man Nehemiah.

When I was in college, I drove a horrible car, a Cherokee Chief. This thing had about 120,000 miles on it, and it had

1

more mechanical problems than I care to list. In short, it was not a dream car; it was a nightmare. One morning I got up, walked downstairs in my parents' home, and walked outside. I got in the car and turned the key, but the car wouldn't start. *Oh, man.*

No one was home but me. My father was out of town. Then I had a brilliant idea. I thought, *Oh yeah, Dad's brand-new Lincoln Continental is in the garage.* It had only twenty-seven miles on it. So I stepped into the garage, started Dad's car, and maneuvered it right in front of the Cherokee Chief. I picked up the jumper cables that I always carried in the front seat of the Cherokee. I hooked up the Lincoln's battery, hooked up the Cherokee's battery, then got into the Cherokee and turned the key. The engine turned over, and I goosed it several times. Then, to my horror, looking through the narrow crack between the windshield and the opened hood of the Cherokee, I saw a little fire flare up under the Lincoln's hood. In an instant the jumper cables exploded. And I sat there and watched helplessly as the fire melted those cables right into my father's brand-new car. In my haste to get the car started, I learned a great lesson that day: Remember to properly ground the cables when you are jumping a car. If you don't, you can fry your car and the cables.

The same thing happens in life when a spark of gossip comes along. If we don't properly ground gossip, it can fry us.

Gossip can melt lives, testimonies, marriages, families, careers—the list goes on and on.

HDP *Leaders ground gossip to avoid getting fried.*

In Nehemiah's story, the gossip begins this way: "Then, the fifth time, Sanballat sent his aide to me with the same message, and in his hand was an unsealed letter" (6:5). An unsealed letter was something that Sanballat's aide read aloud from Samaria or Jerusalem. It was not private. If we put it into modern-day language, it might read something like this: "We have been informed by various anonymous sources that you, Nehemiah, are leading a revolt among the Jews. You are rebuilding the wall around Jerusalem in order to set yourself up as king in Judah."

Nehemiah's enemies were putting some serious wind into the blades of the rumor mill. These guys were good. Let's look at the actual text of the letter in verse 6. It begins, "It is reported among the nations." Let me point out the first characteristic of a rumor: The source is never quoted specifically. People who spread rumors often begin by saying something like, "Well, a bunch of people have been coming to me with this, so let me tell you what the problem is." If you inquire who actually said it, they can never identify the source.

We have a policy in our church that criticism from unidentified sources is not to be taken seriously. Most often it comes in the form of unsigned mail with no forwarding name or address on the envelope, or from unidentifiable e-mail. For security issues alone you should not even open mail without a verifiable return address. But security issues aside, if the sources of a rumor are vague and unidentifiable, you cannot verify the validity of the rumor.

The text in verse 6 continues, "—and Geshem says it is true—that you and the Jews are plotting to revolt, and therefore you are building the wall. Moreover, according to these reports you are about to become their king." This brings us to the second characteristic of a rumor: Rumors are usually exaggerated. While there is often some element of truth in a rumor, you can count on the fact that much of it is exaggerated. People love to embellish the truth and add a little color to a story before they share it, so you can count on a rumor to be pretty far removed from the original source—if you can even identify the source. The longer the rumor has been spreading and the more people who have had their hands, or tongues, on it, the further from the truth it likely is.

Paul exhorted one of the early churches to refrain from gossip. In Ephesians 4:29 he wrote, "Do not let any unwholesome talk come out of your mouths, but only what is helpful for building others up according to their needs, that it may benefit those who listen." Here is your challenge: Tape that verse to your telephone. Every time you start to say something, ask yourself, *Is this constructive? Is what I am getting ready to share confidential? Or is it under the heading of prayer-request gossip?* Ask yourself these questions before you say something like, "We really need to pray for Sally. Do you know what she is involved in?"

Sanballat and Geshem wanted Nehemiah to leave the wall and chase down all this extraneous stuff and miss his purpose. But Nehemiah didn't do it. He didn't play that game. He ignored it for the most part, and he responded to them this way: "Nothing like what you are saying is happening; you are just making it up out of your head" (6:8).

The way you deal with a lie is to deal with the liar. All criticism is not bad, folks. Don't ever think that. But when it comes in the form of gossip, when you feel the wind of the rumor mill breezing by you, you had better run from it. Too many of us feed on gossip like a bunch of speckled puppies eating Purina Dog Chow: "Oh, give me some more!" Then we start to play with it, turning the bowl over, kicking the juicy morsels, and spreading it around.

How do you ground gossip? Nehemiah tells us, "But I prayed" (6:9). When you are struck by gossip, you pray. You talk to God like Nehemiah did. He said, "Now strengthen my hands."

HDP *When you are struck by gossip, pray.*

The gossip was straining Nehemiah, no doubt about it. He was a sensitive person, but sensitive or not, gossip hurts everyone. He asked God to strengthen his hand. Notice that Nehemiah got his strength and his security not from man, but from God. If you are always worrying about what this person or this group thinks of you, you are going to be insecure all of your life, thinking, *I have to wear this, join this, live in this, and drive this just to please people.* Nehemiah was not a man pleaser; he was a God pleaser. He saw who he was in the eyes of God. He saw that he mattered to God. He saw that he was one of a kind. And he knew that he didn't have to go along with what the gossipers were saying.

If you are in the family of God, if you know the Lord personally, you can get your security from the three persons of the Trinity. We get our security from God the Father because we are members of his family. We are adopted into his clan for eternity. That is security. We get security from God the Son when we believe that Jesus Christ died on the cross for our sins, shed his precious blood, and rose again. That signifies our worth. Then God the Holy Spirit enters us and works from the inside out to produce supernatural significance in our lives. We have security because of the power that is available to us in this relationship with the Lord. We get our true identity from the Trinity. And the power of that identity strengthens us to ground gossip to avoid getting fried.

Facing Fears

Do you think Nehemiah was fearful while all this gossip was flying? Oh yes, I imagine he was quite fearful. Back at the beginning of his story, he had admitted that he was scared stiff when he had to ask the king to let him go back to J-town and rebuild the wall. So we know there were times when Nehemiah was afraid. But at the same time, we also know Nehemiah was a man of courage. You see, it's entirely possible to be a courageous person and still be fearful. The important thing is that courageous people are willing to face their fears.

One of the fears Nehemiah faced is mentioned this way: "They were all trying to frighten us, thinking, 'Their hands will get too weak for the work, and it will not be completed'" (6:9). Nehemiah was facing some serious opposition at this point, and his enemies were trying to scare him away from finishing the wall.

When we are afraid, our first reaction is to run. We want to leave the marriage or get out of the company. That was what Nehemiah's friend Shemaiah tried to get him to do. Nehemiah wrote, "One day I went to the house of Shemaiah son of Delaiah, the son of Mehetabel, who was shut in at his home. He said, 'Let us meet in the house of God, inside the temple, and let us close the temple doors, because men are coming to kill you—by night they are coming to kill you'" (6:10).

At first glance you might think Shemaiah was trying to protect Nehemiah, but in reality he had sold out to Nehemiah's enemies. He tells Nehemiah to come on over to the temple, that they can hide there and have a prayer service together. But there was something else going on.

In Hebrew the word *temple* in this passage could be rendered "the Holy of Holies." Nehemiah knew that meaning of the word Shemaiah was using. He also understood, from the Book of Deuteronomy, chapters 13 and 18, that God said no one was to enter the Holy of Holies unless he was a priest.

Suddenly, Nehemiah's discernment device went off. He realized, *Shemaiah is messing around with me,* and then he discerned Shemaiah's true intent: "I realized that God had not sent him, but that he had prophesied against me because Tobiah and Sanballat had hired him. He had been hired to intimidate me so that I would commit a sin by doing this, and then they would give me a bad name to discredit me" (6:12–13). Nehemiah didn't even pray about this one. Why? Because he knew that God had already said not to enter the Holy of Holies.

So many of us waste time and energy discussing, seeking counsel, and praying for things that God already has spoken about and decided upon:

HDP *Discerning leaders don't waste energy debating what God has already decided upon.*

"Is it OK to have sex outside of marriage? We really do love each other." That is a no-brainer. God has already said we are to abstain from sex until we are married.

142

"I wonder if homosexuality is OK. You know, this is the twenty-first century." God has already said that homosexuality is a sin.

"I wonder if adultery is wrong." God has already made it glaringly clear that adultery is wrong.

"I wonder if I can just cheat Uncle Sam out of a little money. The government is so messed up anyway; surely God won't mind." God has already told us we are to pay taxes to whom taxes are due. Cheating is a sin before God no matter how you slice it or dice it.

We waste time debating issues that God has already explicitly addressed in his Word. But Nehemiah didn't waste time; he just said, "No, I will not go."

Persistence Pays Off

The result of Nehemiah's persistence is this simple statement: "So the wall was completed on the twenty-fifth of Elul, in fifty-two days" (6:15). Just think: In less than two months, Nehemiah, in ancient Israel, had completed the construction of a wall two and a half miles long that protected Jerusalem against depression, famine, and danger. Unbelievable!

As I write this book, Fellowship Church is in the last stages of a building program to construct an educational facility for our children. In twenty-first-century America, with the benefits of modern engineering and construction practices and equipment, it took us more than a year to complete the construction of this ninety-thousand-square-foot building. Actually, I thought that was a remarkable feat, but it doesn't compare with what Nehemiah did in sixth-century-B.C. Jerusalem with a ragtag bunch of Israelites on a mission from God.

While I sincerely believe God was involved in our building program, I have to believe that he was at work in a mighty and miraculous way during the building of that wall of protection around Jerusalem. Even the enemies of Israel understood the power of God at work in this endeavor. Nehemiah wrote, "When all our enemies heard about this, all the surrounding nations were afraid and lost their self-confidence, because they realized that this work had been done with the help of our God" (6:16). Once again, Nehemiah was saying the project had been a God thing. God orchestrated it. God designed it. It was his mission. And Nehemiah had asked God for the strength to persist in carrying it out.

Contrast Nehemiah's humble stance with the proud stance of King Nebuchadnezzar over his accomplishments: "As the king was walking on the roof of the royal palace of Babylon, he said, 'Is not this the great Babylon I have built as the royal residence, by my mighty power and for the glory of my majesty?'" (Dan. 4:29–30). God must have chuckled when he saw King Neb stroking his own crown. God told him, in essence, "Because of your ego trip, because you think you did it, because you think you were the catalyst, you, in a very short time, will be out in the fields eating grass with the cows." And sure enough, if you read on in Daniel 4, you find Nebuchadnezzar out there in the field grazing with the animals.

The problem in our lives is that we are great contortionists. When we've persisted through a great challenge, when we've overcome long odds, we sometimes forget where our strength to persevere came from. We get this freaky desire to praise ourselves, and we contort our egos so we can pat ourselves on the back and say, "It's my project. I'm so great. I'm incredible." But then we suffer the same pride problem as Nebuchadnezzar, and it's just a matter of time before we lose it all. We look back on the persistence we showed and we can claim the credit for it, or we can acknowledge the truth and say, "It is by God's mercy and God's mighty power that I am here and am able to accomplish anything at all."

In his persistence, in the way he dodged distractions, grounded gossip, and faced his fears, Nehemiah foreshadowed the life of Jesus. When Jesus was hanging on the cross, dying for your sins and mine, the people around him scoffed, in effect, "Look at him. He's trying to save everybody else but he can't even save himself. He can't even jump down off the cross." Jesus wasn't distracted from his mission by their taunts. He didn't save himself; instead, he persisted in the purpose he had come for: to save you and me.

Similarly, Nehemiah's enemies said, "Nehemiah, come down off the wall. Nehemiah, go to Ono. Nehemiah, what about this rumor? Nehemiah, go to the Holy of Holies." But Nehemiah persisted with dogged determination to accomplish his God-given mission. He said, "No, my purpose is greater. This is God's agenda for me." If Nehemiah had left the wall, he would have missed God's best for his life.

What is causing you to want to leave the wall? Are you ready to jump offtrack when distractions come your way? Do your legs start to falter when you feel the sting of gossip? Are you tempted to cower in fear, unable to persist in your mission, because of the opposition?

It is my prayer for your life and mine that we turn to God daily for the strength to persist on the wall of godly leadership. God has placed you at a certain point on the wall, entrusting that section to your care. Persist in your mission, so that he can accomplish great things in your life and help you make a high-definition impact for him right where you are.

part two

Becoming an HD CEO

Creativity. Enthusiasm. Organization. Do you see the acrostic? CEO. Simply put, these three qualities will enable you to become a CEO in God's economy, a leader in a big corporation, at home, at church, or in school, as you set an example for his glory and praise wherever you are. Creativity, enthusiasm, and organization are the basic building blocks of a high-definition life. They are the foundational characteristics through which godly leaders impact people and events in a positive way. If you possess these qualities, you will demonstrate, from the inside out, that you really want to make a difference in this life. You will be able to inspire others to turn the mundane into the meaningful, apathy into excitement, and chaos into order.

Embrace these fundamental character qualities, make them a fundamental part of who you are no matter where you are, and you will succeed in being a Nehemiah in the world around you. In these next three chapters, I'll help you see how it's done.

HDP
high-definition principles

Working Out the Creative Cramps

- Denying our creativity denies the gifts of our creative God.

- Every personality type was created for innovation and creativity.

- Innovative leaders communicate God's unchanging truth in culturally compelling ways.

- Modeling the teaching style of Jesus means being visual, creative, and contemporary.

- A little confusion in your life will generate creativity.

- Wise leaders know that if you don't invest in your relationships *now*, you'll pay later.

- Leaders who grow creatively, grow spiritually.

- Strap creativity to a strong work ethic and watch what happens.

- Godly leaders catch their vision vertically from God.

- Use your failures as springboards for future successes.

chapter
8

a creative foundation

Working Out the Creative Cramps

Do you ever feel that you go through the same ritual, regimen, and routine day after day, week after week, and month after month? You wake up, take a shower, go to work, have lunch, work some more, go home, eat dinner, watch television, and go to bed. The next day, you wake up, take a shower, go to work, have lunch, work some more, go home, eat dinner, watch television, and go to bed. And, if you're staying home with children, your routine may go like this: wake up, kids, kids, kids, kids, take a shower, kids, kids, kids, lunch, kids, kids, kids, kids, kids, dinner, kids, kids, kids, and collapse (maybe while watching TV).

The net effect of this monotonous schedule is that scores of us feel like we are sleepwalking through life, wondering why we're missing out on vitality and excitement. Such monotony causes us to say things like, "My marriage is in a rut, my career is boring, my surroundings are predictable, and my relationship with Christ is rather routine." You look at your life and know you need to make some changes, but you can't quite put your finger on exactly what is missing, what you are lacking.

Conventional wisdom looks for conventional answers. Sometimes you may think your problem is relational: If you were only married to the right person, with the right look, and the right bank account, things would be different. Or you may think your problem is occupational: If only you had that job with the right company that let you wield the right kind of power, then you would know what you are all about. Or perhaps your problem is geographical: If you lived in the right city, in the right state, or in the right resort or retirement community, then you would have a spring in your step and a twinkle in your eye. Some of us even throw up our hands and say to God, "Well, it must be spiritual. If I came from the right family, if I'd just gotten the right Christian background, if I had the right kind of Bible knowledge, then I would have purpose and a true agenda for my existence."

If you feel this way, you're certainly not enjoying high-definition living! If your life is lacking luster, it's doubtful that you're being the best leader you can be to those around you. If you're bored with life, you could be neglecting one of the most important characteristics in the universe: creativity.

You've Got It—Now Use It

Several years ago I walked into a dingy gym to watch one of the nation's top-ranked high-school basketball teams play. I was enthralled by the skill of the athletes. Flying through the air with lay-ups and slam dunks and shooting three pointers, this team was as good as many of the professional teams I'd observed. But as good as they were, the players were not what held my attention. The cheerleaders definitely stole the show. What caught my attention most was a cheer they repeated over and over again: "You've got it—now use it! You've got it—now use it!"

When I think of creativity, I truly believe that God is chanting that same cheer in our ears. I believe the God of the universe is saying, "You've got it—now use it! You've got it—now use it!" But many of us respond to God's encouragement with a barrage of excuses. I have given him those excuses, and so have you: "Creativity—I don't have it, so I can't use it. Come on, God, I'm not creative. I've never had an original thought in my life. I'm not innovative. I'm not a leader, a polished speaker, or an inspirationally creative writer. Seriously. I don't have a creative bone in my body, God. I can't draw, act, sing, or dance. I'm just an average person doing time on this planet."

 Denying our creativity denies the gifts of our creative God.

Those excuses ring hollow to the ears of our creative God,

because the truth is that everyone can be creative; everyone can be innovative. Sadly, though, many Christians are missing the boat when it comes to creativity. They have lost their luster, because they are neglecting this vital spark in their lives: creativity. Bureaucracies kill it, systems stifle it, schools rarely encourage it, and churches don't discuss it. But you've got it. God gave it to you. You just need to learn how to use it.

Riding the Crest of Creativity

God does not want us to live in a prison of boredom where we are just doing time. So he gave us the gift of creativity. Just watch a bunch of kids, and you'll see creativity at work (or, rather, at play). Watch them naturally use their imaginations and their creativity as they frolic and interact with each other.

Several years ago in the Young household, our four children used our hearth as a stage for the first-annual Young Family Beauty Pageant. Our daughter was ten at the time, our son was five, and our twin daughters were two, and one by one they walked across the hearth and turned around, while one of the others announced what the "contestant" was doing or wearing. Believe it or not, we had four winners. Talk about creativity! One by one they draped a blanket around their shoulders, took turns wearing my wife's old Miss Sports-o-rama crown on their heads, and strutted back across the hearth as the rest of us sang, "There she is..." (or "There he is...").

Creativity is hard-wired into us from childhood. Sadly, though, somewhere along life's journey, most of us get a creative cramp. For some of us the creative cramp struck when we were still very young. We traded dreaming for dogma, the artistic for the analytical, and our imaginations for memorization. I believe this cramped creativity saddens the heart of God, because he cannot stand the thought of his people living regimented, routine, same-ol', same-ol' lives.

That is why God commands us to be creative. I love the J. B. Phillips paraphrase of Romans 12:2: "Don't let the world around you squeeze you into its own mould." In other words, God wants us to stand out from the pack, to ride the crest of creativity as one who is intimately connected to the Author of creativity. But too many of us are content to splash around in the shallows of sameness. We tell ourselves we could never ride that creative wave, because we might fall off. We might feel silly or look foolish; we might even get hurt.

Don't be scared to try new things; don't cower in front of creativity. It won't turn you into something you're not. You can implement creativity and innovation right where you are, no matter what you do or what your personality is.

HDP *Every personality type was created for innovation and creativity.*

part 2

153

Charting a Radical New Course

Several years ago, a generous friend of mine flew me out to Las Vegas to see Mike Tyson face Evander Holyfield for the world heavyweight championship. As we killed time walking around the city together, I couldn't help but notice all the signs. They were everywhere: big signs, little signs, blinking signs, flashing signs, neon signs, moving signs—even talking signs. It was completely dazzling. I thought, *Well, they don't have a lot to say, but they definitely know how to say it.*

It's just the opposite with Christians. We have everything to say, but we don't always know how to say it in the most creative ways. We fail to communicate God's truth in both a biblically based and culturally compelling way. Consequently, many people view Christianity as a dry, stodgy, yawn-filled religion. And too many Christians, even church leaders, are just droning through life—doing the same thing the same way and expecting a unique result. Too many young people are watching these boring church leaders and seminarians and thinking, *If that's what being a Christian leader is all about, then no thanks.*

In 1989 I moved to the Dallas-Fort Worth area to begin a church. I had always told my friends I would never start a church in DFW—after all, there were already so many—but in 1989 I felt a direct leading to go there. We started with 150 people and from there found a core group who shared the same vision: to never compromise God's unchanging truth while communicating it in a culturally compelling way.

IDP *Innovative leaders communicate God's unchanging truth in culturally compelling ways.*

As we reached out to those around us in creative ways, people we never dreamed of reaching began attending our services. And today we have more than sixteen thousand people in regular weekend attendance.

I wholeheartedly believe that, more than any other group of people, creativity should be at its best among those who are most intimately connected with the Creator. Imagine how many people we could reach for Christ if every Christian seriously considered this question: How can I claim to be connected to an innovative God—and be so boring?

Following God's Creative Lead

Creativity isn't just something I'm encouraging you to nurture in yourself because it would make the world a more interesting place and church a less boring experience. Creativity is God's idea. He invented it. Just look at the first sentence in the Bible: "In the beginning God created..." God started this whole process. He thought it up. He initiated it from the very beginning and has been creating ever since. Creativity is part of his very nature. And guess what: God created us in his own image. So if it's in him, it's in us too.

Besides that fact, the Bible tells us in Ephesians 5:1, "Be imitators of God." It doesn't say we're to imitate God in everything except creativity. There are no escape clauses. It commands us to be imitators of God. The word *imitate* means that we are to mimic God. Every time we say we're not creative, we mock God's creative genius.

Jesus provided us with the perfect role model for creativity in leadership. For example, the Bible says in Matthew 13:34, "he did not say anything to them without using a parable." He was always changing his approach, depending on who was listening and what those listeners needed. Jesus spoke from hillsides, boat bows, and beaches. He drew in the sand, turned over tables, and put a child in his lap. He used word pictures and illustrations. He said, "See the sower there scattering seed …See this child…See the key and the lock…See the ground… See the water…See the bread…See the coin." Each time his technique was unique, different, and creative. Everything Jesus taught was visual, everything was creative, and everything was contemporary.

HDP *Modeling the teaching style of Jesus means being visual, creative, and contemporary.*

It's so easy and so tempting to fall into sameness, to ignore

Christ's example and do the same thing week after week until we grow tired of it—and then we keep doing it anyway. It's no wonder so many of us give the impression that the Christian life is boring. We need creativity—not just in ourselves but in others. We yearn for it. We have a capacity for creativity, and we are drawn to creative things. But being boring is oftentimes easier.

Have you thought about the creative process by which God wrote the Scriptures through forty different inspired authors? And how about the innovative ways God talked to and dealt with the great characters in the Bible? He used a piece of fruit to communicate with Adam and Eve. He used the knife to communicate with Abraham. He used salt to communicate with Lot. He used a whale to communicate with Jonah. He used a sling to communicate with David. And, ultimately, he used a cross to communicate his unfathomable, amazing grace to the world.

The Confusion Principle of Creativity

A friend of mine is a personal trainer, and I work out with him on a regular basis at a local gym. A few years ago, when we began working out together, he asked me what I was doing for my workout. I described to him all the different routines I did, from weight training to cardiovascular exercise. Then he asked how long I had been doing the same workout, and I told him about a year. He warned me that if I stayed with the same workout for a long time, I would not make any gains in the strength area or the cardiovascular area. He taught me the confusion principle. He said people who exercise need to change their workout every four weeks so they confuse their muscles. When that happens they experience an increase in strength.

We need to apply and instill this same confusion principle in our daily lives. Confuse your spouse. Confuse your children. Confuse your boss. The confusion principle is a gateway to creativity. Change up your daily routine from time to time. Drive a different way to work. Do something creative with your spouse on your next date night. Spend creative brainstorming time with your kids and find some new games to play. Maybe change your attire a little bit by picking out a fun outfit that is a fashion departure for you. Rearrange your office at work every once in awhile. Go out of your way to speak to people at work or church that you have not had much contact with in the past. Learn new ways to say things, especially relating to your faith in Christ and how you share it with others. You won't believe what will happen, because—I'm not talking about radical stuff now—small tweaks will take you to giant peaks.

HDP *A little confusion in your life will generate creativity.*

Creativity Working

We need creativity in every part of life—especially in our relationships, at work, and in our spiritual walk.

Creativity in Our Relationships

God is a creative, relational God, and we are made in his image. So he intends us to be creative in our relationships. Let's start with marriage. A lot of us married couples were creative when we were dating. Some of us were *really* creative—and innovative. We kept the person we were dating on his or her toes, never knowing what to expect next.

Then, after we walked down the aisle, returned from the honeymoon cruise, and began to live life on the rugged plains of reality, most of us husbands and wives got that creative cramp. We decided we couldn't be creative anymore. It was too much bother. We sat back on the sofa and channel surfed through ESPN, the news channels, and the made-for-television movies while we stuffed our faces with Doritos and whined, "I used to be creative. But I have this cramp. I'm injured now—on the disabled list. I can't be creative anymore."

Well, God wants us to stretch out that cramp. God says wherever we are in our marriage, we are just beginning the creative process. That is why I encourage spouses to continue to romance and to date each other. At lease twice a month you and your spouse should go somewhere to spend time alone together. And make that time creative. Don't just go to a movie and come home. That's boring. And as Christians we should be all about creativity.

Recently I conducted an informal poll among husbands and

159

wives. I asked wives, "In what area do you wish your husband would really show his creativity?"

They told me, "I want him to be more creative in the intimacy and romantic realm. I want him to be more creative in conversation. I want him to be emotionally tied in with me." And I have to agree, we men need to work on that. Every one of us men would probably say, "Yes, I think I could do a better job in these areas."

A little planning and work can go a long way in showing your wife that you are interested in keeping your relationship fresh and dynamic. How about planning a special weekend away just for romance and intimacy? But creativity can also mean inviting your wife to take a long walk with you or to go out for coffee with the express purpose of having an uninterrupted time to share what's going on in each other's life.

Next, I asked the men this question: "In what area do you wish your wives would be more creative?" Here is what the men said, using the one-word answer typical of all men: "sex."

This is not an encouragement to do anything deviant or pornographic. However, without going into details, sex does not have to be experienced the same way every time. Creativity in sex should include being spontaneous, changing your bedroom attire to entice your mate, and sacrificing your needs from time to time so you can focus on meeting your spouse's needs.

While creativity in sex seemed to be the number one response from the men in my informal survey, let me assure you that men appreciate other types of creativity too. I have to give my wife, Lisa, a high-five for a creative idea she had recently. She called me at work and told me we were going to do something special that night for our date night. I told her I would be looking forward to it, whatever it was. I got fired up. She told me to stand outside my office, and she would pick me up. I thought that was pretty cool. So, late that afternoon I stood out there, she drove up in our truck, and I jumped in. We were going somewhere special.

As we drove away I looked around and saw a picnic basket in the back of the truck. I thought it was kind of interesting to be going on a picnic when the sun was going down. Then we drove to a little lake in Irving and Lisa took a coupon out of her wallet. She had arranged to rent a little boat from the marina! We got into the boat, she motored us out to the middle of the lake, and we had a picnic dinner out on the water just as the sun was setting. Now that was creative!

People try all the time to give weak excuses about why they can't be creative in their marriage. For instance, they say that it takes too much money to be creative. Our little creative date on the lake cost us just a few dollars for the boat rental plus a babysitter. You don't have to have a lot of money to be creative. In fact, a lack of money often forces you to be more creative

part 2

and innovative. Let me also suggest something else here. Even if you have to borrow money from time to time to have a creative date (maybe a weekend away), it is worth it. Make the investment now in that relationship or you will pay for it later—in heartache, in regret, or for some, tragically, in divorce lawyers. Don't make excuses; make love by creatively romancing your spouse.

HDP *Wise leaders know that if you don't invest in your relationships now, you'll pay later.*

While creativity in our marriages is ultra-important, we also need to be creative relationally with our children. Talk about something that will stretch your creativity! Each of our children is different, and Lisa and I often see our own personality traits showing up in our children. This was especially obvious one morning before church when we had a pancake breakfast. Our youngest daughters, Laurie and Landra, are twins, but they have very different personalities. Landra is like me. She is loud and wild and eats like a shark in a feeding frenzy. As soon as the pancakes landed in front of her, she had syrup everywhere, in her hair, dripping down her fingers. Laurie, on the other hand, will not even touch syrup. She eats just the plain pancakes. Pray for my creativity as I try to rear these twins!

While children are naturally creative, I don't think they're as creative these days as they once were. Too many children are allowed to park themselves in front of the video screens for noncreative zombie time. Rather than reading books and using their imaginations, they spend countless hours watching television, most of which is not appropriate for them. The other day I asked a little boy if he had noticed how cold it had gotten, and he replied that he hadn't been outside in three years. I'm kidding, but you get the point. When I was a kid I would come home and say, "Hello, Mom, I'm home," and Mom would answer, "OK, Ed, now go outside and play." And off I'd go, spending the rest of the afternoon in creative play, making up my own creative games.

If you're a parent, make sure you have a creative box in your house with crayons and markers and paper and safety scissors, and let your kids go at it. Show them things about God's creation and creativity. Pay attention to the change of seasons and the great diversity of nature. So many parents are such neat freaks that they inhibit the creative potential in their kids. They're afraid someone might spill something on the floor or make a mess in the living room. Now, I am all for keeping a neat house, but if you want to build a creative climate, you've got to let kids be kids. I don't mean they have to paint on the walls, but you have to be flexible. Create an area in your home where they can be free to play creatively without your having to worry that they'll lower the resale value of your home.

And before you buy your child a toy, ask yourself this question: Can he or she do more than one thing with this toy? Steer clear of toys that are meant to perform while the child sits back and watches. Find playthings that foster your child's creativity.

Get involved in projects with them. Help them start little businesses appropriate to their age and abilities so they grow into creative thinkers and well-rounded people. One day we are going to be held accountable for our creativity and how we helped and inspired creativity in others, especially our own children.

Creativity at Work

We also need to be creative vocationally. I'm not just referring to the so-called "creative professions." Creativity is needed by workers in every job and occupation, from secretaries to professional athletes, from real-estate tycoons to people who work in oil and gas. What are you doing in the creative aspects of your career, in the job that consumes so many of your waking hours? What are you doing to bring some vitality to your daily routine? You have to create different ways of doing things if you want to experience growth.

Spiritual Creativity

We also need creativity in another area. We need it spiritually, don't we? Use the confusion principle in your time of prayer and Bible reading. Do things a different way every now and then.

Sometimes in my prayer time I sing to God. Sometimes I write out my prayers in my journal. Sometimes I have my time with God in the office, other times at home, other times while I am driving. Change your time with God. Make it different. Make it unique. You will grow spiritually when you begin to be creative.

HDP *Leaders who grow creatively, grow spiritually.*

I think the most creative place in the world should be the church, and at Fellowship Church we work hard to meet that goal. In fact, our church has received national attention because of our creativity. That is great, but it also saddens my heart. It should not be unique or newsworthy that a church is creative. Every church should be creative.

What should be out of the ordinary is a church that is boring. But I don't think I'm exaggerating by saying the majority of churches out there are boring. And don't ever blame the Bible or God for a church that's boring. Blame the people who are communicating the message and the people who are leading the church.

Church leaders and churchgoers have got to be creative. We serve a creative God. And when we know him personally and are open to him, we should be the most creative people in the world. Christians should be writing best-selling books on

part 2

creativity and excellence, because we are connected with the ultimate source of creativity.

Five Steps to Get Your Creativity Going

We've talked about when and where you should be creative (all the time and everywhere), and now I'd like to share some tips on how you can get started. How can you be creative right now? Here are five steps you can take to get your creativity going.

1. Pray High-Octane Prayers

I didn't realize how often I prayed for creativity until several years ago when I was looking through the entries in the prayer journal I've kept since I was seventeen years old. As I turned the pages, I found prayer after prayer asking God to give me creative energy and ideas. I believe God's answers to those prayers have been very specific because my prayers were focused specifically on creativity. I asked God to help me be creative as I communicated his message, and God has never failed me.

He will enhance your creativity, too, if you pray for it. I challenge you to pray a high-octane prayer like this: "Father, I want to implement what you have already given me. I know I've got it. I've seen that from the words of Scripture, from the theology of creativity. God, please help me to unleash it now. Show me what to do." Begin to ask God regularly for the supernatural power of creativity, then be ready for the answer to blow you away. Watch for creative people God brings into your life. Rub shoulders with creative people to warm up your own creative abilities. I hang out a lot with creative difference makers. We bounce ideas off each other in think tanks and team meetings over and over again. The more you are around creative people, the more creative you will become.

At Fellowship Church I have intentionally hired a diverse group of people who have creative abilities that are different from my own. These folks are hard workers and risktakers who challenge my own creativity and help me learn and grow as we work together.

2. Go through Creative Labor and Delivery

Creation is like a birth. You have conception, you have pregnancy, and then you have labor and delivery. The problem is that so many creative ideas never make it past conception because they are never put into action. As any woman with children can relate, labor and delivery are not easy, but the result is worth the struggle. To bring creative ideas from conception to birth, we may have to go through some difficult times. We may have to struggle. But the result will be worth the work.

God wants us to use our creativity to make an impact in the real world, but it takes work and sometimes involves pain. Many of us conceive unique, creative ideas, but then we stop when we see the painstaking work that lies ahead. Sometimes it involves old-fashioned, roll-up-your-sleeves, dirt-under-your-fingernails, perspiration-everywhere, seeing-an-idea-through type of work. And that can be scary when you're just beginning to make a go of an idea. But the difference in the successful creative person and the frustrated creative person is the ability and the determination to take creative thoughts and bring them to life.

What if God, who had the most creative idea of all time—sending Jesus Christ to die on the cross to pay for our sin problem—had stopped at the conception stage? But God didn't stop, so don't you stop. Jesus lived an earthly life marked by ridicule and insult. Then he died on the cross, and now you and I can be born again because of that action. The struggle was worth the result.

People praise the members of the music and creative staff at our church as creative geniuses. And I agree that God has blessed us by giving us these talented folks. But their talent and creative ideas are just half the picture. Many, many people have creative ideas. Our staff members stand out because they also have an amazing work ethic. It takes hours and hours and hours for our creative staff to put together all the music, the drama, the lights, and the other elements involved in our worship services. But these people are not afraid of work. Nothing we do is as demanding as creativity. Nothing. Strap your creativity to a strong work ethic with commitment to see it through. Then rev up the engine of enthusiasm and watch what happens.

HDP *Strap creativity to a strong work ethic and watch what happens.*

3. Maintain a Vertical Vision

Growing up as a pastor's son, serving on a church staff, and then planting a church, I've seen the ministry from many different angles. And throughout the years, I've found that godly leaders catch their vision vertically from God. When they start applying this vision in a creative and innovative manner, people are reached for the glory of God. No matter where you are in life, this principle applies. Whether you're a businessperson, a father, a mother, a pastor, a teacher, a lawyer, or an artist, you must catch and maintain that creative vision for your life from the creative hand of God. Anyone can be creative from a limited human perspective, but when you get your creative vision vertically from God, the impact of your work will be lasting and fulfilling.

Sometimes you find yourself surrounded by negative people—powerbrokers and naysayers—who insult you, insisting you change your approach and message. But if you give in to them, you move from getting your vision vertically to getting your vision horizontally. And once that happens, you're in serious trouble. If you have a vertical vision from God for your life, your work, your family, and your ministry, let nothing dissuade you.

HDP *Godly leaders catch their vision vertically from God.*

4. Build in Creativity Time

What gets your creative juices going? For me, it's connecting with creative people. Or sitting in a coffee shop with a legal pad and the Bible, just writing. Sometimes it's driving in my truck and listening to good, cutting-edge music. These activities seem to unlock creative thoughts in me.

Creativity often happens at unexpected times and places, when we are out of our usual element. When you change your normal environment and get a different perspective, creative thoughts have fresh, fertile soil in which to grow. In your family and in your work, are you building in time for creativity? During every staff meeting at the church, we push back and say, "OK, now let's take some time to think creative thoughts." Then we brainstorm and discuss whatever ideas come up. Sometimes they're great; sometimes they're not so great. But we write down every thought and then air it out with each other.

To be creative we need to do things out of the ordinary from time to time, maybe even activities that are a little strange; doing something different follows the confusion principle. It gets us out of our comfort zone. When we're doing something different, thinking about something different, then the innovative ideas are most likely to occur.

5. Learn from Failure

You will have progress when you pray high-octane prayers for creativity, when you go through labor and delivery of your creative ideas, when you maintain your vertical vision, and when you build in creativity time. And you'll know you're making progress when your ideas are born and you see how they have changed the company or the church or the marriage relationship or the parent-child bond. Then you'll say, "Way to go! Thank you, God."

There's just one other thing you need to know about the steps toward creativity: You're going to fail. From time to time you're going to mess up, wipe out, go down in flames. It may not be pretty. But it's just part of the process. The important thing is not how hard you fall but how quickly you get back up. Use your failures as positive springboards for future successes.

HDP *Use your failures as springboards for future successes.*

We have had some failures at Fellowship Church, some dumb ideas. One of our most spectacular failures happened when we tried to do simultaneous services. This was when we were still in rented facilities. We had one service going on in

part 2

the auditorium of the Irving Arts Center and another in a smaller theater across the parking lot. I was supposed to speak at one service while, in the other building, the music team was leading the praise-and-worship program. Then we would switch places. I would run across the way and preach in the other auditorium after the music was finished there, and the music team would rush past me to the auditorium I had just left to follow up the message I just preached. It was a dumb idea because it couldn't possibly work. But it was also a great idea because it taught us a lot. You learn when you fail, and you learn when you succeed. Don't be afraid of failure. Get back up and try something else.

When we change our lives, we don't always like it, do we? Change often produces conflict, but if we stay with the change, analyze the conflict, and work through it in love, change can produce growth.

Isn't It about Time?

Just think of what our Lord can do when he takes your unique, creative potential, enhances it, and unleashes it for his glory. How about it? Isn't it time for you to give God your creativity and ask him to use it in incredible, life-changing ways? Go ahead. Ask. Pray to him, "Lord, make me into the creative creature you created me to be."

HDP
high-definition principles

Quashing Enthusiasm Spasms

- Trust is the antidote for worry, stress, and fear.
- When we forget who we are, we forfeit enthusiasm.
- Enthusiasm is a choice.
- Enthusiasm not only motivates other people, it moves the heart of God.

chapter 9

an enthusiastic outlook

Quashing Enthusiasm Spasms

You can see enthusiasm all over the person who has it: the zest, the zeal, the intensity. I believe what we need right now to live high-definition lives is an infusion of outrageous, contagious enthusiasm.

Enthusiasm is a fascinating emotion that is difficult to explain yet simplistic to see. Enthusiasm has the ability to move us from the background into the foreground and from the plain into the passionate. Enthusiasm can lift us from flatness to elation and turn our indifference into excitement.

I am not talking about some sickeningly sweet, syrupy, conjured-up type of feel-good emotion. I am talking about true, authentic enthusiasm. When it comes to real enthusiasm, the eyes have it. All you have to do is make eye contact with someone, and you can tell if he or she has enthusiasm. In contrast there are those perpetually disinterested people whose epitaph could be, "Died at thirty-five, buried at seventy-five."

2

part

In this chapter I want to talk to you not only about the *eyes* of enthusiasm but also about the *I's*—the capital I's—of enthusiasm. I want to show you how making "I contact" with enthusiasm can change the trajectory of your life when you understand that enthusiasm is intentional and inspirational.

Enthusiasm Is Intentional

One winter morning I made my regular trek to Starbucks, and while I was standing in line I overheard a woman talking to one of the workers. She said something like this: "Can you believe this weather? It's horrible. I hate the ice, and the snow makes me sick. The kids get colds, and I just despise it."

The more the woman talked, the more her harangue about the weather brought me down. I began to buy in to her negativity. I started thinking, *You know, this weather really* is *kind of bad. We have to wear gloves and coats and hats. What a drag.* I got my order (a tall coffee with room for cream), jumped in my truck, and headed to work.

The first person I saw at the office was our chief of staff, Preston Mitchell. I said, "Preston, how are you doing today?"

He responded, "I'm great! I am so excited. It's snowing. I love the snow and the change of seasons. My kids love it. My wife loves it. I love it, Ed. I just love this weather." Suddenly the day seemed brighter and my mood seemed lighter.

What was going on in this scenario? The lady at Starbucks

chose not to be enthusiastic, and her dour attitude had rubbed off on me. Conversely, Preston chose to be enthusiastic—he made an intentional choice—and his enthusiasm spoke to me in a great way.

In the last chapter, we looked at creativity and how to overcome an occasional creative cramp. Most of us also occasionally experience what I call enthusiasm spasms, situations and emotions that threaten to tyrannize and paralyze our lives. Enthusiasm spasms come in three basic forms—worry, stress, and fear—but by being intentionally enthusiastic we can overcome these spasms.

Worry Spasms

Worry is an inordinate amount of concern about something that may or may not happen. All of us worry from time to time. Over many years of observing worry in my life and the lives of others, I have come to the startling conclusion that most of the junk we worry about never happens anyway. I suspect you've come to the same conclusion. Yet I've also found that, despite this startling realization, many of us still persist in our worried state of mind.

A few years ago I made the mistake of carrying around a car battery in the back of my Suburban. One day, some battery acid spilled on the carpet. It immediately began to discolor the carpet, so I ran and got a towel and cleaned up the acid spill. I thought I had taken care of the problem—but I was wrong. Over the next few days, I watched in horror as the battery acid ate a Grand Canyon–sized hole in the carpet of my Suburban.

Worry is like acid. It will eat our enthusiasm alive and cause us to have enthusiasm spasms. Jesus said, "Who of you by worrying can add a single hour to his life?" (Matt. 6:27). The irony of Jesus' words is that the accumulated toll of continual worry may actually subtract hours from our lives.

Are you familiar with the enthusiasm spasm of worry? I admit that I tend to be a worrier, and I have learned over the years that my worry grieves the heart of God because it communicates a lack of trust in him. And I know that if I persist in worrying, it can bring on stress, the next enthusiasm spasm, which has the potential to cause even greater mental, emotional, and physical harm. It's enough to make me worry about worrying!

I'm kidding, yet I know what a challenge it can be to do as the bumper sticker advises: "Let go and let God." Worry can eat away at our lives. So we need to consciously rid ourselves of worry and trust God to know what's best for us.

Stress Spasms

I define stress as worry on steroids. It's intense strain about something that seems out of our control in our lives. The

Occupational Safety and Health Administration (OSHA) estimates that stress on the American work force costs our country one hundred billion dollars a year. Stress causes accidents, mental breakdowns, and angry encounters that disrupt work and productivity. It can lead to certain physical and psychological problems that require intensive therapy, medical treatment, and drug intervention. Stress breaks up marriages and friendships. It pulls apart business partnerships and causes people to pull the trigger on freeways. It has even found its way into the church and has the potential to undermine the ministry of both pastors and lay leaders.

The apostle Paul wrote this advice about the stressful spasms that plague many of us today: "Do not be anxious about anything, but in everything, by prayer and petition, with thanksgiving, present your requests to God" (Phil. 4:6). The word *anxious* in this verse literally means "to choke, to strangle, to pull in different directions." Do you ever feel like that in your marriage, with your children, in a dating relationship, or in your business or career—choked, strangled, pulled in different directions?

Anxiety and stress have the ability to choke the enthusiasm right out of you. And continued stress, which often follows from intense and prolonged worry, can lead to another enthusiasm spasm: fear.

part 2

part 2

Fear Spasms

The three greatest fears we have to deal with are the fears of death, loneliness, and failure. Prolonged stress and anxiety in our lives can lead us to live with constant, debilitating fear.

The fact is, we come into contact with fear on a daily basis, and the way we deal with it determines the control it has over our lives. Psychologists have catalogued hundreds of different categories of fear, and the list is still growing. Many, many people today live in constant fear of danger or that something devastating and beyond their control will happen. Our society is also bulging with people who live in loneliness because they are terrified of the prospect of developing new relationships. Others have never taken a risk in their lives out of an intense fear of failing and making fools of themselves. These and many other fears paralyze people and hold them back from experiencing the kind of freedom God intends for them to have as his children.

When I was a child, I was fearful of someone called the "little man." I would walk through our large house, peer around the corner, and scream at the top of my lungs, "Mom! Mom! The little man! I saw him. He's following me."

My mother would come running, then she would assure me there was nothing there. And I would say, "Well, I thought there was a little man following me." This went on for months and months, years actually. I would get my little brother to go upstairs first to check out where we slept and make sure the little man wasn't there. Then, assured that all was safe, I would go up the stairs.

One particular day when I screamed and my mother once again came running, I pointed to the closet, the door of which was mysteriously cracked open. She went over to the closet, opened it, and to my embarrassment revealed the dreaded object that had cast the terrifying shadow I'd seen lurking behind the door: the vacuum cleaner.

Obviously, my childhood fear was unfounded; so are many of the fears we deal with day in and day out as adults. The Bible says in Proverbs 29:25, "Fear of man will prove to be a snare, but whoever trusts in the LORD is kept safe."

If you really take a hard look at the effects of these enthusiasm spasms, worry, stress, and fear, they have caused a large group of people to become Blaming Boomers. Rather than trusting God, Blaming Boomers blame their parents, the government, organized religion, and anyone else they can think of for causing all of the worry, stress, and fear in their lives. And then we also have Generation Excuse. They excuse their lack of trust with a laundry list of reasons explaining that they are not responsible for anything.

BDP *Trust is the antidote for worry, stress, and fear.*

Enthusiasm spasms can wreck our lives. Yet the Bible says if we are in Christ, if we are in community with other believers,

part 2

if we are in church, then we will be in God, and we will be enthusiastic.

No Excuses

The word *enthusiasm* comes from two Greek terms, *en*, meaning "in," and *theos*, meaning "God." So enthusiasm means we are in God. Thus, we believers, those of us inside the family of God, should be the most enthusiastic people in the world. Now and then we forget who we are, what we have, and where we're going in this life, but the truth is, we have no excuse, no explanation, for having long-term enthusiasm spasms. When those forgetful times threaten our enthusiasm, we need to remember the facts: We are in God. Our adoption is secure. We have a constant companion in Jesus Christ.

Our Adoption Is Secure

As Christians we should be enthusiastic because we have been adopted into the family of God. The Bible says that the moment we take the trust step, the moment we receive Christ and turn from our sins, in that moment we are adopted into the family of God.

When he was five years old, our son, E. J., sang a song once a week at the dinner table. It was the chorus of a song done by Sister Sledge: "We are family. I've got all my sisters with me." And then all his sisters would join in. Those kids sang with enthusiasm! They went nuts because in their little minds it was important to be part of a family, a unit. It was important to know one another in an intimate way. In the same way, as believers we can sing at the top of our lungs, "We are family. I've got all my brothers and sisters with me." The moment we put our trust in him, we are adopted into the family of God, and that adoption is secure.

In biblical times a mother and father could disown a biological child, but ironically they could not disown an adopted child. I believe that is why the Holy Spirit chose the word *adoption* to signify what it means to become a Christian. Our adoption is secure, and we can be enthusiastic because of that fact.

We can also be enthusiastic because our eternity is secure. We have a safe and secure home in heaven. The Bible says we have mansions in heaven; it says Christ has gone on ahead of us to prepare a place for us. Have you read the statistics on death? They are pretty overwhelming: 100 percent. One out of every one of us dies. The Bible says we will spend eternity in one of two places, heaven or hell. We have a choice to make. If we are in God's family, our adoption and our eternity are secure. That should cause us to be enthusiastic.

We Have a Constant Companion

Another reason why believers should be the most enthusiastic people around is due to the fact that we have a constant companion with whom we can relate and talk. His name is Jesus. God is omnipresent—he is everywhere—and because Jesus is God, he is with each of us all the time and everywhere we go. We can't fake him out. We can't screen him off. He is right there in our faces all the time.

As believers, we have access to our Lord all the time because he never leaves us. This ability we have to talk to him and rely on him and tap into his power at any time of the day or night should give us great enthusiasm in life.

But sometimes we're not enthusiastic. Why is that? It's because we forget who we are, what we have, and where we're going. We forget that we are members of God's family and that our adoption and our eternity are secure. We forget the omnipresence of God gives us a constant companion. And in this state of forgetfulness, we miss opportunities to enthuse our spouses, our children, our coworkers, and so many others whose lives touch ours. We forget, and in forgetting we forfeit enthusiasm.

HDP *When we forget who we are, we forfeit enthusiasm.*

Enthusiasm Is a Choice

If you want to read something that will really fire you up, just thumb through the apostle Paul's letter to the Philippians, and keep this image in mind: Paul wrote this inspired piece of mail, 104 verses, while he was chained to a Roman guard.

Paul could have whined, he could have moaned, he could have chosen the antithesis of enthusiasm. Instead, he used his experience in prison as an opportunity to write much of the New Testament. Despite his miserable circumstances, the theme of Paul's letter to the Philippians is outrageous, contagious enthusiasm and joy. In fact, joy is mentioned fourteen times in 104 verses. How did Paul do it? How did he muster up this kind of joy in the midst of so much pain and bondage? The only possible answer is that Paul *chose* enthusiasm.

Paul's circumstances didn't dictate his joy; his position in Christ did. Rather than focusing on his negative circumstances and surroundings, he chose to focus on the positive things that were happening for the cause of Christ. Yes, Paul had enthusiasm spasms every now and then, but they didn't last very long. I love what that great man wrote in Philippians 1:12: "What has happened to me has really served to advance the gospel."

Paul's word for *advance* means "to progress" the gospel. An advance was a group of men who would clear out the underbrush for an advancing army. Once the underbrush was cleared, the army could proceed. Paul said that what had happened to him occurred so that the gospel could be preached and more people could come into the family of God.

Paul suffered for the sake of Christ in ways that few of us ever will, yet he chose enthusiasm in the midst of it all.

When I read this enthusiastic New Testament epistle, I think about when Fellowship Church had to make a strategic decision to relocate many of our weekend activities from one rented facility, the arts center in Irving, across the street to another larger rented facility, a high school. (This move came after the failed effort I mentioned earlier of trying to have simultaneous services. In that instance we were using the arts center and another small theater adjacent to an office complex we were also renting across the parking lot.) We really felt like God had been blessing the church, and we were bursting at the seams. We were actually having to turn people away because we had surpassed the art center's overflow capacity. Hundreds were sitting on the floor in both the Saturday night and Sunday morning services. So this decision to move the church was an enthusiastic and visionary decision. It was something we had been thinking about and praying about for nearly three years. We called it Operation Space Jam.

This move was a fabulous opportunity, but it had both an upside and a downside. Let me start with the upside. When we changed venues, we gained several hundred more theater seats per service, meaning that many more people who matter to God would be able to hear the life-changing message of Jesus Christ. The change also meant that our nursery, preschool, and children's churches would be bigger, more secure, and better run. In the new facility, we would have covered walkways and more parking. And finally, we would have more transition and fellowship time between services. You can see why, at this strategic time, we considered this a tremendous opportunity to advance the gospel.

The downside was that this move would not be easy. Because these were rented facilities that were being used as a high school during the week, we had to completely vacate the buildings each weekend. This meant a lot of work for our staff and hundreds of volunteers who every weekend had to set up and tear down everything from the stage to the nursery to the children's church to the areas for our adult Bible-study classes. Toys, cribs, rocking chairs, classroom chairs, sound and lighting equipment, stage props, and even portable wall units that were used to divide classrooms—everything had to be removed and stored away until the next weekend. And then, when the next Saturday morning rolled around, we would begin the moving process all over again. I get exhausted now, just thinking about it.

So, instead of saying we moved into a new facility, I should say we began a perpetual process of moving in and moving out of the same facility every weekend. In addition to these weekend facilities, we still maintained some full-time rental space in the office complex across the street—a major thoroughfare—

part 2

from the high school. We used this space for church offices, some youth and adult classrooms, and for additional parking. Having our temporary church campus split down the middle by a very busy street in Irving meant that we had to deal with the traffic and the safety issues involving thousands of church-goers crossing this street on both Saturday evenings and Sunday mornings. Of course, that meant hiring additional off-duty police officers to direct traffic and asking our regular attendees to park in the remote parking areas so that our visitors wouldn't have to walk across the street to attend the services.

Here's the bottom line: We had an opportunity to advance and clear away the underbrush so that the gospel could be preached, so that lives could be changed, so that fragmented families could come together, so that singles could see purpose in the call of Jesus Christ. We could become a church that continued to reach people in greater and greater ways. Or we could stagnate our growth by refusing to make the move. Going one way would require enthusiastic sacrifice. Going the other way would require nothing more than maintaining the status quo—and in the process turning our back on people who matter to God.

HDP *Enthusiasm is a choice.*

We had a choice. We could have complained, "Oh, man! Why do I have to park so far away and walk across this busy street? I don't like all this extra work every weekend. Do we really have to grow like this? Can't we just stay in our little comfort zone? I really don't have any enthusiasm about this idea for growth." Or we could choose enthusiasm and say, "All right! I love the fact that we're growing. What a privilege to be a part of this church. I don't mind being inconvenienced a little and doing some extra work so the gospel of Christ can be advanced." Enthusiasm is a choice. It is intentional, the first capital I of enthusiasm.

Enthusiasm Is Inspirational

The second capital I is as important as the first: Enthusiasm is inspirational. In 2 Corinthians 9:2 Paul wrote this about the Corinthians' effect on the Macedonians: "Your enthusiasm has stirred most of them to action."

Christians love it when others ask them, "Where do you get your enthusiasm?" "Where does your joy come from?" "What puts that spring in your step?" Think about it. God could have decided that as Christians our prevailing dispositions would be sober, solemn, and sad. After all, God is the Creator, and we are merely the created. He could have given us whatever dominant disposition he wanted to. How wonderful for us that he chose joyful enthusiasm as our default setting.

Jesus must have had incredibly infectious enthusiasm. Read the account in Matthew 4 of how he called Peter, Andrew,

part 2

James, and John to be his disciples. These guys were hard-core fishermen. They were working with their tackle boxes and their nets and their rods and reels, and Jesus said to them, "Follow me." And the Bible says they immediately left all that stuff behind and followed Jesus enthusiastically.

I love to fish, and I know it's not easy to get hard-core fishermen to walk away from a nice boat and a tackle box full of hooks and lures and line. You have got to have some very infectious enthusiasm to cause a bunch of fishermen to close their tackle boxes and leave everything behind just like that. But that's exactly what Jesus inspired these men to do. Suddenly, they were full of enthusiastic focus, zeal, zest, and purpose—for something other than fishing!

The inspirational aspect of enthusiasm is a remarkable thing. It's so powerful it can mark people's lives forever and even move the heart of God.

Enthusiasm Marks the Lives of Others

We are called by God to make a mark, to make an impact, in the lives of others, and enthusiasm gives us the opportunity to do that. Oftentimes as I park my car and walk into the church building to begin another series of messages, I don't feel very inspirational. Week in and week out I walk toward the church telling God, "I feel so inadequate to speak a word from you, Lord." I feel down in those moments, and I ask God what can possibly be done to put a spark in the message I'm about to present.

Then, just in those moments when I'm not feeling very enthused, a man or woman in the parking crew will flash a bright smile my way. Inevitably, he or she gives me a warm handshake and promises to pray for me that day. Or I will see a greeter at the door enthusiastically welcoming the hundreds of people streaming through the doors. Or I will lock eyes with someone in the audience while I am speaking and see God all over them. Suddenly, I've caught the other person's enthusiasm, and that experience happening over and over in my life, just when I need it most, marks me and changes my life.

Others' enthusiasm can change us, and our enthusiasm can change those around us. I tell the people in my church all the time that we have the most enthusiastic church I have ever seen in my life. I thank them for their enthusiasm, because it helps me and motivates me to be a better communicator of God's truth. Enthusiasm is inspirational. It changes us and allows us to mark the lives of others.

Enthusiasm Moves the Heart of God

When I am enthusiastic, I pour out my enthusiasm to God; I worship him joyfully, knowing my enthusiasm can move his heart.

191

Do you realize that God has feelings too? God laughs. God cries. God grieves. He feels the same emotions we do. We are emotional creatures because we have been created in his image. And our emotions, our enthusiastic outlook, can touch the emotions of our Creator. Ecclesiastes 9:10 tells us whatever we do, we are to do it with all our might. Whether you are changing diapers, washing dishes, or staring at a computer screen, whether you are giving shots or making service calls, whether you are carpooling to yet another soccer practice or leading a corporation through a giant merger, whatever you do, do it with all your might. And the most amazing thing happens: As we worship enthusiastically with all our might, we can move the heart of God.

HDP *Enthusiasm not only motivates other people, it moves the heart of God.*

Make "I" Contact

Let me close this chapter with a quick homework assignment. This is something everyone can do every day: When you wake up in the morning and get out of bed, if you're like most people, one of the first things you do is look in the mirror. You may have to put contacts in or find your glasses first, but when you look in the mirror shortly after getting out of bed, before you brush your teeth or wash your face or comb your hair or shave, just stare into your own eyes in the mirror for a minute. Look into your eyes looking back at you, and think about the theme of this chapter: enthusiasm.

As you make eye contact with your own two eyes, remember the first capital I of enthusiasm: Enthusiasm is *intentional*. As you look at yourself in the mirror, say, "Today, I choose to enthuse. I am going to make an intentional choice to give an infusion of enthusiasm to the people around me." Make the decision as it relates to your marriage, to your friendships, to your work. Then think about the second I: Enthusiasm is *inspirational*. Your choice to be enthusiastic can inspire others. It can mark people's lives and move the heart of God. You see, with enthusiasm the "I's" always have it.

part 2

high-definition principles

Navigating Organizational Obstacles

- Godlike leaders mimic God's order and organization.

- As an HD CEO, expect and prepare for organization frustration.

- Don't allow *good* things to keep you from the *best* things.

- The Christ follower's number one priority is a no-brainer—it's knowing God and advancing his kingdom.

- Say no to the things that cause organizational flab in your life.

chapter
10

the organizational framework

Navigating Organizational Obstacles

Just mention of the word *organization,* and most of our minds flood with a myriad of thoughts. You may think, *Organization? Oh yes! That is the name of the game, because life has to be lived in a compartmentalized, digitized, and systematized way.* Or you may think, *Organization? Oh, no!* As you cross your arms defiantly, you say to yourself, *No one is going to take me out of my spur-of-the-moment, off-the-cuff, fly-by-the-seat-of-my-pants mentality. If anything is programmed, preordained, or prearranged, I am not into it.*

Allow me to butt in at this point and interject something. We need to realize the simple reality that our God, our loving and transcendent God, is a God of order and organization. Consider the Trinity, which theologians call the Godhead: God the Father, God the Son, and God the Holy Spirit, three in one, one in three, moving in concert with one another in pristine organization.

2

part 2

Now consider creation. The Bible lays out the order in which God created the heavens and the earth, the plants, the animals, and the human beings in six days, so that on the seventh day he could rest.

Think about your body, how it is organized. You have a muscular system, a respiratory system, and a skeletal system. There is mind-boggling order and precision in our bodies.

Consider the Ten Commandments that were given to the children of Israel. God didn't give Moses a bunch of random thoughts or a couple of suggestions off the top of his head. The Ten Commandments were a perfect summation of what it meant to live in obedience before a perfect God.

Consider the Old Testament description of worship, the details for building the temple, and the description of the sacrificial system.

Then jump over to the New Testament. Think about the organized prayer Jesus gave us in Matthew 6. Think about the organization and the order of the New Testament church: the pastors, bishops, elders, and deacons.

Everywhere you turn, you find that God is a God of order. Organization is woven into the very fabric and framework of who he is. God wants his children to mimic his character and to be known for their order and organization. Thus, I believe, he has built into our beings a need and a yearning for organization.

 *Godlike leaders mimic God's order and organization.*

Many people look organized on the surface but have a completely different character inside. Are you one of them? You may be organized in the way you dress, the way you eat, and the way you take care of your body. You may be organized in the way you run your household and meet your family's many needs. You may be organized at work and precise in the way you keep track of your daily routine. But the truth is, you have a lot of people fooled. Beneath the surface, in your heart of hearts, you live in a state of chaos, a state of disorder. Your soul is screaming for order. So, before we go any farther in this chapter, I want to share with you the first and most fundamental step to building an organizational framework in your life.

The First Order of Order

Let's take a look at what God did to bring order out of the chaos in our souls. God has given us an organized plan; you might think of it as the first order of order. The Bible calls it the gospel. The word *gospel* means "good news." The first part of God's organized plan is this: The Bible says God loves us. The Bible says we matter so much to God that it is beyond our comprehension. The Bible says his love for us is infinite and never failing.

In the second part of the gospel plan, the Bible says human beings live in a state of spiritual disorder and rebellion called

part 2

sin. The Bible says this disorder causes a cosmic chasm between man and God. Now, at this point, God could have said, "Too bad. I am perfect, and you are in a state of disorder. There is no way you can come to me. There is no way you can work your way into my perfect heaven. You deserve hell. See ya." God could have said that. But he didn't.

The third part of this organized gospel plan is this: God commissioned the second person of the Trinity, Jesus Christ, to become man. Jesus Christ voluntarily set aside some of his heavenly prerogatives so that we could identify with him. He lived a sinless life, and when he was thirty-three years old, he hung on a wooden cross and paid the price for your sins and mine. Then he arose from the dead so that we could have eternal life.

The fourth part of the gospel plan involves a decision we must make by faith. God says, "It's your choice." We are not robots. We have freedom. We have the opportunity to receive God's love, his perfect plan, or to reject it. If we receive it, we accept God's organized plan into our lives and allow him to make disorder into order. When we take this step, a transaction takes place that is supernatural. All of the disorder and sin and rebellion that we have been carrying around is transferred in a nanosecond to the shoulders of Christ. And at the very same time, Christ's righteousness and forgiveness and cleansing and salvation are transferred into our lives. That is what happens the moment we express our faith in Christ by praying a prayer of commitment.

So before we go any further with this whole idea of organization, I want to make sure that you have an opportunity to trust Christ and accept his incredible gift of forgiveness and eternal life. You may have already made the decision to trust Christ with your life. But if you haven't, the ball is in your court.

I am going to suggest a prayer for you to pray if want to make a decision right now to accept Jesus Christ into your life, to give your life to him. I have prayed this prayer, and it can be your prayer, too, if you believe in Christ, who died for you. Here it is; if you choose to, you can pray it now: "God, I am in a state of spiritual disorder. I admit the facts about my sinfulness, and I turn from my sin right now. I turn to you. I believe that you died on the cross for all my sins. I receive and accept what you did for me on the cross. Thank you for your forgiveness. Thank you for bringing true order into my life. Help me understand the implications of this decision as I grow and develop into a fully devoted follower of yours. In Christ's name, I pray. Amen."

If you prayed that prayer, it is the best thing you will ever do. Everything else pales in comparison to the decision you just made. My prayer for you now is that you will get involved in the life of a local church so that you can learn more about how to know Christ more fully and how to grow in community with him.

Now that we've dealt with the first order of order, we can talk about additional aspects of organization that we desperately need to learn. First we'll look at the culprits involved in organization frustration. Then we'll take steps to move toward organizational success as we gain organization realization and organization relaxation.

Organization Frustration

Throughout this second part of the book, I have said that most of us, as we move along life's journey, get an occasional creative cramp or an enthusiasm spasm. Now I want to discuss another obstacle, organization frustration, that can keep us from implementing order in our lives and hold us back from our goal of high-definition living. This is an organizational obstacle we should expect and prepare for as HD CEOs.

HDP *As an HD CEO, expect and prepare for organization frustration.*

The fact is, even the most orderly among us occasionally run into organization frustration. I experienced it twenty years ago right after Lisa and I got married. It struck right before we took our first vacation. Let me tell you why. My family would think about a vacation this way: Mom and Dad would say, "Let's take a vacation tomorrow. We'll leave about 9 A.M."

I knew, though, that we would not leave at 9 A.M. We would be lucky to leave before 5 P.M. In fact, it's quite likely that we would still be packing at 5 P.M. We had no clue where we were going, where we would eat, or where we would stay. We just kind of played it by ear.

Conversely, Lisa's family planned their vacations for six months before the big day of departure. By the time they backed out of the driveway, they had the AAA road maps out with their carefully planned route neatly highlighted. They knew where they would eat breakfast, lunch, and dinner everywhere along the route. They knew which hotels they would stay at every night and how long they would stay at the different tourist attractions.

Given this disparity, you can take a wild guess what happened when we got married and took our first vacation together. We experienced a little organization frustration as a husband and wife coming from two very different childhood vacation experiences. Lisa wanted to sit down in advance and plan every aspect of the trip down to the minutest detail. I, on the other hand, was less than patient about this pre-trip organizational process. Lisa, though, has helped me greatly over the years to see the benefit of organizing our vacations, and I have helped some spontaneity emerge out of that organizational framework (something we'll address in greater detail later in the chapter).

Here are some things that regularly occur in my life when I go through organization frustration: My desk is messy and

201

doesn't get straightened up. My car gets dirty, and I don't wash it. I begin to hydroplane over relationships that are important to me, relationships with people like my wife, my children, and my close friends. When I'm stuck in organization frustration, I have good intentions of spending quality time with God and being in communion with him, but I don't really do it.

You've probably experienced many, if not all, of these same problems. Organization frustration afflicts all kinds of people. In Exodus 18 we discover that it even bothered God's man Moses, the leader of the children of Israel during their exodus from Egypt. Moses attempted to be the point man for this task, but he tried to do all the work himself. The Bible says Moses freaked out; he lost it because he was overwhelmed and exhausted. As a result he went through organization frustration. In particular, Moses was besieged by two organizational intruders that you and I still deal with today: the minute muggers and the priority prowlers.

The Minute Muggers

Minute muggers are those insignificant things that steal the minutes from our day. Sometimes we foist them on ourselves, and sometimes they're delivered by other people. They seem to attack me every day. I'm just working along trying to be organized, and *bop!* I get mugged. And then, at the end of the day, I find myself asking, "Where did the time go?"

Moses' minute muggers were unleashed by a bunch of Hebrews who were strong and tough, and because Moses was not organized, they forced their agenda on him. He tried to deal with all their problems on his own, but at the end of the day, he would look back and see that the minute muggers had stolen all of his time.

The Priority Prowlers

The next organizational intruders that afflicted Moses—and that still affect us today—were the priority prowlers. Moses had two priorities. His first priority was to love God, and his second priority was to lead the children of Israel, to cast to them the vision God had given him. But the priority prowlers distracted Moses from what was *best* by getting him to concentrate on things that were only *good*. As a result he got his priorities out of order, and at the end of the day, Moses would question if he had done the best, the ultimate, for God.

As I look for modern-day priority prowlers, I think about the husband or wife who spends hours counseling a friend. This friend drains all this man or woman's emotional energy. Then the "counselor" is too tired to communicate with his or her spouse. This man or woman helped a friend, and that is a good thing—we need to be there for our friends and counsel them in the Lord. But so much energy and resources were spent doing the good thing that the best thing is sacrificed. The most important thing, after loving the Lord, is not counseling friends. It is loving and caring for our husbands and wives.

Then I think about men and women who get on the career track. Wanting to be creative, enthusiastic, and organized, they put all their efforts into this vocational agenda. They get so immersed and enmeshed in their career that when they come home to their families, they are only capable of communicating in one-word sentences: "No." "Yes." "Food." "Remote." "Slippers."

Moses was being distracted by the priority prowlers, and he was losing the battle to prioritize. He didn't know which way to turn until he got a little pep talk from, of all people, his father-in-law, Jethro. One day Jethro knocked on the door of Moses' tent and told him, "What you are doing is not good. You and these people who come to you will only wear yourselves out. The work is too heavy for you; you cannot handle it alone. Listen now to me and I will give you some advice" (Exod. 18:17–19).

In-laws are great at giving advice, aren't they? Well, sure enough, Jethro pinned Moses' ears back, and Moses got it straight. He got rid of the minute muggers and the priority prowlers and began to concentrate on the things that mattered most. He began to be the kind of leader God wanted him to be. He began to do the best and be the best. Jethro suggested an organizational structure that freed up Moses to address only the most important issues, the ones that required his unique authority, and Moses used that system to conquer his organization frustration. He delegated many jobs to others, and he appointed judges to help him arbitrate the problems that were being brought to him day in and day out.

One day, the Bible says, all of us will talk to God as he performs a brief, heavenly audit of our lives. For me, one of the things that scares me most about that audit is to see the opportunities and circumstances I missed because I allowed minute muggers and priority prowlers to keep me from the best.

HDP *Don't allow* good *things to keep you from the* best *things.*

Don't miss out on the best God has for you. Don't let distractions and disordered priorities keep you for being the kind of leader God wants you to be. He wants to move you out of organization frustration into the second aspect of organization: realization.

Organization Realization

In his book *Ordering Your Private World,* G. Gordon MacDonald alludes to the fact that the four Gospel writers described Jesus Christ as a man who was pulled in many different directions. Yet Jesus was never in a hurry. He was never late. He was always on time. He handled all his appointments without a secretary, a Day-Timer, a Palm Pilot, or a computer.

If Jesus were in the flesh today, do you think he would fly in an airplane, take a bus or cab, drive his own car, or walk? Do you think he would use e-mail, faxes, and beepers? I don't know. But we do know that Jesus was pressured for his time in first-century Israel, and he would be just as pressured, or more so, if he had chosen to live on earth in the twenty-first century. Still, we know that Jesus would have pursued his mission with focus, determination, and organization.

In order to follow Jesus' leadership example, we, too, must focus intently on our mission. We must use what I call organization realization to stay on track. We must strive to realize some key elements in organizing our lives for God's glory if we are to be godly CEOs. We have to realize our mission, our limitations, and our priorities.

Realize Your Mission

Jesus modeled organization in an authentic way, a pristine and perfect way. First, as MacDonald points out, Jesus knew his mission. He realized what he had been put on earth to do, and he didn't let anything or anyone distract him from that mission.

Consider the passage in Luke 18 that describes the scene as Jesus was making his final walk to Jerusalem to be crucified. Jesus was about six or seven hours away from Jerusalem, approaching the city limits of Jericho, and as he was walking along he was interrupted by the shrill cry of a blind man: "Jesus, Son of David, have mercy on me!" (v. 38).

The Bible says the crowds tried to quiet the man because they felt Jesus did not have time for him. Their agenda for Jesus was to get him to Jerusalem in time to celebrate the Passover. You see, the crowds around him didn't really get it; they didn't realize what Jesus' real mission was. Even the disciples didn't understand at that point. Jesus, though, was undeterred. The Bible says he stopped and healed the blind man on the spot.

Then, a couple of minutes later, Jesus walked into Jericho, passing beneath the sycamore trees lining the roadway. A little man who had a poor vertical jump was having a hard time seeing Jesus over the crowd, so he climbed up one of the sycamore trees. His name was Zaccheaus, and he was a reprobate, a rich guy who was stealing money from the Jews. The Jews hated him.

As Jesus passed by the tree Zaccheaus was in, he stopped again. The people around wondered what he could possibly be doing this time. Jesus looked up into the tree and said, "Zacchaeus, come down immediately. I must stay at your house today" (19:5). Jesus invited himself over to Zacchaeus's house for the quintessential power lunch, and in doing so, he saved Zacchaeus. But all the while, the crowds were trying to get Jesus to Jerusalem.

From the crowd's perspective, Jesus was not making good use of his time. But if you put yourself in Jesus' sandals, he was doing his mission perfectly: healing the sick and saving the least and the last and the lost. He was a man who realized his mission.

Realize Your Limitations

MacDonald also points out that Jesus realized his limitations. You might be thinking, *His limitations? What are you talking about? Jesus is God, and God doesn't have any limitations.* As I said earlier, Jesus put aside some of his heavenly powers and divine prerogatives when he became man. When he lived on earth, he was fully God and fully man, but he still limited himself so that he could relate to us and empathize with us—and so we could identify with him.

If you read about Jesus' life you see that, right before he chose the twelve disciples, he spent an entire night in prayer with the Father. Right before he began his earthly ministry, he spent forty days in the wilderness with the Father. Before the final week of his life, he climbed the Mount of Transfiguration. Jesus remembered what we oftentimes forget, our limitations. He spent quality time with the Father; he spent time in the relationship that was the source of his strength, praying.

Understand Your Priorities

Organization realization is accomplished by knowing your mission, by realizing your limitations, and finally, by understanding your priorities. You can read entire books that guide you in setting your priorities. You can discuss your priorities with others. You can pray about it. But in reality your priorities as a Christ follower have already been settled. Your priorities are a no-brainer. The Bible says in Matthew 6:33, "Seek ye first the kingdom of God" (KJV). Our number one priority is to know God and to lead out in advancing his kingdom's agenda in the world. That's it. That's number one.

HDP *The Christ follower's number one priority is a no-brainer— it's knowing God and advancing his kingdom.*

We get sidetracked, though, by desiring manifestations of God rather than seeking God himself. For example, we read the Bible and we begin to get a little envious. Moses had a burning bush. Incredible! Isaiah had a vision in the temple. Unbelievable! The apostle Paul had the Damascus experience. Whoa! We read about those amazing encounters, and we want one too. We begin to search for that spiritual quick fix, believing if only we could have an experience like those guys in the Bible, we would hit a new level, a spiritual high.

Some of us go to churches where pastors spray them down every Sunday with the gospel water hose. And they leave feeling better about themselves. They say, "Now I've got a spring in my step, and I feel good." Others look for services that provide an emotional experience—tears, rolling on the floor, that kind of thing. And we go from conference to conference, ministry to ministry, weekend service to weekend service, looking for that mountaintop experience. Some of us search for the spiritual quick fix through doctrine and Bible knowledge. We take courses in seminaries and Bible colleges. We study under great teachers, and we take lots of notes. Still others of us get busy at church. Every time the church doors are open, we are there: I'll serve the coffee. I'll greet. I'll usher. I'll teach a children's class. I'll help with missions. We're busy, busy, busy, busy.

All these things are fine and good. But if you want to grow spiritually, if you want to have Jesus Christ at the top of your priority list, you must first seek to know the person of God. And that means spending disciplined, systematic time with him, getting to know how his heart beats by pursuing a moment-by-moment relationship with him.

I wish I could say it is easier than this. I wish I could tell you to just walk into the nearest field and look for the burning bush. I wish I could tell you that you just need to memorize a few verses or learn church doctrine or serve coffee or usher or have a good cry every now and then during a church service. But that is not what Jesus did as the Son of God on earth. So why do we think we can do any differently? Jesus was involved in ministry, no doubt. He was all for studying the Scriptures in a systematic way. He understood the importance of miracles and spiritual experiences in revealing the power of God. But first of all he understood that his number one priority was to stay in constant contact, in regular communication, with his Father.

I know I have missed the mark many times, and so have you. But that is what it takes to bring godly order into our lives and to be godly leaders wherever we serve in this life. We have to understand our priorities, and our first priority is to know God through a real and vibrant relationship with his Son, Jesus Christ.

Our second priority has to do with the family. Our families should be organized. I refer you again to 1 Corinthians 14:40, one of my favorite verses: "Everything should be done in a fitting and orderly way." If you really pay attention to kids and understand their needs, they scream for order. Some parents, though, let their kids run wild. When these little self-centered banditos test their parents' resolve by disobeying them, nothing happens. What they really want is for their parents to discipline them, to give them order. They are crying out for it.

Many parents think they are making their families a priority, but in truth they are forcing so much stuff, so many extracurricular activities, on their kids that the schedule begins to take priority over the kids. The family becomes so busy that real relationships between husband and wife, parents and children, fall out of this second-most-important priority category. For example, you have got the frustrated All-American fathers who didn't make it on the high-school baseball, basketball, or football team—or maybe they made all those teams. These dads start their kids at four years of age playing every sport available. They make the kids watch ESPN with them, and they read *Sports Illustrated* to them for their bedtime stories. Children of these fathers spend most of their free time in the family minivan perpetually going from one activity to another.

Then there are the mothers who want to live their high-school years over again through their daughters and push them into cheerleading, band, soccer, volleyball, basketball, and every beauty pageant that comes along. Again the kids are so busy that they grow up never really knowing their parents. If you really understand your priorities, if you want to make your family your second priority right behind your relation-ship with God, you will have to simplify. You and your kids have to choose a couple of extracurricular activities they really enjoy and excel in, and then let them be kids.

Organization Relaxation

Once we work through organization frustration and estab-lish priorities to develop organization realization we are ready to move into the place God wants us to be: organization relaxation. Ah, doesn't that sound appealing? There's just a little more work to get to that point. We achieve organization relaxation by saying three *no*s because of three *know*s: We say no because we know our non-negotiables. We say no because we know our rhythm. And finally, we say no to disorganized spontaneity because we've come to know spontaneity that arises from organization.

Know Your Non-Negotiables

The first *no* that we need to say is because we know our non-negotiables, our priorities. If we don't know what our non-negotiables are, there is no way we can say no at the appropriate times. Jesus did not heal everybody. He didn't talk to everybody. He didn't counsel everybody. He didn't listen to everybody. He knew how to say no without an excuse, without a reason.

How many times have you made a New Year's resolution that you were going to eat properly and go on a diet? If you're like me, when you are on a diet, here is what you do: You resolve to say yes to chicken, yes to fish, yes to fruits, yes to vegetables, yes to water, and yes to all of those other good, healthy things. At the same time, you resolve to say no to that double cheeseburger, no to that chocolate malt, no to that chicken-fried steak and all of those bad, unhealthy things. Those things are non-negotiables.

We've all been on food diets from time to time—at least most of us have. Well, now I want you to go on a time diet. I want you to look at your schedule and say, "I am going to dine on those things that matter most: my relationship with God and my family. I am going on a time diet to simplify my life."

When you go on a time diet, you feed on good activities in appropriate quantities, and as a result you build strength, power, and energy. You say no to the empty calories of yet another extracurricular activity for your children. You say no

213

to yet another committee meeting that takes you away from your spouse and children for the third night in a row. You say no to the late-night social outings that keep you from getting up early the next morning and spending time with God. You say no to the things that cause organizational flab in your life. You say no to the stuff and the fluff that robs you of what God wants you to be. To reach organization relaxation, you have to know your non-negotiables and say no when you need to.

HDP *Say no to the things that cause organizational flab in your life.*

Know Your Rhythm

I made a serious mistake one Christmas. I bought my children a little set of drums. (I know the words that are going through your mind right now: What was he thinking?) The funny thing about those drums was that no one, not even adults, could walk by them without banging on them. We had some friends over to the house one day, and one of the guys asked if there were sticks to go with the drums. I could tell he wanted me to give him permission to play, and I did. Eventually, I figured out that what this guy really wanted to know was what kind of rhythm he had—or if he had any at all!

What kind of rhythm do you have? I'm talking now about a different kind of rhythm than beating on some drums. We all have rhythm in our lives, cycles when our productivity speeds up and slows down. We all tend to be better able to accomplish certain things at certain times of the day, depending on our personal rhythm. My rhythm makes me most productive creatively from about 6:30 A.M. until about 11:00 A.M. After that my mind is fried. It's jelly.

What is your rhythm? When you're organizing your life you need to identify your creative rhythm, your work rhythm, your emotional rhythm, and your relational rhythm. Then as you come to know your rhythms, you will be able to say no to those things that don't fit, those things that are out of sync with who you are and how you work.

Know Organized Spontaneity

Finally, to achieve organization relaxation, you need to say no to disorganized spontaneity because you know organized spontaneity. The best spontaneity emerges from organization, not vice versa. Remember, God is a God of order. He is not random or capricious or chaotic. God is organized. Yet, because he is organized, he is able at times to ambush us with something spontaneous. But we can always know that this spontaneity flows from his order and organization.

People ask me at least once a month if I memorize my messages. I answer, yes, I do. It takes me a long time, but I do. I have a system called a message map. It represents hours and hours of

215

work, and it helps me organize and then memorize my message. People also ask me if I improvise at all, if I end up saying things that are not in the message map. And again I tell them, yes, I do. I do not plan on saying everything I end up saying.

After I have written a message, I usually place it on my desk, lift my hands up, and tell God I am submitting the message to him. I tell him I have given it my best, and I ask him to give me promptings and leadings to say what he wants me to say.

Oftentimes I find that the Holy Spirit will prompt me to divert from my planned message temporarily. These times of spontaneity, however, always come from what God brings to mind from my previous study, from the order and organization that come from knowing his Word. I don't just say something off the cuff that does not mesh with the orderly grid of biblical truth. And because my message map keeps me organized, I can easily return to the original message I prepared. I challenge you to get organized and to know the kind of spontaneity that flows from being a person of order and knowing a God of order.

From Nehemiah to Today

Was Nehemiah a CEO in God's economy? Did he use creativity in accomplishing his life's work? Think about the way he handled the king in preparation for his mission. Consider his strategies for assessing the situation before he made his mission known to the Jews in Jerusalem. What about his relational savvy in dealing with those who opposed the rebuilding of the wall? You bet Nehemiah was creative! He knew God intimately, and because he did, he mimicked God's creative character throughout his life.

How about enthusiasm? Where do we see Nehemiah infusing enthusiasm into the lives of others? While he was certainly frightened and downcast, King Artaxerxes could see the enthusiasm, the state of being in God, at the very center of Nehemiah's life when Nehemiah came to make his life-or-death request of the king. Nehemiah's enthusiasm for his work, his people, and his God resulted in his being named governor of Judah. He also must have had great enthusiasm as he cast his vision to the other leaders and workers in Jerusalem. They responded to his vision immediately with the wholehearted enthusiasm he modeled to them.

Do we even need to consider Nehemiah's organizational skills? Well, just for fun, let's summarize what Nehemiah did. After he found out about the problems in Jerusalem, he immediately began praying and planning for the opportunity to take action. When that opportunity came, he knew exactly what he would need to request of the king to make the journey to Jerusalem. Once in Jerusalem, he executed his mission with the precision of an organizational master—from rallying others behind his vision, to delegating the work around natural groupings, to staying focused in the midst of heavy criticism,

part 2

to keeping the exhausted and disheartened workers motivated right to the very end.

What about us? Can we be Nehemiah-like, high-definition CEOs today? Can we be people of cutting-edge creativity, outrageous enthusiasm, and streamlined organization? The answer, without a doubt, is yes. We can be just as effective and influential in this life for one important reason: We can know the very same God Nehemiah knew in such a personal way. And the great thing is that God longs to know us deeply and passionately, and to empower us with his Spirit so we can accomplish great things as Nehemiah did.

Creativity, enthusiasm, and organization are important qualities of the high-definition life. But if you really want to implement these characteristics into your life and make a high-definition difference for God's glory, as Nehemiah did, you must continue to pursue a minute-by-minute relationship with the One from whom all these qualities flow. When you know him in a real and personal way, you will be able to mimic the creativity of our creative Creator, live a life of contagious enthusiasm in God, and understand that organization flows from the very heart of his ordered and organized nature.

FLY FISHING
FOR FRESHWATER
STRIPED BASS

FLY FISHING
FOR FRESHWATER
STRIPED BASS

A COMPLETE GUIDE TO TACKLE, TACTICS, AND FINDING FISH

HENRY COWEN

FOREWORD BY DAVE WHITLOCK

Skyhorse Publishing

Skyhorse Publishing books may be purchased in bulk at special discounts for sales promotion, corporate gifts, fund-raising, or educational purposes. Special editions can also be created to specifications. For details, contact the Special Sales Department, Skyhorse Publishing, 307 West 36th Street, 11th Floor, New York, NY 10018 or info@skyhorsepublishing.com.

Skyhorse® and Skyhorse Publishing® are registered trademarks of Skyhorse Publishing, Inc.®, a Delaware corporation.

Visit our website at www.skyhorsepublishing.com.

10 9 8 7 6 5 4 3 2

Library of Congress Cataloging-in-Publication Data is available on file.

Cover design by Daniel Brount
Cover photo credit: Henry Cowen

Print ISBN: 978-1-5107-3501-9
Ebook ISBN: 978-1-5107-3502-6

Printed in China

Contents

Foreword
by Dave Whitlock

Freshwater striped bass pioneer and fly-fishing icon Dave Whitlock with a striper. *Credit: Dave Whitlock.*

Freshwater, landlocked striped bass are truly an outstanding quarry for flyfishers who want to experience saltwater-class battles but don't live conveniently near brackish or ocean coastal shorelines. I discovered these breathtaking Atlantic natives while living in Maine and conducting the annual L. L. Bean fly-fishing schools in the early 1980s. Stripers immediately struck me with their awesome beauty, shape, aggressiveness, and fly-rod-wrenching, long, and powerful runs. Upon returning home to Norfork, Arkansas, in the fall of 1983, while stopped at a gas station, I noticed a small group of men peering into the bed of a pickup truck. It was late October, so I assumed someone had bagged a big whitetail deer. My curiosity moved me to join the group. What a shock I got! It was not a deer but, instead, five really big stripers laying there. They had just been caught that chilly, fall morning barely five miles from my home near Lake Norfork! The chance experience of seeing that limit of huge stripers was, for me, the beginning of an exciting, lifelong fly-fishing addiction to freshwater stripers.

I went out the very next day, but even after many chilly, predawn trips to Norfork Lake in hunts for these super bass, I was not successful. To add insult to disappointment, I had to endure the remarks of conventional tackle striper guides while I was out there. I'd hear, "Hey flyfisher, the trout are below the dam, not up here!" and "Flyfisherman, that fly pole is way too scrawny to hold up a striper!"

The stripers had been stocked on Norfork Lake in the 1970s and 1980s from brood stock of the Santee-Cooper landlocked stripers. When I began trying to catch one, these relatively unknown residents had enjoyed very light fishing pressure in this extremely popular largemouth and smallmouth fishery. Norfork Lake's ideal depths, temperatures, size, and almost limitless forage of striper favorites—shad and crayfish—had helped these fish quickly reach double-digit proportions. From October to May, huge schools of stripers roamed the shallows in this thirty-mile reservoir from sunup to sundown, feasting at the surface on football field–size school of thread fin and gizzard shad. This was my quarry—and it was eluding me.

One day, as I was putting my boat in, a Norfork bait guide gave me some advice about using more realistic shad flies and approaching the surface-busting fish quietly and with stealth. I had been using the flies, approach, and presentation that I had used successfully along the coast of Maine—but Norfork stripers wanted no part of it. That helpful guide's advice was exactly what I needed. Nearly five months after I had begun, I hooked my first Norfork freshwater striped bass! I started out early one morning, in the bitter cold, using an 8-weight and size 4 thread-fin shad flies—and hopeful with my newfound knowledge. My very first Norfork Lake striper emptied my big Tibor reel spool of 215 yards of backing in just seconds. I chased it across the arm of the lake using my electric motor and finally, after a long, hard fight for what seemed like hours, I brought that gorgeous, leg-long, exhausted bass to the surface. I had no net big enough to come close to lifting it aboard, and I feared I'd get pulled overboard trying to lip the monster. So, I held it alongside the boat and motored to the nearest shoreline, beached my skiff, and then the striper. It was forty inches long and I estimated its weight at twenty-three to twenty-five pounds!

Over the 1980s and early 1990s, I fished for Norfork's stripers every time I could and often landed three to four per morning, averaging fifteen to eighteen pounds. My best weighed thirty-eight pounds, but I hooked several that I'd estimate would go fifty pounds. Over time and with much trial and error, I taught myself how to catch Arkansas, Oklahoma, and Texas stripers. During the 1990s, a similar experience was being carried forward. I was only one of a handful of freshwater striper flyfishers that I knew of. However, through fly-fishing shows, I had gotten word that a guy named Henry Cowen was giving striper fly-tying demos and slideshows on catching stripers on fly rods. These bits and pieces of positive news about Henry and his Lake Lanier guiding success had me really looking forward to meeting the young man. I finally got my wish at the Atlanta Shallow Water Fly Fishing Show. Before I actually met him, I watched his outstanding presentation of tying his popular Coyote striper fly he had developed and an information-packed slideshow on how and where to catch southern freshwater striped bass. I learned so much that day, and as soon as I met this neat and personable young man, I decided I'd like to be friends.

A year later, at the same show, Henry invited Emily and me to a day on his home water, Lake Lanier. From the moment we pulled away from the dock, I knew we were in very professional and capable hands. His equipment, method, and system for locating and approaching stripers was flawless. Henry truly excels in guiding for freshwater stripers.

Fast-forward to last spring, at the Atlanta Fly Fishing Show. Henry told me, in a low-key statement, that he had been asked by a publisher to write this book. My first thought was what awesome news for flyfishers and striped bass, because I can think of no one more qualified than Henry to compose this important book. His perfect prospective of this magnificent gamefish has now produced for us the definitive system to help every potential striper flyfisher be successful encountering freshwater stripers in the North American reservoirs, tailwaters, and rivers in which they roam. He has precisely what it takes to produce this long-needed "classic" for fly fishing striped bass.

I was honored when Henry asked me to write the foreword, especially after I reviewed the book. I am so pleased at how very thoughtfully he has covered for us all the aspects needed to locate striper fisheries, choose the flies and tackle, and use methods of presentations to assure success catching them. Henry's book has distilled for you the information and instruction that will help guide you to success in one season. I predict this book will become the standard reference for fly fishing for freshwater stripers. Enjoy!

—Dave Whitlock

Preface and Acknowledgments

Fly-fishing guide, tier, and author Henry Cowen. Photo *Credit: Henry Cowen.*

This book has been in the making in my mind for over fifteen years. When I moved to Georgia back in 1997, I never had previously fished for freshwater striped bass with a fly rod. I had been a striped bass fisherman since the mid-1970s and became a fly-fishing saltwater striped bass fanatic in 1990. Once I moved south from the tristate fisheries of New York, New Jersey, and Connecticut, I needed to learn an entirely new fishery: landlocked stripers. The problem? There was little if any information available on sodium-free (landlocked) stripers with regard to fly fishing. It took a while, but eventually I was able to figure out the fish and this type of fishery, which differs in many regards to that of saltwater stripers. Over time I began to meet and talk to a few folks who had the same burning passion to fly fish for these great freshwater gamefish. Folks like Dave Whitlock and Dan Blanton became good friends, and I was able to compare notes as to how these fish behave and the patterns that are prevalent to our respective fisheries. Our fisheries were over a thousand miles apart from one another, yet we seemed to all encounter the same types of patterns year after year. That also meant we had to solve similar problems regarding this fishery. I cannot say enough how much I appreciated our talks and their friendships over the years. My good friend O'Neill Williams once made the most important observation I had ever heard about freshwater striped bass: "Henry, striped bass do not know where they live." I took that to mean a striper in Virginia is no different than a striper in California or Oklahoma, and they can be patterned all the same. Those words resonated with me like no others when it came time to write this book. Thank you for those words, O'Neill.

As time went on, my "brother from another mother," Kevin Arculeo, would pester me, saying, "You need to write a book on freshwater stripers." He's been saying this for over ten years. I think Kevin was like a fishing Nostradamus. In 2017, my dear friend Lefty Kreh called me on the phone to have one of our thirty-minute chats, as we did about every two or three weeks. Lefty said it was apparent to him that freshwater striped bass fishing was a powder keg ready to explode. He was getting emails and letters constantly asking about this fishery, and there was little if any information on it. He said the industry needs a book to be written on this subject and I needed to be the one to write it. He further hoped that this book would be a "how to" on everything you need to know about these fish, as folks just do not know where to begin. I was honored he would think of me to take on this project. For that reason, I feel he is one of a handful of folks I would like to dedicate this book to. Unfortunately, he passed away before this book's completion, but his character and spirit were with me the entire time, pushing me to complete this project he believed in.

When I called Dave Whitlock to tell him of the book project I was about to undertake, he simply said, "Marvelous." He then said he would love to help with any information or illustrations needed for this project. His illustrations were simply the icing on the cake. Our publisher, Skyhorse, was delighted that Dave and Emily Whitlock were going to be a part of this book. For those of you not personally familiar with Dave and Emily Whitlock outside of their vast knowledge of fly fishing, they are simply two of the nicest and kindest people you could ever meet. Thank you both for your help and participation in this book.

I briefly want to thank my photographer, Josh England, for all his help with this book. For me, writing is the easy part of the project. Pictures, well, that's an entirely different daunting task. Josh is one of the best and most talented photographers there is as well as a striped bass junky. He has no ego, which means when you question a photograph, whether he or anyone else took it, you get a straight answer. I am not quite sure if this book would have happened without his participation, so for that I say, thank you buddy.

I would also like to thank my dear friend and outstanding outdoor photographer David Cannon for allowing me to have use of his entire photography library. I am lucky to have friends like that. I remember David catching his first striped bass with me many years before he carried a camera around with him.

Now that this book is completed, there are a few people I would like to thank for their time over the years discussing freshwater striped bass or simply having the patience to put up with my affliction of this great gamefish. I would like to first thank my parents for exposing me to fishing. My dad started taking me fishing when I was four years old, and the spark from that first trip has never been extinguished. We spent many days in a rowboat either fishing for fluke on the South Shore of Long Island or in the Catskill mountains tossing artificial lures for largemouth. Years later he showed me the art of fly fishing, and our trips eventually landed us on the fabled streams of Roscoe, New York, fishing for trout. I would give my eyetooth to have one more trip on a boat or in a pair of waders wetting a line with him. I would like to quickly thank my mom for never feeling left out of these trips and always suggesting, "Why don't you two go fish for a bit and come back for dinner." She understood the bond between parent and child that fishing can bring forth.

I would like to thank Gary Merriman, owner of the Fish Hawk fly shop in Atlanta, Georgia, for never letting up the pressure on me to become a guide for this fishery. It is one of the things I truly love and look forward to about the sport. I have witnessed its growth over the past twenty years, especially on Lake Lanier as well as throughout the entire United States. Gary and all the folks who work at the Fish Hawk continue to play a huge role in getting the word out about this great fishery.

When I first showed up on Lake Lanier back in 1997, there was no one to discuss the fishery with. There was, however, a conventional tackle guide whom I would first hire and then commiserate with; I'd pick his brain to help figure out the certain twists and turns these crazy fish can take from time to time. Captain Mack Farr became a great friend, and to this day I think he is quite possibly the most adaptive and versatile fisherman I have ever met. I was with him when he caught his first striper on a fly nearly twenty years ago while we were making a video on freshwater striped bass on the fly. This book certainly has his fingerprints all over it.

Just like Mack Farr, Captain Clay Cunningham is a dear friend who fishes freshwater striped bass over two hundred days a year. He is a top striper guide on one of the best striper lakes in the country. He and I have had many conversations over the years comparing the current patterns these fish display. We are continually trying to figure out our next best move in order to be successful on the lake. I appreciate all of what seems like a daily chat during striper season. Although Clay has not caught one on a fly yet, I know it is on his bucket list.

While I do fish for striped bass in rivers, I am certainly way more comfortable when I am fishing reservoirs. With that said, I could not give enough credit to friends Rob Smith of The Fish Hawk fly shop and angler Bill Butts of Springfield, Missouri, who are both river rats when fly fishing for striped bass. These two guys will forget more than I will ever know when it comes to river fishing. If you look closely, you might find that they both have gills behind and under their ears.

I would also like to thank dearly departed friend and angler Tommy McCue, who I met back in 1999 on Lake Lanier on his first ever day fly fishing the lake, when I was still green myself and learning the fishery. Tommy and I became good friends, and I taught him all he needed to know about fly fishing in exchange for thirty years' worth of his knowledge about conventional fishing on Lake Lanier. It's obvious that I got the better of that deal.

There is positively no way I could have ever written this book without the help of the folks at the Georgia Department of Natural Resources. These guys put their lives' work into our fisheries here in Georgia. Establishing relationships with these folks many years ago allowed me to call and get answers to the scientific data questions discussed in this book. I am grateful for their years of friendship and, to the extent that when our hatcheries produce a few thousand extra striper fingerlings, that they consider giving them all to the Lake Lanier fishery (grin).

I would also like to thank anyone who reads this book and finds that it helped them become better at figuring out how to catch freshwater striped bass on the fly. As anyone who fishes for these animals knows, they are not particularly easy to figure out, especially on fly! My wife has made a believer out of me with regards to karma. When it comes to fishing, I have always tried to put an effort into paying it forward. If I can help one or one thousand people make their fishing more successful, then I have done right by what I was fortunate enough to have learned over the years.

Lastly and most important, I would like to thank my wife, Tina, for putting up with all the lost time spent on the "pond" over the last twenty-three years and for never saying no if I wanted or needed to go fishing. When we were first going together back in the mid-1980s, she knew what she was getting into regarding the role fishing played in my life. She was with me in the beach buggy when I fished the tip of Breezy Point Jetty in Jamaica Bay; in a pair of waders alongside of me in the surf off Staten Island, New York; and even walking out and under the girders of the Marine Parkway Bridge in Brooklyn, New York, when we would sight cast to forty-plus-pound stripers moving in and out of the shadows of the lights cast from above the bridge. After thirty-two years of marriage, she has been, and continues to be, one hundred and ten percent supportive of my fishing obsession, for which I am eternally grateful.

The author (right) with photographer Josh England (left) and Dave Whitlock.

Chapter 1

About the Fish

HOW THE FISHERY STARTED

Freshwater striped bass fishing has become one of the hot topics in communities throughout the United States. *Photo Credit: Josh England.*

Everyone knows that striped bass have thrived along the East Coast of the United States for centuries. Heck, the Pilgrims talk about how their survival in the New World was due to being able to harvest striped bass out of New England waters. Fast-forward to 1942: A dam was completed on the Santee–Cooper reservoir in South Carolina that essentially closed the Cooper River's natural flow. Striped bass that made their yearly spawning pilgrimage up the Cooper River were trapped behind the newly built dam and thrived in fresh water. Most folks believed the trapped stripers would just die off. But, to the contrary, they found the stripers were thriving and still reproducing in the lake. This was the birthplace of striped bass in fresh waters. Since then, many lakes around the country have been able to produce a quality freshwater striped bass fishery. If we fast-forward into the 1950s, we see a few lakes where biologists started small stockings of striped bass. Their survival rate increased, and more and more states started looking into and producing striper fisheries around the country. This fishery really began to take hold in the 1970s when departments of natural resources (DNR) or fish and game departments around the country concluded the abundance of forage fish in a given lake can be best utilized by stocking a predator species, and that species became the striped bass. There was obviously a dual purpose as the DNR realized that they would also be sponsoring the use of a brand-new recreational fishery. Talk about foresight! Biologists learned that some fisheries could reproduce on their own merits while others needed the help of hatcheries to keep them going.

For striped bass to reproduce in fresh water, they need to have their eggs tumble in the current of a flowing river for at least forty-eight to seventy-two hours to avoid suffocation. Then the eggs hatch after being fertilized, and the lifecycle begins. This usually occurs in early spring through early summer. The water temps in our lakes will warm to about 57°F, and the pre-spawn will take place. Ideal spawning temperatures will be in the 60° to 65°F range.

For lakes that have rivers running into them, this occurrence will begin sometime in March or April. Once the surface water temperatures on the lake hits that magical high-50°F mark, the striped bass go

A striped bass's colorful markings are like none other in the freshwater fishing world. Their silvery sides along with striped lateral lines are admired by anglers in both fresh and salt water. *Photo Credit: Josh England.*

into what we call the pre-spawn phase. Fish will become extremely active and will start feeding aggressively. This is a time when you might see some very good surface feeding activity going on. The fish are all storing up weight to make that run up the river very soon. Fish expend many calories during the spawning run, so a good feed prior to that is in order. On many lakes, not all fish will run up the river. Some will make spawning runs down near the dam where there is major current. Others may run into the backs of creeks where there is a source of water running into the lake. Obviously, these fish's eggs will not reproduce due to the fact that they must be in constant moving water. However, the fish are always looking for opportunistic conditions to try to find a place for reproduction. The only chance of reproduction is for those that run up the rivers to spawn. The males will get out and onto a lake's points, near the river channel, and wait for females to journey up the river. The males will then be in hot pursuit of the spawning females. Once upriver, the females will drop their eggs and the hope of new life begins. Some lakes (like Lake Lanier, officially called Lake Sidney Lanier) will have striped bass making the spawning run up both rivers that feed the lake (in this case, Chattahoochee and Chestatee rivers). However, neither of the rivers are long enough to have successful spawning runs. The eggs released upriver will tumble down and settle in at the bottom of the lake and never hatch. It is these lakes, with the help of a proactive department of natural resources or US Fish and Wildlife Service and their hatcheries and stocking programs, that help keep the supply of striped bass thriving in lakes. Here in Georgia, our DNR has hatcheries that produce in excess of 2.5 million striped bass fingerlings a year. We will discuss this later in this chapter.

The only place where a different type of spawn occurs is in some of the north-central lakes of Southern California. This is where California's famed San Luis Reservoir is located. San Luis gets its water from the Sacramento–San Joaquin River Delta. This is a pump storage reservoir, and how their striped bass get into the lake is fascinating. Juvenile striped bass and many other forage species are pumped into the lake from the delta. Even striped bass eggs and larvae are pumped into the lake. However, biologists have determined that stripers already in San Luis will spawn and drop their eggs in the springtime. Interestingly, these eggs have enough current from the water being pumped out in the spring along with the cool winds coming off the ocean to create enough current for stripers to successfully reproduce in this watershed without the use of a river system to carry the eggs until a fry is hatched. Amazingly, this system once produced some of the country's biggest freshwater striped bass on record and on occasion can still produce some quality fish for anglers wanting to pursue a sodium-free striper.

DIFFERENT STRAINS OF FISH AND THEIR RANGE

Striped bass, along with their close cousins (hybrids), have become the target for fly-fishing anglers throughout the country. *Photo Credit: Josh England.*

While the markings of all striped bass and hybrids might vary slightly depending on their makeup, there is no mistaking that pronounced spiny dorsal fin. *Photo Credit: Josh England.*

Most freshwater stripers are managed by either US Fish and Wildlife or a state's department of natural resources. Many states that stock their own fish get them from local hatcheries sourced through local lakes and rivers. However, these fish came from somewhere originally, long before they were supplanted in that state's fishery. California got its original striped bass from the East Coast and had them shipped across the country. Any stocking that might happen today would come from local fish. However, to my knowledge, California is getting its fish from natural spawning and has not stocked striped bass in over twenty years. Florida and some parts of southwest Georgia are using their brood stock from fish that originated from the Gulf of Mexico brood stock. I have heard that over time this strain of fish has gotten used to being in warmer water, but this has not been proven scientifically. While these Gulf-strain fish are striped bass, they originated from waters that empty into the Gulf of Mexico and genetically are slightly different from what we call the Atlantic strain of striped bass. Our DNR prefers to use Gulf strain of stripers for reservoirs whose waters eventually go into the Gulf of Mexico. However, the fish that are stocked throughout the rest of Georgia

Striped bass fall into the category of temperate bass, which is depicted in this illustration by Dave Whitlock. Top left: white bass; top right: white perch; center: striped bass; bottom left: yellow bass; bottom right: hybrid striper. *Credit: Dave Whitlock.*

are stocked by raising striped bass that are considered the Atlantic strain of fish, which originated from the Savannah River basin. Those are basically the only two strains of fish available to all hatcheries throughout the United States, either originated from the Gulf stain or the Atlantic strain. Most states are using fish from their local area to produce hatchery raised stripers, as it is simply more cost effective. While there are some federal hatcheries where fingerlings are transferred into certain watersheds, most states prefer to rear their own if they can get the brood stock. Some of the hybrid stocking programs may have a hard time finding white bass and, in that case, will find hatcheries that can help get them the brood stock needed to produce a hybrid fingerling. No matter where the brood stock is coming from, most anglers need to know that the dollars that they are paying for a state fishing license helps pay for these hatcheries and the cost involved with freshwater striped bass and hybrid stocking programs. This is proof of your dollars at work and a thank you should go out to those state and federal agencies that help with the production of these wonderful gamefish.

GROWTH RATE AND LIFECYCLE

Stripers can grow very quickly in freshwater impoundments. The reason for this is that the forage is landlocked and if there is a consistently good spawn and

Most striped bass take three years to grow to a catchable size of three to four pounds. *Photo Credit: Josh England.*

hatching of threadfin shad, the young stripers have an excellent food source from which to thrive. Stripers when stocked are put in as a very small. Here on Lake Lanier, our DNR (which manages our stocking program) will collect sperm and eggs from local lakes throughout the state and then send them to the hatchery, where they are reared into fingerlings. At one inch in length, the fish are released in several areas of our lake around mid-April through May. The release is planned around that time so it can coincide with the lake's shad spawn. If we have a successful shad spawn, the stripers will at first feed on insects, plankton, and shad larvae. Should a good shad spawn occur, the stripers will grow rapidly and start feeding on the newly hatched shad over the next year. When all goes right, the stripers can grow up to one foot (give or take) in the first year. Everything is dependent on water quality and having a good food source to feed on. Stripers can grow extremely fast after their first two years and can put on between two and four pounds a year after their first two years. That kind of growth is usually not seen in salt water. While they can live far longer in salt water than fresh water, their average size is generally larger in fresh water during the earlier years. Again, this is because living in an impoundment makes feeding easier as the forage cannot get away. If you look at photos of freshwater stripers compared to those out of salt water, you will notice the freshwater (sodium-free) stripers have these enormous pot bellies. A thirty-inch fish in salt water will typically weigh about ten pounds while that same thirty-inch fish in fresh water will typically weigh twelve pounds and have that deep belly. Since water quality can play such a tremendous role in a freshwater striped bass's growth, there is really no standard we can look at for consistency due to the year to year changes in a lake's water quality. Some years our one-year-old fish are six inches long and we never see them, and other years they can be ten to twelve inches long and they will show up in a lake's fishing catch more frequently.

The life cycle of a freshwater striped bass can vary from lake to lake and varies hugely from that of their saltwater brethren. Once again, it all comes down to water quality. Typically, it appears that fish living in

Fly-fishing icon Lefty Kreh along with Georgia freshwater striped bass angler Dennis Ficco holding a two-and a half to three-year-old striped bass. *Photo Credit: Henry Cowen.*

Freshwater striped bass can grow to enormous sizes, but it is their girth that allows them to achieve these massive weights. *Photo Credit: Henry Cowen.*

impoundments that are generally cooler can grow faster and live longer. Stripers living in fresh water typically can live a maximum of fifteen years of age. What is interesting is that here in Georgia that age would be a tad generous. Most of the time we see our fish living ten to twelve years. Yet our neighbors in Tennessee have stripers that grow bigger and live a little longer. That is why you will see that Tennessee consistently records some of the largest striped bass catches here in the South. If you were to look up the lifecycle of a saltwater striped bass, you will find it is considerably longer. Stripers living in fresh water out West in northern California have been recorded at some enormous sizes. While both San Luis and the O'Neill Forebay have their share of large fish, it is those found in both the Sacramento and American rivers that are truly impressive when it comes to size. The reason one watershed can have fish that push the limits of fifty-plus pounds while others struggle to hit the forty-pound mark is just a measure of the fishery's water quality and food source. Give a fish an additional two or three years of life and you can understand why that watershed yields bigger fish.

Hybrids are a completely different story. While hybrids typically do not reproduce and, because they are bred to be crossed with white bass and striped bass, we see that their growth is smaller for the most part. An untypically large hybrid will push the mid-teens in size. However, most hybrids found through-out the United States will typically be in the two- to five-pound size. Hybrids pushing the limits of double digits are considered highly prized by anglers fishing for them. The general life cycle of a hybrid would be in the four- to six-year range. They simply do not have as long a life cycle as striped bass do. Once they get past their first two years, they can grow relatively fast during the time they have left in their impoundment. As previously stated, water quality is tied to their growth rate and life cycle too.

FISHERIES MANAGEMENT FOR FRESHWATER STRIPERS

Freshwater striped bass fisheries are managed by each individual state. In salt water, there is a federal fisheries commission (National Marine Fisheries Service) that manages migrating coastal stocks but gives each state the oversight to manage their fishery while complying with federal rules and regulations to conserve those coastal stocks. In fresh water, there is little if any federal involvement in any one specific fishery. There may be some regulations where a national parks service might be involved with regards to when an angler might have access to a specific reservoir or river, or where the Corps of Engineers has oversight to an impoundment's access or flow of water, but not to the specific oversight of the fish itself. In fresh water, state wildlife agencies have the primary responsibility

Freshwater striped bass can live into their mid-teens and can put on three to four pounds of weight a year if they have the food source. *Photo Credit: Josh England.*

for managing any inland striper fishery. Department of Natural Resources, Game and Fish, Wildlife Resources, and Department of Fish and Wildlife are some of the names these agencies may go by. Essentially, they are all the same even though their names may differ.

It all started back in the 1950s and 1960s, when the construction of many large reservoirs offered fishery opportunities throughout the country but particularly in the Southeast. It started with the Santee-Cooper (South Carolina) stripers. Once fishery biologists saw that not only were the Santee-Cooper stripers surviving, but also thriving, they became more and more interested in the hatchery culture of both striped bass and hybrids. The construction of many dams trapped striped bass in the reservoirs, making them landlocked. Even though the striped bass were trapped, biologists soon learned that they could complete their lifecycle in fresh water. Due to the overpopulation of certain forage species, such as gizzard and threadfin shad, scientists thought about how to best manage those populations. They came up with the idea that by introducing striped bass into freshwater impoundments through stocking programs, they could both manage the forage as well as create and provide sportfishing opportunities for their resident anglers. Nearshore species like black bass and crappies created great shallow-water fisheries, but most lakes lacked an offshore (pelagic) predator that could take advantage of the shad abundance. That essentially is how the birth of all inland striper fisheries began.

Reservoir biologists from the state will sample their reservoir's fish, water quality, and anglers' opinions to best determine where these programs might best work. Essentially, it's all determined at the state levels and based on both supply and demand with a biological basis. When decisions are finally made, they must be biologically sound and publicly supported. Here in the Southeast, the states all work together and share information by communicating with each other. It's essentially a technology transfer of information with each other to get the latest and greatest in aquaculture and reservoir management techniques. If one state finds a certain win in their fishery, then it is passed on to other agencies. An example of this is that Georgia used to stock stripers for the year and release their fingerlings in one or two specific areas. Another state found that their mortality rate of fish stocked was lower when you spread the released fish out into more areas. Georgia now releases its fish in up to ten areas in a season. Another shared experience is when the so-called summer squeeze begins. This is when the reservoir's water temperature and oxygen levels were affecting survival rate of the fish. Once identified and shared with other states, you learn how to best deal with that phenomenon. Much of this is done through the state's fisheries biologists as well as a state university's fisheries biologists. Through cooperative efforts and

Most freshwater fly anglers still practice catch and release with these prized gamefish. That allows some impoundments to sustain a trophy fishery. *Photo Credit: Josh England.*

information sharing, fisheries management improves, and our striper fishery is enhanced.

So how is all this funded, you might ask? It seems to me that nearly all these state fishery agencies are vastly underfunded. Some of the monies come directly from your fishing license purchases, as they help fund the wildlife agencies. Sales of fishing equipment and other items provides tax dollars that go into the federal Sport Fish Restoration account, which is administered by the US Fish and Wildlife Service. Then those dollars get redistributed back to the states based on the number of licenses sold in a state as well as some other factors, including the size of the state. It's this information that helps the feds determine how many dollars a state will receive. Basically, it's your tax dollars at work, as the number of licenses sold allows a state to capture back those tax dollars. It is set up as a user pay program. At the end of the day we know that anglers are a major player in the freshwater striper game too, through their opinions, catch data gathered, and especially their dollars.

How the Fishery Happens (Natural vs Stocking)

As previously discussed, there are many lakes and rivers throughout the country that simply cannot produce a self-sustaining wild striped bass population. This is

Many impoundments throughout the United States have striped bass fisheries where anglers can catch double-digit-sized fish with regularity. *Photo Credit: Josh England.*

where the government steps in. Through either a state's DNR or the US Fish and Wildlife Resources department, hatcheries are set up to continuously populate the lakes and rivers with striped bass. Most of the states will rear their own fish from within the state. However, there have been times when some states will buy the hatchery-produced fish for their impoundments. We see this more frequently when some fisheries are stocking hybrid striped bass (*M. chrysops*) rather than a striped bass (*Morone saxatilis*). The difference is how the eggs and sperm are cross-bred. A natural striped bass is bred by getting both the eggs and the sperm from a striped bass. A hybrid striped bass is bred by getting a combination of a striped bass along with a white bass. Some other common names for these hybrid bass are wipers, vipers, sunshine bass, Cherokee bass, and palmetto bass. In order to make a hybrid, biologists will use the fertilized eggs from a striped bass and cross them with white bass sperm. Or they might do the opposite and use the fertilized eggs from a white bass and cross them with a striper's sperm. Which combination is used can determine the size of the hybrids as well as the warm-water tolerance of the hybrid. A sunshine bass is a cross between the fertilized eggs of a white bass with the sperm of a striped bass. These hybrids tend to grow smaller and slower than their palmetto bass cousins, whose eggs come from the striped bass and sperm from the white bass. White bass can live in more temperate waters then striped bass, so lakes and rivers that cannot maintain a cool comfortable water

Most fisheries around the country will have a sustaining population of fish in the three- to five-pound class. *Photo Credit: Josh England.*

temperature required to sustain striped bass may opt for hybrids instead. Hybrids, unlike striped bass, cannot reproduce. They must be crossbred and reared in a hatchery environment. Hybrids also do not live as long as striped bass do. The average life expectancy of a hybrid is somewhere around five to seven years. The average life expectancy of a striped bass is around fourteen years.

In order to produce both striped bass and hybrids, biologists must go through a series of steps in order to produce these gamefish. It starts by electroshocking fish and keeping them alive and comfortable in order to bring them back to their hatcheries. This is usually done in the springtime, when the females are full of eggs and the males are full of sperm. Once back at the

For fisheries that need stocking, it is the Department of Natural Resources or a state's wildlife management agency that helps keep the fishery alive. *Photo Credit: GADNR.*

hatcheries, the fish are managed so the eggs from the females and the sperm from the males can be removed. It takes about two days to get the eggs to turn into fry. Once hatched, the fry are boxed up in oxygen-filled bags of water and shipped out to various hatcheries in the state, where plankton-filled ponds support the growth of the fry for thirty days. Then, once they reach a measurement of about one inch, they are harvested and stocked in reservoirs and rivers across their state or sold to other states.

Striped bass that are stocked are usually done so at the one- to two-inch size. These fish will have the chance to grow to fifty pounds in some freshwater lakes and rivers. *Photo Credit: GADNR.*

Chapter 2

Where to Find the Fish (Top Reservoirs in the USA)

Reservoirs offer anglers an opportunity to catch stripers in a freshwater environment while having a saltwater experience. *Photo Credit: Jim Klug.*

Stripers and hybrids can be found across the United States. You can go as far west as California or as far east as New York State and nearly everywhere in between to find lakes and rivers that have either naturally reproducing or stocked striped bass and hybrids. The farther north you go, the less likely you will find states that manage them, as the water is simply too cold for a sustainable population.

However, the farther south you go, the more likely it is you will find impoundments that have recreational fisheries for one or both species. Once again, water temperature seems to play a significant role in which species are found where. The hybrids can tolerate much warmer water temperatures throughout the year then striped bass can. As of last count, there are over thirty-two states in the US that have a recreational striped bass or hybrid fishery. Some states may only have one or two lakes with these fish while other states may have as many as a dozen or more impoundments that carry either or both species. If you speak to folks in the know, most of your southern states from Texas to South Carolina have multiple reservoirs and river systems with plenty of fishing opportunities. Not all these reservoirs have self-sustaining populations of striped bass. Many are supported by the Department of Natural Resources or their state's fish and wildlife department. Hybrids, of course, must be managed by one or the other organization as they (for the most part) cannot reproduce and must be hatchery replenished. The reason we see these fish in so many areas across the country is that they serve as viable recreational fisheries for a large number of anglers. Some of these fisheries were started to help control the overpopulation of certain forage species, but in the end the recreational fishing benefits have become huge pluses in the angling world (and especially for flyfishermen). Where else can anglers have a saltwater-like gamefish and fishing experience miles and miles away from the ocean? Here are some of the more popular striper lakes that can be found in the US:

San Luis Reservoir—California
Smith Mountain Lake—Virginia
Lake Murray—South Carolina
Lake Sidney Lanier—Georgia
Lake Martin—Alabama
Ouachita Lake—Arkansas
Lake Texoma—Texas
Lake Texoma—Oklahoma
Cumberland Lake—Kentucky
Cherokee Lake—Tennessee
Lake Powell—Utah
Lake Mead—Nevada
Raystown Lake—Pennsylvania
Lake Gaston—North Carolina
Bull Shoals Lake—Missouri
Wilson Reservoir—Kansas
Sangchris Lake—Illinois

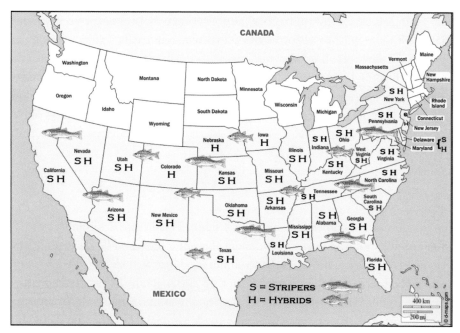

This Dave Whitlock illustration of a map of the US shows which states have a striped bass or hybrid fishery. *Credit: Dave Whitlock.*

There are also many rivers throughout the country that support thriving land-locked striped bass fisheries. Stripers in the salt will run up freshwater rivers to make their spawning runs. That is why many states on the Atlantic Coast have thriving freshwater fisheries. One of the more popular runs is in Virginia, when the fish make their spawning run in the area of Roanoke Rapids. New York and Pennsylvania have their run of fish when the run is made up the Hudson River and the Delaware River. However, these are saltwater fish, and I am not including them in what we deem "freshwater striped bass." There are landlocked stripers that make their spawning run up rivers in states throughout the country. This same type of spawning run also holds true for hybrids. Both species will make a spawn-ing run up their respective rivers and then move back down into their home res-ervoirs at the end of the spawning run. Some may run back up and live extended periods in these rivers, when the water temperatures in their home waters become too warm. Whether they reside in their river system or reservoir, these fish are landlocked, and it is these fish we are deeming true freshwater striped bass. These fish are free to move in and out of their reservoirs, and many anglers in the know will follow these movements throughout the year so that they can have an oppor-tunity to continually catch these great gamefish. It is this writer's opinion that when fly fishing for landlocked stripers, it is easier to be successful in rivers than it is in reservoirs. Most river systems are just smaller and narrower than open reservoir. Locating and successfully catching these fish is made easier when you need to cover less water, and a river usually allows you to do just that. I hear many anglers throughout the country say that their success rate is consistently much higher in a river system than of reservoirs. Suffice it to say that if you are new to the striper game, starting in a river will bring you more instant gratification. However, it is the reservoirs that provide fishing over a longer period. Most river fishing for stripers is short-lived, as the fish eventually move back to their respective reservoirs. Many areas of the country offer fishing for both reservoir and river stripers. The western part of the United States, for example, offers many options, wtih California standing out as a prime example. California has striped bass fisheries throughout its lake aqueduct as well as in its river systems. Both the Southeast and Southwest offer anglers many choices as to where to fish for striped bass and hybrids. The south-central part of the country is teaming with some striper lakes and many hybrid lakes. Longtime striped bass angler Bill Butts has spent nearly a lifetime chasing these fish and figuring out their eating habits throughout much of the south-central region of the United States. Having chatted with Bill many times about his fishery, it is obvious to me that striped bass really do not know where they live (as stated by television and radio show host O'Neill Williams). Nearly all the patterns we look for here in the deep South, which is my fishery, also occur in the south-central part of the country.

Chapter 3

The Food Source (What Striped Bass Eat)

FORAGE FISH

Striped bass are some of the most opportunistic fish found in fresh water. They have been known to eat of host of different things, including forage fish, crustaceans, aquatic insects, and worms. I have a buddy who once witnessed a late-morning feeding frenzy on the Oconee River, where stripers were gorging on a *Hexagenia* hatch on the surface. While I've never seen anything like that on my home water of Lake Lanier, I will say that once stripers enter a river, they may not have quite the same or same amount of dining choices that they have on lakes. Lakes usually hold more types of forage species then rivers do. No matter where you go in the country, the two most popular forage species for striped bass are threadfin shad and gizzard shad. Both species are in the herring family and serve as the main course for nearly all lakes and many river systems throughout the United States. Looking at these forage species, you will notice immediately that there is a size difference between the two.

Threads (as they are routinely called) tend to be much smaller in size, and on average will be found in varied sizes ranging from one to five inches in length. While threadfin shad can get into a river system, most of the time we find them in lakes. They can travel in massive schools and have a similar look to that of a juvenile bunker (or what saltwater anglers call peanut bunker or simply peanuts). They have a somewhat wide profile to start and then gradually taper down to being narrower at their rear. Threadfin are sort of a silvery gray color with a hint of blue or lavender along the sides. The very top of their back is sort of a dark peacock green color. They are not too hard to imitate with a fly. They are a slow-moving baitfish that, when attacked, become denser as a school. They can be found both shallow and deep at times in lakes. However, threadfins can tolerate warm water very well and can be found near the surface at times when striped bass need to stay deep in the comfort of cooler, more oxygenated water. During the late fall and winter months, it is the young-of-the-year threadfin that seem to attract the most attention of striped bass. When this occurs, lakes will see their best topwater opportunities, with blitzing striped bass having a field day with these baitfish. Threadfin are also the more likely forage species anglers will find when fishing dock lights at night. The lights attract plankton that the shad feed on. That is one reason why dock light fishing is gaining in popularity across the country. Find a dock light and you are likely to find it covered up with threadfin. Once again, find the baitfish and you are likely to find striped bass. One thing you should know about threadfin shad is their lack of tolerance for cold water. Once a lake's surface water temperature drops below 50°F, the threadfin become very uncomfortable and look for the warmest water they can find. They will ball up in big schools as they search for warmer water and become extremely lethargic. This gives striped bass an opportunity for an easy meal. If the water temperature drops to 46°F or lower, this colder water increases the likelihood of a threadfin kill. Should that happen, you will be able to see massive schools of dead threadfin lying on the bottom on your fish finder. One way to determine if the threadfin are uncomfortably cold is to keep an eye out for them on or near the bank in the dead of winter. If they are swimming super slowly and even moving somewhat erratically, it is likely that the shad are in trouble. This is usually an opportunity for anglers, as the striped bass sense this and will feed more aggressively during these periods. Threadfin are simply not very hardy fish.

Another thing to know is that when the cold weather sets in and the water temperatures really plummet, if you can find an area where the surface temperature might be a couple of degrees warmer, you will likely find a ton of shad there. And, the stripers will positively find them too. Another interesting phenomenon is that threadfin tend to stay higher in the water column on overcast days. Those overcast days tend to lead toward more surface feeding. I always tell my customers that if you fish with me in the fall or winter and you get an overcast day with light winds, you will likely hit the jackpot. That's not to say you will not find them feeding on top during sunny days, but cloudy days rule when threadfin shad are on the menu. If you ever come across a school of striped bass blitzing a bait ball of threadfin shad near the surface, it is interesting to see how the stripers attack and eat the threadfin. When the stripers come near the surface to feed, they will turn on their sides and glide through the school of shad, inhaling as many as they can fit in their mouths. An angler in a boat looking down into the water will never see the striped bass's back (top of the fish) but rather the stripes along its sides (the sides of the fish). The fish are feeding on their sides as they cruise through the school of shad. It's one of nature's coolest feeding patterns I have ever witnessed. Finally, one more thing worth noting is that those anglers who like to fish above and under water dock lights for striped bass will find that threadfin shad are the primary forage under the lights. That's because the lights attract plankton and the threadfin shad will gather on the lights for an easy meal. While there are a host of other forage alternatives for striped bass to feed on, threadfin shad seem to be one of their top choices and quite possibly their favorite meal.

Threadfin shad are a smallish type of forage species found in nearly all lakes around the country and some rivers. Matching the hatch is the key to fooling striped bass into taking your offering. *Photo Credit: Henry Cowen.*

Gizzard shad is the other forage species found throughout the lakes and river systems in the United States, and striped bass have taken a liking to them as well. Gizzards (as they are routinely called) are high on the value list of a striped bass's palate. When it comes to targeting a striped bass's preferred forage species, gizzards certainly rank high due to their larger size. Since gizzard shad are generally larger than typical threadfin shad, a striped bass gets more nutritional value when it eats a gizzard versus eating a thread. While gizzards can be found on nearly all striper lakes throughout the country, their real value comes into play when targeting them on river systems that have striped bass. Gizzards can be as small as three inches in length but can also grow upwards to twelve—and even fourteen—inches in length. The old saying of big bait catches big fish applies to striped bass and gizzard shad. Saltwater anglers would equate a big gizzard shad to that of a large menhaden (bunker). Anglers that are true trophy hunters would be advised to imitate a large gizzard shad if they ever want to catch that twenty- or even thirty-plus-pound striped bass on a fly. Gizzards are also very gray or silvery along their sides and have a blueish or lavender hue to them. However, they are not as metallic looking on their sides as threadfin are. Their backs are a very dark green and almost black on top. Gizzards on a lake are usually best targeted in the

Gizzard shad are found in reservoirs and rivers throughout the country. They can grow upwards of fifteen inches in size as they mature, and large striped bass can't resist a big gizzard. *Photo Credit: Henry Cowen.*

fall and again in the spring when they appear to be more active. One of the major patterns for striped bass when they are eating gizzards is the nighttime bite as well as their April spawning period. Gizzards will get up shallow on sandy beaches and flats and stripers will follow them into these shallow areas. It is best to have flies that are both five to six inches in length as well as those that are at least one foot long. Striped bass can sometimes be extremely fussy and size-specific when they are feeding on certain baits. Matching the hatch is certainly the best tactic to employ. When fishing a river, most of the time we find gizzards in the five- to seven-inch length. They also feed on plankton, just like threadfin shad. They tend to be a hardier species than the threadfin and really thrive in the cooler, highly oxygenated waters. Gizzards as a forage species seem to be able to handle the faster currents, so they do quite well in river systems throughout the country.

Depending where and what body of water you are fishing, there are a host of other forage species that stripers will feed on. While both threadfin shad and gizzard shad are common to nearly all lake and river systems where striped bass thrive, certain bodies of water have additional forage species that must be accounted for. In California, some other prominent forage species are American shad, Japanese smelt, sculpin, and various panfish. Here in the South, many of our lakes have blueback herring (also known as bluebacks). Along with bluebacks, stripers will feed on panfish, crawfish, and any other smaller fry-type fish. Folks in Tennessee will have skipjack herring as an alternative forage species along with gizzards and threadfin. Trout are yet another species that striped bass feed on. As a fly angler, it pains me to go into a tackle shop and see live trout in their bait tanks to be legally used to catch striped bass (especially in the winter). One thing is for certain, striped bass may be one of the most opportunistic feeders in fresh water. As anglers, it is important to know not only what the fish are feeding on, but also what time of year they feed on them. Throwing a blueback herring pattern to stripers on my lake in January will likely yield you few if any bites. However, toss a juvenile threadfin shad pattern that is two inches in length, and you are now in the game! That is part of the secret to cracking the striper code.

Striped bass and hybrids are opportunistic feeders. They will eat whatever forage comes their way. Blueback herring are a favorite in many reservoirs in Georgia and South Carolina. *Photo Credit: Josh England.*

HOW TO FIND THE FORAGE IN RESERVOIRS

As I have stated throughout this book, the key to finding landlocked striped bass is to first find the forage fish. Stripers have a voracious appetite; all they do is swim and eat. So, when trying to put the pieces together of how to catch them, you just need to find their food source. It is just that simple an equation. However, it is easier said than done. Both gizzard shad and threadfin shad can move around to different areas of an impoundment as well as move to different parts of the water column. What determines where you will find them is water temperature. Forage fish need to feel comfortable and need to find food for their survival. Since shad do not know where they live, finding the bait generally is the same for all impoundments. The only change is that water temperatures vary from lake to lake due to climate differences. In other words, what happens on an Oklahoma impoundment will happen nearly identically on a Virginia impoundment.

However, the water temperatures on an Oklahoma impoundment may warm up more quickly in the spring due to its being farther south. Conversely, in the fall Virginia impoundment waters will cool earlier due to their more northerly climate, which means their fall bite should occur earlier than that of an Oklahoma impoundment. There are times of the year where the forage fish will be shallow, and that's what fly anglers wait for during a typical striper season. However, most of the time the forage will be down deep, and anglers will need to adjust their fishing tactics to the water column where the largest concentration of forage will be. That is where the stripers most likely will be too. Just to give you a snapshot of where the forage may be, let me give you a list of places you might consider looking for baitfish. Forage could be in the backs of the creek up on the bank in super shallow water. Or they may possibly be in the creeks and under docks in water that's ten to fifteen feet deep. They may be in the mouths of the creeks that might be twenty to thirty feet deep. You might find them in open water over a very deep bottom, like a lake's river channel in twenty to thirty feet, or possibly super deep in forty feet of water or deeper. For fly anglers, when the bait and fish go deep it's time to look for something else to fish for. It's also possible the forage fish may be hiding up shallow on points that are on the main lake or just off those points, ten to fifteen feet down. Sometimes they are not found on what we call main lake points but are found congregating on secondary points near the main lake. There are many times throughout the year that the forage will be congregating on humps that are twenty to twenty-five feet deep. The forage themselves may be stuck to the bottom of those humps or halfway up to the surface. Note that when the forage relates to humps, it's always best to try to find humps that have brush piles on them. The forage will use those brush piles to hide in and camouflage themselves. Forage at certain times of the year can be hiding up on shallow rock piles or on a lake's deep man-made seawalls (usually near marinas). Other times they might be on sandy beaches in very shallow water. Lastly, you might find the forage milling around pilings or blowdown trees that they use for cover. So, you see there are many places where forage can spend their time hiding and eating, and it's our task as anglers to find those places where they might be.

Once you find the forage, you are likely to find the striped bass. We term all these different areas where the forage may be as "forage patterns." As the patterns change, so must a striped bass angler's strategy as to where he or she might decide to fish. The anglers that figure out these forage patterns on a yearly basis are the ones that are most successful in catching freshwater striped bass. This is no different to that of a bass fisherman's fishing strategy. If you have ever watched a pro bass fishing show on television and seen the professional anglers fishing all over a lake during a tournament, they are clearly trying to dial into a pattern that tells

Using wildlife to help locate the forage will also lead you to the ultimate prize, striped bass. *Photo Credit: Josh England.*

them where the fish are hiding. Striped bass fishing is like that too. The biggest problem I see is too many anglers simply like fishing up shallow and pound the banks with their flies. While that strategy will work during certain times of the year, it is generally not the best strategy to use day in and day out. Most of the time, fish are not shallow but deep. You just need to know where to look and employ a strategy that helps you find that forage stacked up in a certain water column.

Threadfin shad tend to congregate in big schools throughout the year. In the summer they can tolerate warmer water then most stripers can, so they are relatively safe from being eaten by the stripers at that time. As the water temperatures start to cool off in the fall, the threadfin will be found high in the water and usually out over open water, mostly on the south end of an impoundment. Now is the time to look for humps that are twenty to twenty-five feet deep with some brush attached to them. The shad will tend to congregate on these humps for a few weeks. Many of the open water shad will just hover out over a bottom that may be over one hundred feet deep. This trend or pattern will continue until a lake's surface water temperature drops down to the low sixties, and then the fish will start migrating farther north. While most of the threadfin will still be found in open water, you will start seeing some schools migrating into the coves. Most of the time they will be fifteen to twenty-five feet deep, although at low light you might find the threadfin high in the water column. As winter approaches, the threadfin can be all over a lake, but the big schools will certainly have moved to the northern end of the lake and will be moving into the creeks as the surface water temperatures drop into the fifties. Once again, most of the threadfin will hover in twenty to thirty feet of water. Note they may be in the mouth of a cove over a sixty-foot bottom but will hover in that twenty- to thirty-foot water column. Your fish finder can help you locate this forage. Remember that threadfin shad are extremely temperature sensitive and once a lake's water temperature drops into the forties, the fish will become somewhat uncomfortable. If it drops into the mid-forties, the likelihood of a threadfin kill will occur. As the water temperatures get to 50°F, it's time to start looking in the backs of the coves, as the shad will look to find the shallow water that gets heated by the afternoon sun. Just one degree of water temperature is good enough to allow these temperature-sensitive fish to feel a little better. Once the springtime temperatures start allowing a lake's surface water temperature to rise, the shad are once again on the move. It is this time of year that the shad start to migrate south again, and we look for the shad to be on a main lake's points or in the mouths of the coves that are located farther south. As the temperatures continue to rise into the sixties, the fish will get up shallow on the main lake points as well as on secondary points located just off the main lake. Shad will start to move into some of the more southern coves on a

When things are not as obvious, driving around slowly and using your fish finder can help you locate a school of baitfish. *Photo Credit: Josh England.*

lake and can be found in big groups under docks. If there is a marina nearby, that is a great place to locate the forage. With the season progressing into late spring we find the water temperatures rising into the seventies, and now is the time the forage is using a lake's structure to eat and hide. Look at seawalls, saddles, blow-throughs, and long tapered points as areas of interest to find the shad. The shad should be getting shallow especially early and late in the day.

This is also the time of the year that the shad will spawn on the new or full moon phase. The shad spawn is an awesome sight to see if you hit it just right. It will occur up shallow and usually in an area of heavy rocks or blown-down trees on the water's edge. The shad need to release their eggs and have them adhere to something, so the shallow structure is where they do much of their spawning. Look for a twinkling on the water's edge and, if you see it, then it is likely you have found the spawning shad. When the surface water temperatures hit the high seventies and above, the shad leave a lot of the coves and migrate out to the deeper water. This is when you want to locate the humps of the lake that are twenty to twenty-five feet deep and have brush on them. Next, we hit summertime, and the pattern makes no difference as the stripers have gone deep for the summer or have moved into the river systems attached to the lakes. You might find some smaller groups of juvenile stripers eating threadfin, as they can handle the warmer water temperatures better than the mature of the species. So hopefully, this will help you pattern the threadfin forage on nearly all reservoirs. The sooner you figure out the

Seeing forage spraying on the surface is a sure sign that something below is making them very nervous. *Credit: Dave Whitlock.*

threadfin pattern on your reservoir, the quicker it will allow you to crack the code for catching freshwater striped bass when they are targeting one of their favorite forage species.

Gizzard shad are like threadfin shad in that they are another favorite forage species that freshwater striped bass love to target as a food source. However, the big difference between these two forage species is that gizzard shad are not nearly as sensitive to the cold-water temperatures as threadfin shad are. They do much better in colder environments, which is why we find gizzard shad in nearly all reservoirs and rivers throughout the US that have striped bass in them. Gizzard shad offer a higher degree of protein for striped bass, in that they are generally larger in size, so bass don't need to eat as many to satiate their appetites. When it comes to targeting gizzard shad, once again water temperature plays a huge role in where you will find them. During the summer, gizzard shad are not as tolerant of warm surface water temperatures as threadfins are. Gizzards can be found in waters ranging from ten to thirty feet deep but are mostly found hovering in schools that are twenty to thirty feet deep, especially in river channels. You might be sitting over a one-hundred-foot bottom and come across gizzards in that twenty- to thirty-foot range. However, for striped bass anglers who are tossing flies, it doesn't really matter, as we generally do not fish to freshwater striped bass when the water temperatures reach above 80°F. As we come out of the heat of the summer and enter the fall, as northerly winds start to cool lake surface water temperatures, the gizzards are still mulling around in that twenty- to thirty-foot water depth over the river channels or over some of the deepest water found in a reservoir. Once the water temperatures start to drop and drop below 70°F, we start to see the gizzards moving back into the creeks and going up higher in the water column. Now you might find the gizzards in ten to twenty feet of water. In the evenings (after dark), you might find the gizzards getting shallow, and look toward tapered points and sandy beaches to find them. By the time winter arrives, the gizzards are in the coves and will start migrating to the north ends of most reservoirs, as north ends are usually shallower than the south ends, especially if there is a dam on the southern part of the lake. If the dam is on the north end, then the reverse would apply. The forage will now be in that same ten to twenty feet of water, but can be found in the mouths of the coves and even all the way back toward the backs of the cove. This pattern will continue throughout the winter. Once the warmer spring weather starts to come into play, the gizzards may be found all over a given reservoir; however, this is when it is time to start looking for them on flats and shallow points in the coves. This time of year, we will see gizzards anywhere from just below the surface to ten feet deep. This pattern will last throughout the spring, when the water temperatures are in the sixties and on up to 70°F. Nighttime will see the gizzards get super shallow. We also see the gizzards spawning up shallow at this time of year, and you can target your biggest striped bass of the year when the gizzards are getting ready to spawn. Once the water temperatures of the lakes start heading northward of 70°F, the gizzards start to move out of the coves and back out over the river channel. The shallow water you were previously targeting is not where they will be found any longer. This should give you a starting point on where to target gizzard shad on nearly all reservoirs throughout the United States.

Chapter 4

Tactics Used to Locate Striped Bass in Reservoirs

SEASONAL PATTERNS USED TO FIND STRIPED BASS

The key to targeting striped bass in freshwater impoundments is to first understand their movements throughout the year. We term these movements as "patterns," and the angler who figures out these patterns will have more success than those who just go out and blindly fish for them. Striped bass are always looking to feel comfortable in their environment (water quality/temperature) as well as always looking for where they will find their next meal. So, when trying to pattern striped bass, it is usually done through both water quality (oxygen and clarity) as well as water temperature. Patterns will change throughout the year, which means stripers will be found in many different places on an impoundment during different times of the year. Sometimes a pattern might even repeat itself during different months. All this has to do with where they are going to get their next meal or where they will feel comfortable. Let's look at some different patterns that may occur during the year on a striper lake.

Stripers are happiest in lakes when water temperatures range between 50°F and 75°F. While they can easily survive in waters cooler than 50°F, they become more lethargic feeders when the lakes surface water temperature drops to around 45°F. When a lake's surface water temperature rises above 80°F, on the other hand, the stripers tend to look for cooler, more oxygenated water. Let's go through a typical calendar year to explain what tendencies anglers may experience when trying to pattern striped bass. Using my home lake (Lake Sidney Lanier), we can explain what you might see on a typical striper lake. Keep in mind that other striper lakes around the country will experience similar patterns, but they might not be during the same months due to varying climate differences.

In January and February, water temperatures are hovering in the mid-forties to low fifties. At this time of year, stripers can be expected to be feeding at the north ends of most impoundments. That's where much of the bait will be. You might see them feeding on the surface or find big schools twenty to thirty feet below the surface, but rest assured the north ends are where you will most likely find the big schools of fish if the dam is on the south end. The shallower northern waters not only cool down more quickly, but will heat up slightly faster too during the cold winter months. Baitfish will look for these shallower areas where the water can heat up one or two more degrees more than that of the deeper south end of the lake, and will migrate there. Another area to pattern during the coldest part of the year would be any hot water outflows on the lake. Some lakes may have power plants on their shores, and you can expect that bait and stripers will be stacked up there.

March is a tricky month to pattern stripers. As the surface water temperatures start to rise, the fish will make their way south again having lived their last three to four months on the northern parts of the lake. A couple of patterns will overlap during the month. Baitfish will start piling up in the backs of the coves as the shallower water warms up from the afternoon sun hitting its banks. Look for stripers

Fall is a great time to find stripers feeding high in the water column. *Photo Credit: Josh England.*

feeding in super shallow water at this time. Another area to fish would be flats. Most lakes have flats (shallow water with no defined drop into deeper water), and the fish will get up onto these flats and feed during March. As the surface water temperature heats up even more toward the end of March, we see fish leaving the backs of the creeks and the flats and going out into open water. This can even happen in early April. What we are seeing during this pattern is that the fish are staging for their pre-spawning run up the rivers. The fish will be high in the water column during this period. You might find fish two to five feet below the surface over a bottom of forty to eighty feet of water, and in the main lake. It is during this period that fly anglers tend to strike out, as there is simply no way to find the fish. Not all the fish do this at the same time, but a good many do, and if you are not finding fish on the flats or in the backs of the coves any longer, the likelihood is that they are in the first stages of the pre spawn.

Once the surface water temperature hits 57° to 58°F, the fish are getting ready to head north and go through their spawning period. Anglers can start running up the lake and into the mouths of the river where the fish will look for running water to drop and fertilize their eggs. This is the one time of year where anglers can cash in on some tremendous fishing. Again, not all the fish run upriver to spawn. Some will do so in the backs of coves where there is a good supply of fresh water coming into the lake. Others will go south and down to a dam or even a culvert where water comes in and out. Now is the time to get up and into the river itself. Look for fish to be anywhere, but especially in deeper holes in the river. If your river has an average depth of two to four feet, then target the stripers in holes of six to twelve feet. They will usually be stacked up in those holes this time of year. Just remember that running water is the key to the spawn. Another pattern to look for during the spawning run is that when the stripers are heading up lake, you can target them on the points near the river channel in that lake. The males will sit on the points waiting for the females to make their run upriver. Once the females are moving upriver, the males will follow them. Just keep in mind that once the fish are on their spawning run, food is not their focus.

Once the spawning run ends, the fish will move back downriver and back into the lake again. This usually will occur by mid to late April. When the fish are done with their spawning run, they are usually hungry, which makes this a great time to target the stripers on those same points you fished while the males were waiting for the females to head upriver. Now is the time when the fish will spread out all over the lake. Structure is certainly the key to the post spawn pattern. Now is the time to start looking shallow. Look for fish up on reef markers, flats, blow-throughs, saddles, points, secondary points, and humps. Surface water temperatures should now be in the sixties, and the fish will be content and eating. Another

Winter is one of the best times to locate stripers feeding both high in the water column or subsurface to about twenty five feet below. They are much easier to fool on the fly during the early part of the winter. *Photo Credit: Josh England.*

pattern that occurs in April is the gizzard shad spawn. When gizzards spawn, you can find stripers eating like it's their last meal. Gizzards are usually found spawning on the bank up shallow and especially on or around sandy beaches. This is a go-to pattern, and fly anglers will find the spawn by seeing striped bass crashing big baits on the surface usually just after first light. It's also a good time to fish to them after dark on sandy beaches. This is also a great time of year to see the fish all over dock lights at night. Both underwater and above-water dock light patterns will be on fire this time of year.

The month of May in the South is usually the last month of striper fishing for anglers using a fly rod. The same pattern as occurs at the end of April applies now. Look for fish early and late in the day (low light) on the same structure as previously mentioned. The fish are spread out all over the lake, but the tendency is to see them moving south, where the water temperatures are a tad cooler than the north end of the lake. Surface water temperatures will now be in the seventies and, depending on how warm a spring we have, can even push upward of 80°F. The fish are getting set to go deep, and while they will be easy to locate, many of the schools of fish will hover between thirty to fifty feet deep (too deep for fly rod anglers) toward the later part of the month. However, the first part of the month brings about the shad spawn. Threadfin shad as well as blueback herring can be found spawning early in the morning. When the shad spawn occurs, fly rod anglers can look on the bank, inside marinas, or on sea walls for stripers feeding on the surface while the bait is tight to the structure. This is a yearly occurrence, and is a money-in-the-bank pattern for anglers to look for. Certain lakes may have other baitfish that stripers will feast on, and springtime is usually the spawning season for nearly all forage fish. Keep an eye open for this opportunistic feeding pattern.

Here in the South, the months of June through September will see our lakes' surface water temperatures range between 80° and 87°F. It feels like bath water to most of us. The striped bass cannot tolerate that warm temperature and will spend these months deep in the lake where cooler water prevails. The oxygen content in many of our southern impoundments disappears too. This makes life nearly intolerable for stripers, especially in July, August, and September. A thermocline will set up at a certain depth (usually around thirty feet). This is a narrow band of water where the oxygen content is livable, and the stripers and even certain baitfish will spend their summer months in the thermocline. During these periods it is advisable not to fish to stripers while they are trying to survive the heat of summer. While the fish will surely be bunched up in large schools during this time, it is best to just leave them alone. Most of the striped bass will be on the south end of a lake, as this is where the deepest, coolest water can be found (especially if you have a dam attached to the impoundment). Lakes farther north or even out West may not experience this summer pattern of the fish lying super deep. Studies have shown that fish caught while surviving in the summer thermocline have nearly a 100 percent mortality rate even when caught, handled, and released properly. The bottom line is that if you want to preserve and protect your resource, it is best to leave the striped bass population alone in the heat of the summer.

If you simply must continue to fish through the summer, then your best pattern to target would be to head upriver into the colder, more highly oxygenated waters of the river system your impoundment is attached to and fish for those striped bass that summer over in the river. This is when river fishing for stripers is best! While there may not be as much food for them in the river system, striped bass are opportunistic feeders and can make do hunting what forage is available. The river systems throughout the entire South are full of fish by the end of June, and they'll usually stick around through most of August before making their way back down the river and into the lake. Patterning the fish in the rivers is not that difficult, as the fish seem to find comfort in the deeper holes or where creeks dump into the river. River fishing—due to its smaller size compared to an impoundment—will allow you to more successfully target stripers in a kayak or even wading. The fish are in a more confined space, so finding them should not be as difficult as in a lake.

Once the cooler September nights and more northerly winds start cooling the surface water temperatures of the lakes, the striped bass will begin to appear higher in the water column again and the fall bite pattern starts to take shape. The first pattern to appear occurs by the end of September or early to mid-October. The surface water temperatures drop back into the mid-seventies and stripers can be patterned by fish humps that are twenty to twenty-five feet under the water. Bait starts to congregate around these underwater humps, allowing the stripers to find easy meals. Using your fish finder should help you locate underwater humps. By the time the surface water temperatures drop to the low seventies, top-water pattern will take shape. Stripers will feed in large groups on the surface especially during lower light conditions. An interesting note is that when I fished salt water for striped bass, I found that the nastier the conditions (especially windy) the more the fish fed on top and blitzed the bait. On my lake, the pattern is just the opposite. Stripers feed more aggressively on the surface, blitzing bait when the conditions are calm. In fact, we rarely see them on top when the wind is blowing hard. Most of the activity takes place on the south end of the lake. This is due to having just finished summering over on the south end of the lake due to the deeper and presumably cooler water. This pattern will occur earlier in lakes where their temperatures cool more quickly. My top-water pattern that begins in mid-October may start in Virginia a full two to three weeks earlier. Again, it's all about water temperature.

By the end of October, another pattern starts to take shape. This is what conventional anglers call the bomber bite. The bomber bite pattern is nothing more than going out at night and fishing these lures called a Bomber Long A. It is a six-inch-long plastic swimbait that can be fished one to three feet under the surface on structure-like points, blow-throughs, saddles, and sandy beaches. Fly anglers can do the same using an intermediate fly line and a gamechanger-type streamer. This is a very consistent and reliable pattern that can be used once the surface water temperatures start to drop under 70°F. This pattern can last well up to one month.

November and December see our lakes' water temperatures starting to fall from the sixties to the fifties, and the fish will start migrating to the north end of the lake again due to the baitfish moving north as well. There are a few patterns to look for at this time of year. Top water is in full swing. This will continue until the water temperatures plummet to around 47° or 48°F. Then the fish will stay deep and become more lethargic feeders. On warmer days, or if there is a string of warm days together, you can look for fish feeding in the very backs of the coves in super shallow water. On other days, look for fish on points that are close to the channel or anywhere near deep water. You can see big schools of fish hovering in twenty to twenty-five feet of water; they are easy pickings once you locate them with your fish finder and toss a fast-sinking line at them. Remember, as the water gets cooler, the stripers usually target small young-of-the-year threadfin shad in the one- to two-and-a-half-inch range.

WATER TEMPERATURE: HOW IT AFFECTS STRIPED BASS FISHING

In saltwater striped bass fishing, knowing the tides and how to use them may be the single most important factor in order to successfully catch striped bass. The tides can tell you where to fish and not fish depending on their stage. Fish use tides to help find their next meal. In freshwater striped bass fishing, we do not have use of tides to tell us where to find the fish. What dictates to us where the fish will be is simple: Where are the forage fish staging? That is all we really need to know. You see, striped bass for most of their lives only care about two things: when do I go on a spawning run and when do I eat—the latter being a near everyday occurrence. In order to find the forage fish that striped bass dine on, anglers need only know one thing: water temperature. Surface water temperature will allow anglers to annually pattern the forage fish that striped bass feed on. In order to figure out the stripers' feeding pattern, you must first figure out where the food source is. Keep in mind that striped bass do not know where they live. So, a striper in Georgia or Tennessee is going to feed similarly to a striper in Virginia or Texas. It is the surface water temperature on a reservoir that will determine where the baitfish are concentrating. Once you find the baitfish, it is much easier to find the stripers. Please note that just because an area has a lot of baitfish doesn't necessarily mean you are going to find big schools of striped bass. However, once you locate areas of concentrated baitfish, you are likely going to find striped bass nearby.

While all striper lakes may differ slightly on their makeup, nearly all of them have both threadfin and gizzard shad as a forage species. Learning how the bait travels and moves throughout the year will give you a heads-up as to where to look for striped bass. Most striper lakes that have a thriving fishery will find that striped bass are comfortable in water temperatures that range between 55°F and 75°F. That doesn't mean that water temperatures may not spike into the high eighties in the summer or drop into the mid-forties in the winter. They most surely will. It is these fluctuations in temperature that create the different feeding patterns we see on reservoirs throughout the country. Nearly all patterns on all lakes are similar. It

As a reservoir's surface water temperature drops below 60°F, striped bass become more aggressive feeders. *Photo Credit: Josh England.*

just may be that the water temperatures for that pattern may be one month earlier or later depending on what part of the country your striper lake is located. Here is an example:

On Smith Mountain Lake, Virginia, the fall top-water bite may begin as early as mid-September. However, on Lake Sidney Lanier, Georgia, that same top-water bite will likely start in mid-October, a full month later. That is because the lake surface water temperatures drop earlier in Virginia due to being farther north than those in Georgia. Even with a four-hundred-mile difference separating the two fisheries, the same pattern will occur at different times. The pattern is the same, but the time range varies slightly. Still, the common denominator is water temperature.

Let's peek at a typical year of threadfin shad movement patterns and how water temperature plays a role in that pattern. I will base this on my lake, Sidney Lanier, so any angler can plug in water temperature to his or her home lake and more than likely witness the same pattern. Let's begin in the winter when water temperatures in December, January, and February typically put our surface water temperatures at 50°F or below. Threadfin shad can handle some widening degrees of temperature and still thrive, but when the water temperature drops into the mid to high forties the shad become lethargic and extremely uncomfortable. Here in the South, most of our reservoirs have rivers running through them and have dams attached to the most southern ends. While both forage fish and striped bass can be found all over a given lake, most of them will be found on the northern end. The deepest water in a reservoir (especially if a dam is attached to its southern end) is on the south end of the reservoir. That is where most of the water is stored. One reason why the bait migrates north during the coldest months is that the shallow water on the northern end will warm up more quickly. As the afternoon sun hits the banks of a reservoir, that shallow water can heat up by as much as one or two degrees. That makes threadfin shad more comfortable. While there will always be shad throughout the entire lake system, it is the north end in the winter that will hold the biggest schools of shad. Striped bass know this and follow the food source. Shad may be found both in big schools in or near the river channel, or possibly in the very backs of the creeks near a freshwater source coming into the lake, or even on a red clay bank. These red clay banks heat up rather quickly from the sun's exposure to them. Once the springtime comes into play the lake's water temperatures start to rebound and will get up into the mid to high fifties. This is a trigger for striped bass, not for shad. The pre-spawn is forthcoming.

Striped bass will start to eat vigorously and store up enough protein to make the trip upriver to spawn in the coming weeks. Once the spawning run begins, many fish will run upriver to spawn. Not all do, but most will. When the fish are done spawning upriver, they will come back down to the lake and start to make their way south. Water temperatures are now pushing into the sixties and the shad are comfortable and moving south again. Look for bait on points near the river channel at this time. They will be leaving the backs of the creeks and traveling using the river channel like a highway. They start by staging near the mouths of the creeks and, once the water temperatures hit 75°F, they head southbound in big schools. Again, not all the bait heads south, but a large portion of it will. By now we are in April, with May fast approaching. Now is the time to concentrate off points on the south end of the lake and on humps that are twenty to twenty-five feet deep. The bait will continue to stay there until the water temperature pushes into the high seventies and even 80°F. At this point it doesn't really matter what the shad is doing, as the water temperature is starting to become uncomfortable for the striped bass, who will start to go deeper to find the cool, oxygenated waters. This will continue throughout the summer as water temperatures push into the mid and upper eighties. It is at this time of the year that I lay off the stripers as they are stressed by the lakes unoxygenated water. Striped bass stay in the thermocline at this time of the year and should really be left alone. The lack of oxygen in the lake makes them a candidate for high levels of stress until the lake turns over and carries good levels of oxygen throughout the entire lake. By end of September or early October the cool northerly prevailing winds will once again

As water temperatures begin to warm during the springtime, striped bass can be found feeding in more shallower waters. *Photo Credit: Josh England.*

start pushing the water temperature down into the low to mid-seventies and the stripers will come up to feed on threadfin shad that are concentrated on the southern end of the lake and are high in the water column. This is just one example of how water temperatures can help you find striped bass throughout the entire year.

WEATHER PATTERNS: HOW THEY AFFECT STRIPED BASS

I spent over twenty years fishing for striped bass along the eastern seaboard. Having grown up in Brooklyn, New York and living within walking distance to the entrance of New York Harbor, I spent many a day huffing it to the water to toss lures at stripers. As I got older, my bicycle became my vehicle to allow me to fish waters a little farther from home. Eventually, a beach buggy was in my future and that opened up much of the New England and mid-Atlantic coast to pursue these fish all year long. I was lucky enough to meet and fish with some of the best and brightest striper fishermen on the coast—guys like Nat Piazza, Dominick and Vito Battaglia, Steve Campo, and a host of others who were known as the "sharpies" during the seventies and eighties. I was a sponge to it all. One of the best lessons I learned from these anglers was how to let the weather help define when and where to fish for striped bass. Striped bass in salt water seem to eat best during the snotty weather. Get a

Fishing to striped bass during a prefrontal weather pattern usually leads to a successful outing. Some of the best prefrontal conditions happen during a winter snowstorm. *Photo Credit: Henry Cowen*

nasty, windy, cold day in the fall and these fish will put on the feed bag. It's not that they won't feed in calm weather, but if it is pre-frontal and blustery, the likelihood is that these fish are feeding somewhere. Like many animals, stripers are affected by barometric pressure. Take a trip on a pre-frontal weather pattern and you'll notice that the barometric pressure will start to drop. As the pressure drops, the fish will become more active and feed more aggressively. Wait until after the front goes through and you will find the pressure has bottomed out and has started to rise. Once this occurs, the feeding pattern of the striped bass will usually shut down until stable weather becomes the norm again. Back in the early eighties I spent many a night fishing the tip of Queens, New York's famed Breezy Point Jetty. Breezy (as we called it) was at the entrance to Jamaica Bay from the Atlantic Ocean, and that jetty put more thirty-plus-pound fish on its rocks than any other. I learned quickly that to stay home on an easterly blow meant I probably missed out on some tremendous striper fishing. We also learned that if you fished prior to a major storm surge (like a nor'easter or a hurricane), the fishing would likely be epic. Fishing on the backside of these storms usually meant dirty water and a very lackluster feed.

When I moved down to Georgia in the late nineties, I learned that weather patterns played a significant role in freshwater striper fishing too. Some of the same patterns I had known about from fishing the salt water applied to the freshwater striped bass game. However, some of the patterns I had savored and relished in the salt water were just the opposite when fishing in fresh water. With regards to the pre-frontal storms, freshwater striper fishing is very similar to that of the saltwater fishery. Striped bass in fresh water will feed like it's their last meal prior to a storm. I believe the bite is even more predictable in fresh water; as the barometric pressure starts to fall, nine times out of ten the fish will

Anglers need to dress for success. Weather on reservoirs can change in a New York minute, and it always pays to layer under a rain jacket to account for all conditions. *Photo Credit: Josh England.*

feed vigorously. Once the clouds start to roll in on a pre-storm weather pattern, you need to drop everything and get out on the lake. The bite will surely be coming. However, fishing on the backside of that storm, as the pressure starts to rise, will shut down the fishery as if you had just flicked off a light switch.

The big difference between the freshwater pattern versus the saltwater pattern is in watching the fish feed on the surface. I have witnessed countless days on the ocean in snotty, windy weather and had striped bass tearing it up on the surface. Blitzes that stretched as far as your eye could see would take place during a blow. Sometimes it was blowing fifteen miles per hour and sometimes it was honking at twenty-five miles an hour and the fish just didn't seem to care. Birds were diving, bait was spraying, and the water was erupting with surface-feeding hungry striped bass. Take those exact same conditions and move the local from salt water to fresh water and you likely will not find a fish feeding on the surface. During these conditions on area lakes around the country, stripers seem to honker down deep and wait for the system to pass. However, get a windless or near windless day and

When fishing for striped bass or hybrids that are eating threadfin shad, all anglers pray for overcast days. *Photo Credit: Josh England.*

you'll have a different story. For some reason, the stripers we fish to in reservoirs and lakes seem to like to feed on the surface in calm waters. I am not sure why that is, but it just is. During the fall here in Georgia, Lake Sidney Lanier has one heck of a top-water bite that can occur several times a day. It's almost a rite of passage that when mid-October arrives, so does the blitzing striped bass on Lanier. This pattern will stay for four to six weeks. Much of Atlanta's fly-fishing community waits for this bite and plans its schedule by it. If the weather is cloudy and light winds prevail, the top-water bite will likely be epic. If the winds pick up, however, then you'd better find an area of calmer water if you want to see surfacing stripers blitzing shad.

Depending on the forage fish in the reservoir or river you are fishing, weather can always help dictate the feed of stripers. This is especially true in reservoirs, even more so than in rivers. Many reservoirs have a mix of both threadfin shad and gizzard shad in their system. Weather helps determine where that forage bait will be. Threadfin shad seem to stay higher up in the water column on cloudy days and go a little deeper on sunny days. While I have not found gizzards to be as predictable to the sun or the clouds, I will say that on my lake, Sidney Lanier, we have a tremendous population of blueback herring. Herring seem to do just the opposite of the threadfin shad. Herring seem to get higher in the water column on sunny days but lurk a little deeper on cloudy days. Knowing this information can help determine what the fish are eating on any given day (especially when they are seen feeding on the surface). This is when it is best to keep a fishing diary so you can figure out the feeding patterns of your fishery. Every time you make a trip to the lake or river, it's best to document your day for later use as reference. Fish and patterns repeat themselves year after year. For your diary, mark the date, time you fished, how many you caught or didn't catch, the wind direction and speed, water temperature, moon phase, and any other pertinent information you may have noticed on that day of fishing. Eventually it will

Fishing for striped bass during a prefrontal weather pattern usually leads to a successful outing. Some of the best prefrontal conditions happen during winter snowstorms. *Photo Credit: Henry Cowen.*

all become second nature to you, but having a diary and paying attention to weather patterns will positively affect your success rate.

Moon Phases: Their Effect on Striped Bass

Saltwater anglers have known for a long time that certain species of fish seem to feed better on specific moon phases. Science tells us that that gravitational pull has a direct effect on animal behavior. For example, deer tend to move in the woods more during certain phases of the moon. Deer hunters know this and use those specific moon phases to give them an edge when looking to take a buck.

Fishermen do the same thing with moon phases. They know that more movement due to the moon improves the likelihood of their running into feeding fish. While this is never a sure thing, fishing certain moon phases is like putting another chip on your side of the table when it comes to locating feeding fish. The full and new moon phases will have a direct effect on tides for saltwater anglers.

Peek at any tide table and, when you look at the height of the tides around both the new and full moon phases, you will see there will be stronger tides, which means more water will be in each area. This all creates movement, which allows anglers to find more aggressively feeding fish. In-the-know anglers have used moon phases to be successful for years. Having fished for saltwater stripers since the mid-1970s, I can tell you this is 100 percent accurate.

Moon phases play a big role in the movement of freshwater stripers too. One of the first things I learned when I started fly fishing for freshwater striped bass is that the new and full moon phases heighten fish feeding activity. Because of this, I always try to fish three days before and the three days after the new moon.

Fishing around the new and full moon phases always heightens the chances for success when hunting for striped bass. *Photo Credit: Josh England.*

Anglers need to be prepared to share the water when fishing around the best moon phases. *Photo Credit: Josh England.*

Fishing the day of the new moon can sometimes lead to slow fishing in lakes. The days just before and after seem to ring the dinner bell for fish. What I have experienced is that if you are going to fish the day of the new moon, it is probably best to fish in the dark (nighttime). The full moon is slightly different. I have found that fishing as far out as seven to eight days before and up to three days after the full moon will get you an enhanced bite. Just as with the new moon, fishing the day of the full moon has often been disappointing to me. I will say that, over the years, I have found that while most of my striper fishing occurs during the lower light stages of the day (early morning just after sunrise) or late in the day (just before sunset), if you must fish the day of the full moon, then on rare occasions you might get lucky and find some decent fishing in the middle of the day. This by no means states that fishing any of the other moon phases will not produce fish. On the contrary, I have caught fish in freshwater lakes no matter what the moon phase is. However, these moon phases just mentioned have time and time again proven to have an enhanced feeding period associated with them. It just makes sense to use that information to help you find feeding fish.

When it comes to striped bass fishing in rivers, I have not really found any correlation between any enhanced feeding when fishing any moon phase. Fishing striped bass in rivers has way more to do with water levels and water clarity than moon phases.

WATER CLARITY IN RESERVOIRS: HOW IT AFFECTS STRIPED BASS

While we know that water temperature plays what may be the most central role in finding freshwater striped bass in both lakes and rivers, water clarity plays a major role as well. Talking in the most general of terms, water clarity can be clear, stained (mildly versus heavily), or dirty. Stripers act differently in different water conditions. How an angler fishes to stripers in clear water will differ from fishing to them in heavily stained water. What flies we choose to fish, what color we decide to throw at them, and how we retrieve the fly will all play a part, depending on the water clarity. Let me start by saying it is extremely difficult to fish for freshwater striped bass when the water is completely dirty, or what we term "chocolate." The fish are not comfortable in dirty water and they do not see the fly very well. While you might mark fish in dirty water in an impoundment, it is not recommended that you spend much time fishing for them, as it is nearly impossible to get them to hit a fly, or even a conventional lure, in such conditions. If you simply must fish dirty water for stripers, your best shot is going to be to throw up and into shallow water. I have had some decent fishing on occasion by tossing flies and bucktail jigs (yes, I do fish conventional tackle too) in water that was dirty due to heavy rains that had muddied up the back of a creek where the fish were previously holding. The key is to find the mudline where the dirty water meets the stained water. Let's say you were going to fish a certain cove where fish have been recently residing. Now let's say you had three to four inches of rain and that cove got muddied up and looks chocolate when you get back in there. Just slowly turn around and drive out of that cove until you see the visual mudline that goes from brown to off-colored green. There is a good chance that the stripers will have moved out of the back of the cove to find food in the slightly clearer water. Stripers also generally do not like to feed in cold, muddy water. Many times, I will fish the points or structure on the mudline and stick a few fish on what otherwise might be some challenging hours of fishing.

Anytime you fish water that is not clear, your choice of which fly to fish and how to retrieve it can make all the difference. In dirty water conditions, I prefer to use flies that make some noise. Such flies either have bulky heads to push water or have spinners or rattles that create vibrations in the water. As for color, go with a dark fly for dark water and something lighter in water that's somewhat clear. Whether I am fishing a river or a lake, my strategy on color does not change when

Striped bass can be found feeding in clear water as well as stained water. The fish can be tougher to fool when fishing the clear water. *Photo Credit: Josh England.*

the water is dirty or heavily stained. I like black as a first choice in heavily stained water, though I would also consider two-toning a fly's color combination like blurple (black and purple). If the water is clear or slightly stained, I am a staunch believer that chartreuse works the best. As for retrieves, the dirtier or more stained the water, the slower you need to fish. That may mean retrieving your fly with longer pauses between strips, as well as using shorter strips.

I like the clarity of slightly stained water best of all. I believe striped bass can be fooled into eating a fly or lure through instinct. There are many times they see something moving and just cannot help themselves. This is especially true when you're fishing an area that does not have a lot of bait or forage around. A striper may need to make a quick decision to eat or not to eat, and in slightly stained water it may not get that good a look at your presentation. This is when I might fish a fly a little more quickly. However, remember that even in slightly stained water a striped bass is more likely to eat on a slight pause than with no pause at all. As for color, when fishing slightly stained water matching the hatch is always your best bet. If there is no discernable hatch, use a fly that incorporates some gray, olive, white, chartreuse, or yellow into the pattern.

The last type of water clarity we need to discuss is clear water. Everyone loves to go out and fish gin-clear water, as the lake or river is so pretty from an aesthetic point of view. That may very well be true, but it also makes it more difficult to fool a freshwater striped bass into taking your offering. The problem is that in clear water, fish can take a longer look at your presentation and decide whether to eat or pass. When fishing in clear water, I have always found it best to fish a tad faster. We do not want the fish to get a really good look at your fly, as that will often lead to a refusal. I also find that a sparsely tied fly will often perform better in clear water that a bulky fly will. This is when I prefer to use flash rather than noise to entice a hit from a striped bass. Lastly, when fishing clear water, it is my opinion that matching

Matching the hatch is always your best recipe for success when fishing clear water. *Photo Credit: Josh England.*

the hatch by size is critical. However, now is the time when you also may want to consider using a chartreuse colored fly. Occasionally pausing your retrieve in clear water may or may not make sense, and only trial and error will allow you to figure out how to retrieve the fly in the cleanest of waters. Me, I am still a believer in having pauses during your retrieve, though maybe only very short ones now. What you need to remember is that you must change your tactics based on a river or lake's water clarity.

DAMS, POWER PLANTS, AND PUMP STORAGE RESERVOIRS

When fishing for striped bass in tidal waters, one of the best ways to figure out where the fish will be is to use the tide tables in any given location. All gamefish, and especially striped bass, can be better targeted when you put tide charts in play with your strategy of where to fish. Fish use tides to ambush their prey, and when saltwater anglers figure out what locations are holding fish at certain parts of the tide, they can virtually guarantee themselves a more productive fishing trip.

Unfortunately, freshwater anglers targeting striped bass do not have the luxury of having tides to help them locate productive feeding patterns. However, lakes and rivers do have man-made dams that they can use to help them figure out feeding patterns. While nearly all lakes have some sort of current running through them, it is important to know that the stronger the current the more likely there will be a good feeding pattern. A stronger current usually elicits or triggers a more solid feeding pattern for striped bass. The question is, where do we find the strongest currents on a lake? The answer to that is simple. If there is a dam attached to the lake you are intending to fish, the creeks or coves nearest the dam will have the most current.

On my home lake, Buford Dam is located on the southern end of the impoundment. There is always water flowing through the dam into the Chattahoochee River below. However, the US Army Corps of Engineers (which controls the dam) publicly releases a daily generation schedule, which tells you when additional water releases will be made. Sometimes the generation will be for only an hour and other times it may last up to seven hours. When the lake has received a lot of additional rainfall, the Corps of Engineers can decide to release around the clock. However, most of the time an average release is anywhere from two to four hours. These releases will increase the current on the lake, thus triggering more feeding activity for striped bass. The farther away you are from the dam, the less likely these releases will trigger any additional feeding activity. So, in the winter months, when I am fishing the north end of the lake, I do not concern myself

When water is being pulled from a dam, the stripers usually feed better, as the increased current can accentuate their feeding. *Photo Credit: Josh England.*

with the water releases. But in the early fall and late spring, when I do most of my fishing on the southern end of the lake, I follow the water release schedules like clockwork.

When anglers are looking to fish to stripers that are feeding on or near the surface, keeping a close eye on water release schedules can put extra fish in the boat. Once the scheduled water release begins, it will normally take twenty to thirty minutes to get the current flowing enough to start the enhanced feeding pattern. I will plan my guide trips many times around the water release schedule. This has really helped me determine when a top-water pattern will occur on any given day.

Some impoundments may have hydroelectric power plants on them. These plants are there mostly to help create energy for people who live in that area. For anglers, this is a bonus if there are striped bass in that lake. Power plants will often create currents through the water discharges they give off. These discharges will keep fish nearby throughout much of the fishing season, as the bait will stack up near these plants. There will always be some sort of current being generated by these plants. The real bonus is if these plants produce a hot water outflow.

When I grew up fishing in and around New York City, I learned about how effective fishing a hot water outflow could be. While our typical saltwater striped bass season started around mid-April and lasted through November, I learned how a hot water outflow could help extend my fishing season. Once the waters around New York City cooled down to sub-45°F water, the forage fish would leave and move south during their fall migration. The striped bass would follow the forage and move south too. Yet what always happened would be that some baitfish would stay too long in the area where a hot water outflow was occurring, and then would be trapped there for the entire winter. Some of the stripers would consequently stay all winter and feed on that bait until the following spring, when the waters would start to warm up and the bait as well as the stripers could venture out into the surrounding waters and migrate north again. We would fish all winter long in the area of the hot water outflows and catch fish the whole time. There were times when we would wade into these areas and feel like being in a sauna.

Lakes with hot water outflows work in a similar fashion. Once the surface water temperatures drop down to below 50°F, there is a good chance that large amounts of forage fish will migrate to the outflow. This in turn will cause striped bass to congregate around that hot water too. Hot water outflows can produce some fantastic fishing on lakes throughout the United States. In fact, the end of November through March can be a good time to fish around any hot water outflow. If you fish these outflows during the day, you might find fish feeding on the surface at first and last light. However, most of the time hot water outflows produce best when you locate the fish with your electronics and by tossing

Cloudy days coupled with dam generation makes striped bass fishing with a fly rod easier.
Photo Credit: Josh England.

fast-sinking lines around or near the warm water. Using hot water outflows to help locate and catch fish is one of the best and easiest ways for fly anglers to find honey holes. One final mention about power plants and striped bass fishing is that since striped bass are nocturnal feeders, fly fishing to them at night around hot water outflows in the winter produce some of the best fishing you will find anywhere.

Not all reservoirs have dams with rivers running through them or have power plants attached to their system. Some watersheds were created as pump storage reservoirs to hold water for the area. Many of the lakes throughout California use this type of system. The California aqueduct, which runs from north-central California down through southern California, is made up of a few pump storage reservoirs. The pump structure brings water and allows water to flow out, which allows the water to be manipulated throughout the entire system. A couple of great striper lakes using this system would be O'Neill Forebay and the San Luis Reservoir. Both freshwater lakes are pump storage reservoirs, and their pump structures create current both when water is coming into the lakes as well as when they are pumping out of the lakes. The areas around the pump structures are where anglers should start hunting for stripers. Some of the biggest freshwater stripers ever caught on fly have come from these two reservoirs.

STRUCTURE FORAGE FISH USE TO HIDE IN A RESERVOIR

Locating certain structure in a reservoir can be a big help in your overall success when fishing for freshwater striped bass. Striped bass will often set up and ambush targeted forage fish. These gamefish can be extremely strategic at times, and it is important for an angler to be strategic as well. Knowing which structure to look for can shorten the curve needed to catch striped bass. Striped bass will continually locate specific structure and use it to their advantage when on the hunt for a meal. If you were to empty a reservoir of its water and look from above, you would clearly see why certain areas of structure continuously hold fish year in and year out. Those areas become "hot spots," and should be marked on your GPS for future reference. It is also a good idea to keep a journal of successful and unsuccessful days to help you identify patterns for future reference. In the journal, you can reference such things as water height, weather, wind, time of day, number of fish caught, specific areas where you fished, which flies were successful and which ones weren't, and much more. There just is not any substitute for time spent on the water. Of all the info supplied in your journal, describing the structure where

Once you locate the forage, there is a good chance the striped bass are not far behind, traveling in schools where multiple hook-ups are possible. *Photo Credit: Josh England.*

you found the fish is probably the most important piece of information you can supply. Let's identify some of the more popular pieces of structure found on many reservoirs throughout the country.

Tapered points are one of the best pieces of structure that an angler can find and fish. There are both long tapered points and short tapered points. Basically, these are high spots near the shoreline that gradually drop off into deeper water. Some tapered points may be one hundred feet long while others may be as much as three hundred feet long. Forage will get up on these points for feeding, warmth, or safety. Usually forage will get up on these points in low light conditions and then, as the sun gets high in the sky, back off into deeper water. Stripers may get up shallow on these points or lay in wait on the drop-offs to attack their prey.

Seawalls are usually found on reservoirs where large marinas may be found. The forage will use these wooden or metal seawalls to find food or hide from predators. It is always best to throw your flies on both ends of the seawall, as those seem to be the most reliable spots for finding bait and striped bass.

Humps are also great areas to fish. These are underwater pieces of land or mounds surrounded by deep water. Forage will look to hide on humps that are mostly twenty to twenty-five feet deep. If the hump you fish happens to have brush on it, then you have hit the jackpot! Always fish around brush or brush piles.

Many brush piles are man-made, and include such things as discarded Christmas trees that have been weighted and sunk onto humps by savvy anglers. Forage will gather on those brush piles in big concentrations. Some humps may be as small as thirty feet in circumference while others can be five times that size or larger. No matter what the size, always try to find any brush piles and fish them hard.

Blowdowns are yet another structure we find on reservoirs. These are basically downed trees that are near the bank. Forage use blowdowns to hide from predators. When the forage and stripers get shallow, these are great pieces of structure to fish.

Standing timber is also worth checking, as it can often attract forage fish. This is especially true with gizzards during certain times of the year. For most fly anglers, standing timber is rather deep and difficult to key in on. However, some man-made lakes have trees that have been cut to twenty or thirty feet down. If the lake levels ever drop by any significance, then tossing flies into and around the remaining treetops is a great way to find fish.

High grass can also be good structure to find both the forage and the stripers. This is especially true when the grass is either on a point or when it's along a flat. Either way, you might see forage dimpling near the grass early and late in the day,

Georgia striped bass angler Steve Dean located a large school of threadfin and then proceeded to find a good-sized school of striped bass on Lake Sidney Lanier. *Photo Credit: Josh England.*

as well as striped bass blowing up on the surface eating threadfin or gizzards near this type of structure.

Saddles (also known to some as "blow-throughs") are structures that start on a piece of land and go across to an island or another piece of land. The water may be deep on both sides, but the high spot that attaches from one piece of land to another is called a saddle. Saddles are some of the most consistent pieces of structure an angler can fish on a reservoir. The only difference when referencing a blow-though versus a saddle is that some anglers find that a shallow sandbar between two pieces of land would deem it a blow-through as the land is shallower on both sides of the sandbar. They are very similar, and should you find this structure, make sure you fish it thoroughly.

Pilings are yet another structure that anglers should consider fishing, as they are great hiding areas for forage fish.

Along the same lines as pilings are docks. Docks, especially marina docks, can offer great hiding places for forage species. Gamefish like striped bass will get right in there and feed in and around the dock structure. Some docks have pilings to keep them secure, while others docks are floating. Both will have a lot of shade around them, and that's where the forage will gravitate to.

Rock piles and riprap are other types of structure that forage will be around at times. On reservoirs that have a lot of rocks, I have found that the forage's spawning season is when I'll see a lot of shad around the rocks. For that matter, you will find that a lot of juvenile fish use rocks as cover throughout the year.

Ledges are deep-water structures that need to be addressed as well. Ledges are usually found where the river channel meets some rising topography. We usually find threadfin using this structure in the fall and sometimes in the late spring when you might encounter a top-water bite. As you move about, watching your depth finder, you might see the water quickly rise from a bottom of one hundred feet to sixty feet in a matter of seconds. If you see that, you just went over a ledge.

Culverts are easily some of the most reliable structures on any reservoir. Why is that? Simple: Culverts are large round pipes that allow water to flow into the reservoir from another source. Because of the current coming through, forage love to hide around areas with culverts. When I look for striped bass in any reservoir, culverts are always one of the first things I try to locate.

Any new incoming freshwater source is also good structure to fish, as forage fish will always congregate near highly oxygenated water. If you see a waterfall or a spot where a creek flows into a cove, you can rest assured that forage will be there at some time of the year and that the striped bass will not be far behind.

Lastly, I would include mudlines as good structure. After a hard rain, a reservoir can get very dirty and muddy, to the point where the forage can handle the dirty water better than the striped bass. However, the stripers will not venture far from where they were previously feeding before the water muddied up. So, fishing a mudline is an opportunity to find fish in a confined area and should be considered as structure.

Gulls are the perfect giveaway that striped bass or hybrids may be harassing forage and busting the surface. *Photo Credit: Josh England.*

WILDLIFE AND HOW IT CAN AID ANGLERS

Birds can help anglers find stripers on impoundments throughout most of the season. Impoundments around the country have a variety of birdlife that will eat fish as a mainstay in their diets. While eagles and ospreys can be found on many impoundments throughout the country, these are not the birds we are looking for, as they are looking for predator fish to eat. They eat bass, stripers, trout, bream, and so on. The birds we are looking for to help us find baitfish and, therefore, striped bass, are herons, loons, kingfishers, gulls, and terns. These birds love to eat small baitfish like shad and herring. Finding these birds is a sure sign that baitfish are close. Remember, find the bait and you find the striped bass. What's most important is that you find these birds while they are hunting for their next meal. Just finding gulls sitting on the water and not flying much isn't going to give you any clues as to where the bait is. Here are a few clues in cracking the code on how birdlife can help you find striped bass.

Great Blue Herons

Herons may very well be the best fishermen on your lake. They are stealthy and walk softly when hunting for a meal. They move very little water when standing shallow on a bank and stalking their prey. They are sort of a prehistoric-looking bird, with a long neck. While they look kind of gawky due to their appearance, they are anything but. I have seen them roost in the very tops of the trees on thin limbs. When a heron is seen on the bank with its neck tucked into its body, it is clearly resting. A resting heron will not help you find baitfish. However, if you see a heron with its neck extended and either walking along a bank or standing stationary at the water's edge, you've just found a bird that is hunting. If I see a heron with its neck extended as I am running up or down the lake in my boat, I will immediately slow down and watch for a few seconds to see what it may have found. Sometimes it's nothing, but many times it has found some baitfish close to the bank. This is exactly what you need to see when trying to locate striped bass. Sometimes the heron may just be hunting along a stretch of shoreline that seems like a regular piece of land with no identifiable structure around it. Many times, you'll find a heron sitting on a point of land or an entrance to a cove. These are the places that really catch my attention and need to be watched. You might even consider dropping your trolling motor and making a few blind casts where the heron

The best fishermen on any reservoir or river are great blue herons. When their neck is extended, they are hunting for their next meal, and this can aid anglers in finding both forage and striped bass. *Photo Credit: Josh England.*

is hunting. There are also times when you will see a heron sitting in the back of a pocket or the back of a cove. That is usually when you have hit a homerun, as that bird has probably found some shad or herring in the shallow water. There is a good chance that stripers are close by too.

Loons

Loons are migratory birds that can also help you find baitfish in reservoirs. These birds start to show up on my lakes in north Georgia once the fall weather begins in October. They will stick around until the weather warms in early May or possibly slightly before if we have a warmer than normal spring. Loons are cool birds that many of us associate with on the lakes of the upper Midwest and Northeast. When I think of a loon, I think of a bird singing aloud on a calm lake in Minnesota. These birds migrate north and south, and even the deep South will have these part-time residents for six or seven months of the year. Loons are positively baitfish eaters. They can be one the best birds to help you find baitfish and striped bass. A loon can dive down twenty feet or more to gather up a meal before resurfacing. To me, they almost swim like penguins! Loons can travel solo or can be found in groups of as many as a dozen or more. If you watch them closely, you can see them swimming on the surface and then dipping their heads in the water looking for bait. Suddenly, they'll go completely underwater for up to one minute before resurfacing. That tells you that the loon is hunting. If a loon goes subsurface and pops back up one hundred feet away from where it originally went underwater, then that bird is searching but has not yet found a school of baitfish. However, if that loon goes underwater and pops back up in a confined area and then goes down again and comes back up in nearly the same place, there's a good chance your loon has struck gold and found a school of baitfish. Sometimes you see the loon go down and, before it resurfaces, it will push the bait up to the surface and spray the bait like a little blitz. This is the time to stealthily make your way up to that

Many reservoirs have loons that migrate and stay for part of the season. Loons can be incredibly helpful in finding feeding striped bass. *Photo Credit: Josh England.*

loon or loons and throw a fly to that area. There is a good chance there may be a striper or two in with those loons. I cannot tell you how many times I have seen a loon working a bait ball only to then see a striper come up and pop the baitfish on the surface. The loon and the striper are working together to ball up the bait and then take turns feeding through the bait ball. It's some of the most fascinating feeding I've seen on my impoundment. Just remember there are also going to be times where the loon is working alone, and you may not have any striped bass working with them. Making up to a half dozen casts into the feeding loons is called for; if I do not get any takers, it's time to move on.

Kingfishers

Kingfishers are very cool birds whose range stretches throughout the country. They are generally blue in color, and you can hear them squawking around impoundments throughout most all lakes that have striped bass in them. Kingfishers love eating forage fish. Most of the time I use kingfishers to help me find bait and striped bass in the colder months when the fish are in shallow water and in the backs of the coves. While kingfishers are around all year long the colder months are when they seem to give me the most help. If a kingfisher comes swooping in from a tree limb or off the top of a boat dock, it's usually a good bet that it has found a school of baitfish on or near the surface or in shallow water. While these birds are fish eaters, they are not always going to aid the angler in finding bait and

The kingfishers is another important bird that can help anglers locate threadfin shad. *Photo Credit: Keegan Corcoran.*

striped bass. That's because they are so prevalent on area lakes and they can be found in nearly every cove. However, if you are wondering whether there is bait in a certain cove or not, find a kingfisher working and you've found your baitfish.

Terns and Gulls

Most saltwater anglers know what to look for when hunting for many species in the ocean. Locating a flock of diving terns and gulls can be one of the most exciting ways to find and fish to feeding fish. It's what makes saltwater fishing so exhilarating. Well, the same thing can occur on impoundments. Terns and gulls are also migrating birds and, while some lakes get more than others, suffice it to say these guys are the easiest wildlife found to help you locate striped bass. Here in the Southeast, we get our terns and gulls flying down from the north in mid fall and staying through the entire winter before heading back up north again in the middle of spring. While our terns arrive first, they do not really stay very long. It's the herring gulls, ringed-bill gulls, and Bonaparte gulls that stay for a good five months. While any and all these gulls can be tremendous fish finders, it's the Bonaparte gulls that are the superstars in helping us locate forage fish and striped bass. Sometimes all it takes is one single gull to help locate fish, but obviously it's when a flock of gulls is diving and trying to land on top of the water in a confined area that gets every angler's attention. What's most important is that you approach a feeding frenzy of gulls diving on the water quietly and slowly. Give the gulls their space and they'll stay and continue to feed. Run up on top of them with the big motor or get too close with the trolling motor and you will spook them off. I have found that the gulls will only go back so far when fish are feeding in the backs of the coves. I'm not sure of the reason for this. It's almost as if they are claustrophobic. Fish can be busting baitfish in the back of cove in shallow water, but if there are lots of trees in a confined area the birds will only go back so far before they just circle around the area, even if the fish are feeding. Gulls just like their freedom of space. It's also important to try to read the gulls' posture when they're flying. By doing so, you can almost always tell whether the gulls are seeing baitfish or striped bass. When you see gulls flying high in the sky and going around and around in a circle over a very confined area, its nearly certain they see baitfish that are deep. However, if the gulls are flying low to the water in that same confined area, it's likely the gulls have found high bait. That's what should tip you off as to whether to toss a slow-sinking intermediate line versus a fast-sinking line in an area. Another tip to look for is if you go to an area and happen to see a bunch of gulls just sitting on the water and not flying, make a point of looking around to see if there are a bunch of feathers floating on the water. Just after a feeding blitz, many times the gulls will sit and rest on the water. However,

This is why we see gulls or terns diving on the water. They are hunting the forage for food just as the striped bass are, and can be an angler's best indicator to help find feeding fish. Photo Credit: Keegan Corcoran.

when a feeding frenzy is really going on, the birds will often land on top of each other as they try to grab baitfish and, in so doing, will actually knock off each other's feathers in the melee. What those feathers floating on the water will tell you is that you just missed a feeding period. I've also noticed that gulls will start flying right at first light, but a massive feed at that time is unlikely. Birds diving early in the morning are usually just picking up baitfish that are high in the water column. Give it thirty minutes or so, and wait for the feeding to begin. First light bites usually occur in the backs of the coves and in shallow water, like up against a reef marker. In other words, don't worry about gulls right at first light. Give the light a little time to get up before looking for gulls and terns to help find your fish. The same holds true for last light. It is rare that I see gulls blitzing bait at this time either. The fish may be feeding, but watching the gulls and terns at this time will usually not lead to your finding feeding stripers.

Nighttime Fishing

Striped bass are nocturnal fish, meaning that they hunt and feed vigorously at night. Throughout the entire fishing season, anglers can take advantage of this trait by tossing flies to striped bass in the dark. All you need to do is home in on

Bomber Long A lures have developed a huge following for nighttime fishing of striped bass in freshwater reservoirs. *Photo Credit by Josh England.*

the nighttime patterns available throughout the season and you can be very successful fishing. While fly fishing at night for any species is a different game altogether from daytime angling, the rewards for fishing in the wee hours of the evening can be tremendous. There are three distinct nighttime patterns that anglers should learn if they want to catch stripers in the dark. The first is known as the "bomber bite."

Once the heat of the summer is over and the cool weather starts to arrive, a special striped bass pattern develops. Conventional anglers in the know start going out and fishing impoundments after sunset around shallow structure on lakes throughout the country. These anglers are fishing in waters that are three to fifteen feet deep along shorelines and tossing a lure known as a Bomber Long A. It is a six-inch-long plastic lure with a molded lip on the front, and when retrieved slowly it makes an S-like wiggle under the water that can drive stripers crazy. It resembles what conventional freshwater anglers call a jerk bait, but saltwater anglers call a swimbait. If you fish a Bomber Long A in dark colors like black, purple, or even bubblegum pink, you are almost assured of eliciting a strike. What triggers this bite is when a lake's surface water temperature drops into the 70°F range or slightly below. The key to fishing the bomber bite is to find productive shallow structure where the stripers are searching for an easy meal. Long tapered points, sandy beaches, and areas where shallow water drops quickly to deep water are the places to target. If your lake has reef markers on it to alert boaters to shallow obstructions, those are good places to start. Fly anglers can follow suit by tossing intermediate fly lines with Gamechangers, Snake Flies, or any larger fly that offers some movement. The key is to run from place to place and hit as many spots as possible. You may have to hit five or six spots before you find the fish. Once you do, it's game on. One of my favorite tactics is to fish a hookless Bomber Long A and move from spot to spot until I get an eat on the hookless lure. Then I simply put down the conventional outfit and start tossing flies on that spot. I use the hookless lure as a bird dog to flush out the stripers since I can fan cast an area much more quickly and effectively using a conventional outfit. All it takes is half a dozen casts on a spot and then I move on. The more places you hit over the course of an evening, the more likely you are to run into the fish.

Another time you can employ the bomber bite is in the spring, when the lakes' surface water temperatures are coming out of the fifties and moving into the sixties. Stripers just seem to love the nighttime bite when the water temperature is somewhere in the sixties. Once the temperatures go above 70°F, the nighttime bite on artificial baits is over. There is also a time in the spring when the gizzard shad move up shallow and onto the banks to spawn on impoundments throughout the country. This is yet another opportunity for anglers to go out in the dark and toss flies to striped bass that are feeding in the shallows. This usually occurs in

Anglers can sight fish to large striped bass when fishing a dock light. *Photo Credit: Josh England.*

April in the Southeast. The water temperature on the surface is usually hovering in the mid-sixties for the gizzard shad spawn to start. Once again, the key to this pattern is to get up on sandy beaches and using slow-sinking intermediate fly lines along with longer and larger profile flies that have some movement to them. This pattern will usually last a couple to three weeks before the gizzard shad move out of the shallows post spawn.

Finally, one of the most exciting ways to fish at night is to go out and find dock lights to toss flies to. What we term the "dock light bite" is a good way to catch freshwater stripers on lakes throughout the country. I've never met a striper in any lake that didn't like to feed on forage fish under a well-lit dock light. Anglers who fish for snook in Florida regularly employ this pattern to their fishery. The only difference is that snook can be awful spooky when you're trying to coax one into taking an artificial bait (fly or lure). Striped bass, on the other hand, are suckers for artificial baits on dock lights. I used to fish lights very effectively back in my youth when I fished the lights shining down off the Marine Parkway Bridge in Brooklyn. The lights from the bridge were there to aid drivers driving from Brooklyn to Queens over Jamaica Bay. Those streetlights would cast a shadow onto the water and large striped bass could be seen swimming in and out of the shadows. The key was to sight cast to stripers from the bridge stations above. I caught many a large striper that way and to this day my personal best forty-six-pound striper came from using that method of fishing. If you see a striped bass swimming around on a dock light, you are almost surely going to get them to eat a fly! Here is what basically goes on with dock lights in fresh water. First you must either put out a light or know where other lights on your lake are. The easiest way to locate dock lights is to go out on an exploratory trip and just drive all over your lake in the dark, looking for lights on docks that are shining down onto the water. These lights will attract plankton, which will often attract forage fish like threadfin shad, which will attract gamefish like striped bass. It's an entire ecosystem going on right at the dock in the dark. Pull up stealthily to these lit docks and toss either an intermediate outfit or a fast-sinking outfit with a fly. I tend to always toss the fast-sinking line, as the bigger fish usually hover a little deeper on the lights. Fly selection on dock lights is not that important, although I will say that if fish are feeding on small young-of-the-year threadfin shad during the daytime and tossing small flies is a must in order to elicit strikes, at nighttime I'd still toss a larger fly like a full-sized Clouser minnow. You must be able to feed the fish even on a dock light. That means employing a strip-stop technique. Toss your fly around the light and let it sink some, then use a series of short strips followed by a three-second pause and then a few short strips again. This strip-stop technique is easily the most effective for fishing to freshwater striped bass. Once you hook a fish, you'll find that the fish will immediately run back to the light and try to wrap you around a dock piling or some other obstruction, and any other fish on or around the light will be spooked from your hooking that first fish. Sometimes it's a one and done deal, especially with larger fish (over eight pounds). If you pull the fish off the light and get it to the boat quickly, you might have an opportunity to fish to more stripers before they eventually spook off. Once that occurs, it's time to go to another light. If you rest the light just fished for an hour, you can come back later and find fish hovering around the dock light. That is why your best strategy is to find three or four lights in a fairly close proximity that you can bounce around to fish throughout an evening trip.

There are basically a few types of lights you need to know about. Let's break them down into two groups: above water and underwater. Above-water lights are simply just halogen lights folks use around their docks to keep them lit. If a dock owner's lights are facing down and toward the water, that is your best scenario. Anywhere you see a lighted glow on the water can hold striped bass. One other factor is the color of the light. It has been my experience that yellow lights do not attract the forage bait to them as much as white lights do. I'm not sure if this is because yellow lights do not attract the plankton, but I suspect that may be the reason. So always try to find the white lights when looking for above-water lights at nighttime.

Striped bass in reservoirs will find dock lights to feed on threadfin shad after dark and are much easier to catch versus snook, which in salt water can be more finicky under dock lights. *Photo Credit: David Cannon.*

The second lights you should look for are underwater lights. These are the home-run lights that are put out by dock owners specifically to attract gamefish. Many of the lights will have large green hues to them, and are fish-attracting magnets. Some of the more well-known makers of underwater green lights are Hydro-Glow and Green Monster. These lights are plugged into an electrified dock with a waterproof cable and a large waterproof LED bulb. There will be a converter on the dock so that the voltage going into the water is extremely low, making it safe for people swimming around the area. These underwater lights can have a cord up to one hundred feet in length so that dock owners can set them out fifty feet from their dock so they can cast and fish from the dock itself. Usually the dock owner will sink the cable into the deepest area out from the dock and use dumb-bell weights and zip ties so that the light floats up to just under five to seven feet below the surface. The higher the light is to the surface, the more easily it is to see fish hovering around the light. However, the higher the light is to the surface, the bigger and brighter is the glow. That means it's easier for other anglers looking for lights to find it from greater distances. If you find one of these underwater lights, it is best to toss your fly to the edges of the light, as fish seem to swim around and through them. A fish hooked on the edge of a light is less likely to spook off his friends, thus allowing you to fish to more stripers before eventually spooking them. I have gone to lights and found as many as thirty to forty fish on one light.

Fishing dock lights, especially underwater lights, is a sure way to find hungry striped bass on nearly any reservoir. *Photo Credit: Josh England.*

Dock light fishing usually begins around Thanksgiving on my lake (when water temps are around 60°F) and continues through most of May. While most folks like to fish lights after dark, I prefer to fish lights early in the morning. First, there is less pressure on lighted docks after midnight. Second, most dock light owners are usually sound asleep when I am fishing their lights. Dock lights can be legally fished, as they are not private property, but the dock light owner is the one who owns the light and may shut it off if he sees you fishing his light. If someone is already fishing on a light when you arrive, it's best to just turn around and leave and come back later, when they are through fishing it. Dock light courtesy is basically first come first served unless it's the dock owner. They trump all others. A final word about dock light fishing is that it usually takes about forty-five minutes to an hour after dark to get the fish swimming around the light. Next time you want to try something completely different, give dock light fishing for striped bass a try. It'll ruin you for life!

Chapter 5

Tactics Used to Catch Striped Bass in Reservoirs

How to Target Surface Feeding Fish

One of fly-fishing's great moments is experiencing a true top-water surface feed. It happens in many saltwater fisheries as well as some warm-water bass fisheries

A good pair of binoculars is indispensable when trying to locate fish that are feeding on the surface. *Photo Credit: Josh England.*

during certain times of the year. If you were a trout fisherman, you might liken it to an all-out insect hatch, which usually occurs at dusk. To be on a cold-water river and see trout rising as far as the eye can see is one of those magical moments in the sport of fly fishing. On striper reservoirs, there are those magical moments when an area is teeming with what looks like white-water explosions on the surface that can be seen from nearly a half mile away. You might see an entire fish coming out of the water or just a tail kicked up from beneath the surface. It is the type of explosion that one could replicate by dropping a cinder block out a second story window and into the water. Now multiply that surface boil by twenty, thirty, or even one-hundred and you are experiencing an all-out feeding frenzy or what many saltwater anglers call a "blitz." It can happen on many lakes when the forage gets high in the water column and the water temperatures start cooling down after a long, hot summer. These blitzes can continue throughout the fall and through some of the winter. They can also occur in the springtime, but are more likely to happen in the fall as far as freshwater striped bass are concerned.

There are some measures an angler can take to take advantage of these blitzes. First, make sure you do not get too close to the surfacing fish. Stripers can be easily spooked, and staying thirty to forty feet away from the surface feed will help ensure that the fish stay up longer and continue their feed. Next, it is always best to shut the big engine down at about one hundred to two hundred feet away from the feeding fish, and approach the school using your electric trolling motor. If the fish are going up and then back down in short order, not allowing you to get close to them, then pulling up to them with the big engine is all you can do. Do not waste your time trying to get near them with the electric motor, as that is all but impossible to do. I have seen stripers come up and feed for thirty seconds and then go down and come up again within a couple of minutes, only to feed for another thirty seconds and then descend below the surface. That is a hard and frustrating game to play. On my lake, it happens when the stripers are gorging on blueback herring. When they are on threadfin shad, the stripers seem to stay up on the surface much longer, so employing your stealthy electric trolling motor is a much better strategy then. Always try to cast your fly into the middle of the school or at the very least in the direction the fish seem to be moving. Also remember that if you simply must catch a fish feeding on or near the surface, it is always best to toss a subsurface fly and work it back to the boat with pauses in the retrieve. If you want to catch a striper on a surface fly like a popper, then have at it, but remember that if you do not get an eat after a good half dozen casts, it's best to go back to tossing a subsurface fly that sinks slowly. Even though it may appear that the fish are feeding on the surface, the stripers actually may be feeding on forage one to three feet down. When you see a splash or blowup, what you may be seeing

Once a school is located feeding on the surface, anglers need to be stealthy and quiet as they approach the fish. *Photo Credit: Josh England.*

is the fish coming up and feeding just under the surface, then kicking its tail to turn and go back down to deeper water. Many anglers mistake this feeding pattern as a top-water feed while it is truly taking place a few feet below the surface.

Angler etiquette can play a vital role when chasing surface feeders. You see people tend to get too excited when fish are blitzing on top and, as Lefty Kreh used to say (via Mark Twain), "common sense isn't all that common." This is true during top-water season as folks just lose their sense of fairness and politeness during this pattern. Even though there may be multiple boats chasing and fishing to these surface-feeding fish, it's always best to use caution and politeness and to not cut off other boats off or throw across someone's line. I have seen many an incident turn ugly when anglers throw etiquette to the wind. Many of the guides on my lake refer to this pattern as "combat fishing." I personally do not mind a boat getting within seventy-five to one hundred feet of me if they are not casting over my lines or moving up and into the fish. It is okay to be close, but just not too close. This is where common sense comes into play. There are folks who are newbies to this and will unknowingly blow the fish out by getting too close or running into them hard with the big motor. My suggestion is that while you will be upset or at the least frustrated, it is best to politely advise them of what they did by stating, "You probably didn't realize this, but these fish are spooky and you need to approach more cautiously next time." Politeness always wins out in these

If the gulls and terns have returned to your reservoir, then finding the surface feeding stripers is made easier by their arrival. *Credit: Dave Whitlock.*

situations. Lastly, always remember that fish are probably feeding on top in more than one place. Many times I have left five or six boats fishing one school on top to go and find another school that is getting less pressured. It is all about being strategic when it comes to the top-water bite.

When waiting for a top-water blitz, it never hurts to run and look for surface feeding activity. The guy or gal who burns the most gas is usually the one who is most rewarded. Just because the fish were up yesterday in area "A" does not mean they will be up in that exact spot again the next day. If you can work with another boat to cut the area that you feel is in play in half, it will allow you to expand your search and double the odds of finding fish on top. Another tactic is to look for the calmest water in the area you will be hunting. If the wind is up, the likelihood is that the fish will show up on top in the calmest water. This is exactly the opposite of what I experienced in my thirty-plus years of striper fishing in salt water. We always found that fish fed best and in the highest water column when the weather was nasty. Reservoir stripers like calm water when they feed on the surface.

While a top-water feed can occur at any time, anglers should look to sunset as one of the prime times to see surface feeding fish. *Credit: Josh England.*

Another good tip is that fish tend to feed on top during lower light stages. It is best to look for them on top during the first three hours after first light or the last three hours before dark. You will also notice that the fish feed best on overcast days when they are on threadfin shad versus sunny days or when you are closer to a new or full moon phase. Finally, if your reservoir has a dam attached to it, then try to plan your fishing around the water generation schedule. When they pull water from the reservoir, it creates a current that gets the stripers and shad moving around more, which tends to promote surface feeding activity. When the top-water surface feed begins on my lake, it is easily the most popular time for anglers to be out striper fishing. Lake Lanier has no fewer than ninety boats that specifically fish for striped bass with fly rods. Rarely do we see more than a dozen fly fishermen out at a time, but when the word gets out that the top-water bite has begun, it gets more crowded on the pond.

HOW TO USE ELECTRONICS TO FIND SUBSURFACE FISH

For reservoir fishing, the one question I get asked by more anglers is: How important is it to spend a lot of money on buying a fishfinder? The answer is not as simple as one might expect. It all depends on what you are going to do with that fishfinder. If you are strictly fly fishing for striped bass, then going out and buying the latest and greatest the industry has to offer is fine, but probably not necessary. If you plan on fishing for striped bass using both fly and conventional methods and you would even consider fishing live bait, then buying the industry's best will positively add a few more bites to your day's fishing. You see, when the fish are down deep and hiding in the trees, most good fishfinders will not show you the stripers hiding out in that structure. However, a top-of-the-line fishfinder will separate the stripers from the trees more easily, thus allowing you to know where to drop your bait. This is especially true when anglers fish to stripers over the summer months. The fish can be found as deep as one hundred feet or you might find them at forty to fifty feet down. Personally, I recommend leaving these summer fish alone, as the hotter water temperatures combined with the depleted oxygen levels can stress out the stripers to the point of killing them once brought to the surface and then released.

For anglers strictly fly fishing, however, a good electronic fishfinder is a must. You will also need good mapping technology as part of your electronics package, and a large-screen, dual-mode fishfinder/GPS combination is a must for helping

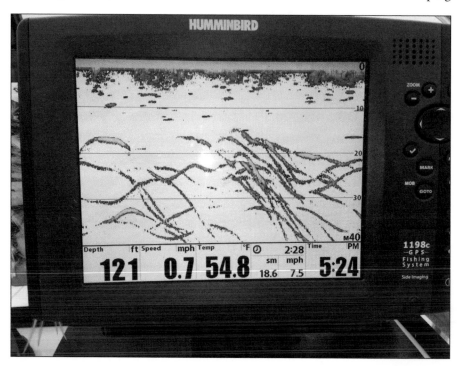

This photo shows that the fish are moving more slowly and are bunched up between eighteen and twenty-five feet over a 121-foot bottom. These stripers can more easily be caught on a fast-sinking fly line. *Photo Credit: Henry Cowen.*

to locate and catch freshwater striped bass. Many companies make great fishfinders today, and the technology seems to get better year after year. The biggest difference is the mapping technology that's available. I, for one, am a fan of Humminbird electronics, as they have the best in mapping technology (Lake Master) as well as excellent fishfinding capabilities. Combine that with the fact that their parent company, Johnson Outdoors, owns Minnkota trolling motors, and you can have your electronics synced to your trolling motor. Working together, this combination provides some of the greatest technology available, and helps an angler really tailor his fishing tactics to every situation. No matter which company's electronics you buy, however, the key is setting everything up correctly and learning how to use it.

Once you have decided where to mount your fishfinder (helm, bow, or both), it is important to play with it and configure it so you can have everything you need for a day's fishing. Many of the larger screen fishfinders offer a "favorites" button that allows you to have three or more screen settings shown with a simple push of a button. My ten-inch Helix has three preset favorite buttons that I have set up as sonar (fishfinding), GPS (mapping), and split-screen sonar/GPS (fishfinding and mapping together). Some folks might like down imaging or side scan as a favorite if their electronics offer those options. I also do not like to keep my fishfinder set up on automatic (which is how it comes preset from the factory). I prefer to manually configure my settings of clarity, depth levels, and sensitivity to my own likings. One presetting tip that has worked well for me is to keep my lower depth range reading to forty feet. I might be in one hundred feet of water, but only need to see what is on my fishfinder from the surface down to forty feet. The reason for this is that I really do not care what is below forty feet since I can only target fish from the surface down to about thirty feet anyway. If you can catch them on a fly below that, then set your lower depth range to that number. If you want to see deep bait, then it might pay to lower your depth range. My experience tells me that I do not need to fish below thirty feet, so I have my sonar set at forty feet in case I want to chart some deeper bait.

When looking for fish using your sonar, it is always best to slow down and look at near idle speed. I try to run my boat at approximately 1000 to 1500 rpms, which translates to about 5 to 10 mph in speed. This way I can take a good look at whatever I am running over. Once I find a good-sized school of fish, I will shut down and use my electric trolling motor to try to stay with them. It is at this time that I might change my screen to go from all sonar to a split between sonar and side scan. This will allow me to see not only directly under the boat but also out to both sides. If I see the fish under the boat and to my port side, I will cast accordingly. You can set up your side scan (if your fishfinder offers that feature) to

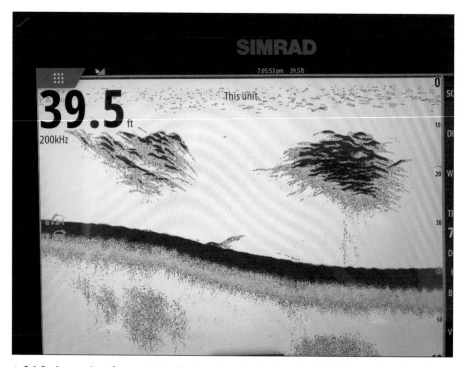

A fishfinder can be of great aid in finding schools of subsurface fish. You will not be able to catch these fish, as the marks are bunched together or on top of one another, meaning the fish are moving fast and likely uncatchable. *Photo Credit: Keegan Corcoran.*

go out approximately 120 feet on both sides. However, the closer in you set the side scan's outer range, the more powerful and detailed a picture you will see. I like to set my side scan out to about ninety feet maximum. I rarely throw a fast-sinking line at fish that I find on my fishfinder if I am not seeing at least ten or more arches on the screen. If I see only a few arches (fish) on the screen, I find it very hard to hook these fish. You really need to see many arches on the screen (multiple fish) to be successful at catching deep-water striped bass. One more tip for anglers using electronics is that when you locate the fish and the arches are nearly on top of one another, that means the fish are on the move. These are very hard fish to catch, as the fish will likely have moved on by the time it takes for your fast-sinking line to get down to the depth where you located the stripers. You want to see a screen shot where there are many arches, but they are spread out over most of the screen and not all clumped together.

Another tactic is to find a group of gulls or terns flying low to the water and then, using your big engine or trolling motor, idling around that area looking at your sonar to find that school of striped bass. Sometimes it may just be a large pod of baitfish but sometimes you might find a big school of stripers. Then you can toss your fast-sinking lines using the countdown method, discussed below. I will do the same thing if I find a loon diving down in a very small or confined area. Many times, you can find schools of striped bass that you would never see by using your fishfinder in conjunction with the wildlife.

When I am blind casting for stripers on humps in the fall and late spring, I always have my electronics set to a split screen of sonar and GPS or to side scan and GPS. This way I can see if there are any fish under the boat while always making sure I am casting on the hump while I am encircling it. If you split the screen to side scan, you might just set the side scan up to show only one side (the side the hump is on). This way you can see if there are fish on the hump while maintaining your course of blind casting onto the hump. These are just a few ways that your fish finder can aide you in finding stripers that are subsurface.

The same can be said when fishing a long tapered point. Set your fishfinder up so that you show a split screen of sonar and side scan. Have your side scan set to only go out to the side you are fishing, and you can peek at what may be under

Kevin Arculeo caught this teen-sized striped bass using a fast-sinking line after locating the school on his Humminbird electronics. *Photo Credit: Henry Cowen.*

the boat as well as what may be up onto the point. Your fishfinder is your eyes under the water, and anglers who become adept at learning how to use it will be more successful in catching striped bass when they are not feeding on the surface.

HOW TO FISH THE COUNTDOWN METHOD

West Coast striped bass fly-fishing pioneer Dan Blanton, along with the iconic Lefty Kreh, showing off a couple of fish they caught out of Lake Sidney Lanier using fast-sinking lines and the countdown method. *Photo Credit: Henry Cowen.*

One question I often get from freshwater striped bass anglers is, "How do I catch fish that are deep." This always seems like the most intimidating of all the patterns to anglers. In reality, it is probably the easiest and potentially the most successful of all patterns to fish. I have had my best days on numbers of fish caught when I am targeting fish that are deep. When I say deep, I am talking about fish that are in anywhere between fifteen and thirty feet of water. Let me say that the best part about fishing to deep fish is that it is nearly impossible to spook them. That gives the angler a distinct advantage. Another advantage to the angler who fishes to deep feeding stripers in fresh water is that a long cast is not necessarily required. Of course, a fifty- to sixty-foot cast is always desirable, but when fishing to deep feeding stripers, I have had customers catch fish regularly by throwing thirty- to thirty-five-foot casts. The key to catching deep feeding striped bass is to take a page out of our saltwater brethren's tactics, which is first being able to locate the fish and second being able to present the fly to the fish, no matter how deep they are.

Locating freshwater striped bass that are feeding in deeper water is not always that simple. However, there are certain times of the year that this pattern is as easy as it gets. In the winter when the fish are making their way to the northern end of most reservoirs you will find the fish might feed on or near the surface during low light periods. However, after the sun rises over the treetops on most reservoirs, the fish will usually feed deeper in the water column. This is where both birdlife and your electronics become your best bird dog. Gulls, herons, and loons can be your best indicator of where to start looking underwater. They will lead you to the fish. Once you think the wildlife has led you to the fish, you will need confirmation of this by seeing the stripers on your fish finder. Your fish finder will show what we call spaghetti-like marks on the screen of your fish finder. That will confirm you have located a big school of stripers. I usually have my fish finder set to a forty-foot bottom. I do not really care about anything deeper than that as it is nearly impossible to fish to subsurface striped bass below thirty feet. It simply takes too long for the fly to sink to that depth.

Now that you have confirmed that there is a school of fish under the boat, it is time to take out your fast-sinking fly line and make as long a cast as possible

Anglers fishing to deep fish must be patient while using the countdown method, as they must wait for their fly to reach the depth where stripers are shown on their fishfinder. *Credit: Josh England.*

behind the boat. I am assuming the transducer to your fishfinder is placed on your transom. If there are two anglers in the boat, then your best bet for both anglers to fish to these stripers is to turn the boat on a 90-degree angle (a hard left or right turn with your trolling motor) so that you both can cast to where you located the fish on your electronics. Using your fast-sinking fly line, you make the cast and count down several seconds so that your fly is sitting in the same water column where the fish are. Fast-sinking lines have different sink rates. The lines I use sink approximately six inches per second. So that means my fly will sink at a rate of one foot every two seconds. The best way for me to get my fly to the fish is to simply double the number of feet where the fish are and then count down that many seconds. So, if the fish are sitting in twenty feet of water, I count down forty seconds. If they are grouped in up to fifteen feet of water, I count down thirty seconds. This is what we mean by fishing the countdown method to get your fly to the deep feeding fish. Once the fly is in what you think is the strike zone, it is time to retrieve the fly and wait for a bite from ole lineside. Fly fishing using the countdown method works like a charm and is incredibly effective. I also use the countdown method in the late spring in a similar fashion, only I will be on the southern end of my reservoir. The countdown method will work anytime you are tossing a fast-sinking line to fish that appear to be feeding deep. This tactic also

The countdown method, coupled with his electronics, allowed this angler to locate and fish to stripers that were in ten to fifteen feet of water over a twenty-five-foot bottom. *Photo Credit: Josh England.*

works when you're casting flies from long tapered points near the deeper end of the point as well as when you're fishing humps.

How to Fish a Point (Uphill and Downhill)

Striped bass use points on a reservoir to seek out food. These anglers were blind casting in hopes of finding a hungry fish. *Photo Credit: Josh England.*

Fishing a large freshwater reservoir for the first few times can be an intimidating and daunting task. You see, to most anglers fishing new waters, everything basically looks the same. At least in a river you can easily look at the banks and pockets and kind of plan a strategy, but a reservoir can look like one giant puddle. As in a river, you must try to break down the large body of water into smaller, more manageable areas to fish. The first places anglers should look to are points, which are pieces of land that jut out farthest into the water. They may be areas where you can make sharp left or right turns from a straightaway. These points of land tend to hold plenty of forage fish, and the striped bass are usually not far behind. Points can be broken down into three types: long tapered, short, or secondary. What is important is to learn when and which points fish will congregate to and hold on with some regularity. On any given lake, there may be more than a thousand points an angler is able to fish. Certain points are well known for catching fish while others may be more obscure. Fishing the well-known points

Points located at a creek mouth are some of the best areas to look for striped bass. *Photo Credit: Josh England.*

on a weekend may require you to take a number and get in line as you would in a bakery. These points are targeted by many anglers. However, finding and successfully fishing the more obscure points will have you finding a honey hole all to yourself. The well-known points will be obvious to the angler trying to figure out which points to fish. One way to learn is to mark all the points or make a mental note of the points that you see being regularly fished by other anglers. As Yogi Berra once said, "You can learn a lot by observing." Some lakes that are managed by the Corps of Engineers have points that are defined by reef markers or buoys. What you might see is an aluminum pole with a white float-like marker affixed to it. This tells you there is an obstruction of some sort, be it low water or rocks. Many of these are put out on a lake's points. These are fish-catching markers as far as I am concerned. Points can be fished a few different ways, so let's look at the different points we may find on a reservoir and describe how best to approach them.

My favorite points to fish are those that are long and tapered. In other words, these are points that start off shallow near the land and may go out as far as two hundred feet or more before dropping off. That two-hundred-foot-long point may be three feet near the bank and, as we go out another fifty feet, may drop to ten feet. Then, as we go fifty feet farther, the water depth drops to fifteen feet. Finally, the last one hundred feet may gradually drop to twenty feet under the water before it gets to the channel or simply deep water. Striped bass love to hunt up on these long tapered points. On my lake, most of these points have clay bottoms. On other lakes, the tapered points may have sandy or rocky bottoms. Either way, what is most important is that you notice the gradual drop in the water depth as you start to head farther out into the lake. The best approach is to fish the point in from the deepest water to the shallowest water. Start with a fast-sinking line that will allow your fly to get down five to fifteen feet deep, which is most likely where the fish will be. As you get closer to the bank, you may want to switch to a slow-sinking intermediate line when targeting water that may be six feet or shallower. If the long tapered point is also a very wide point, you may opt to fish perpendicularly across the point rather than up and onto the point as previously discussed. The last piece of advice was given to me by my good buddy and striper guru Dan Blanton, who once told me to try fishing a point uphill in the springtime. You see, when we toss flies from deep to shallow, we are working our flies downhill as we pull it back to the boat. Dan's advice was to try starting shallow and work the fly in so you would be fishing your fly uphill on the point. I have since tried that approach and there have been times where it worked like a charm. When fishing uphill, your offering is being presented in a different manner. Sometimes forage is going deeper as the sun raises up over the treetops and other days the forage is climbing up and onto a point and getting shallower. Thus you are presenting your bait uphill and sometimes downhill. Changing things up can be the difference between success and failure.

There are also points that are not long and tapered but rather short with drop-offs close to the land. We call these types of structure simply points and can find them to be extremely fishy at times. These types of points are usually found where a cove or creek comes off the main lake. If you ever see a blue heron sitting on one of these points, give this structure a good look-see. Points like this usually are less than one hundred feet in length before the bottom drops out into deep water. However, fish will often find forage on these points, which is why they are worth looking at.

Finally, the last point worth discussing is what we call a secondary point. Secondary points are usually found inside or just behind a main lake point or the second and less defined points when you're looking inside a cove or creek. Secondary points are not as obvious to anglers and get overlooked by many fishermen. However, they can be incredibly productive and must not be passed over when you're trying to figure out where fish are holding. There are times of the season when fishing points may be the only way to find fish. This is especially true if you are fishing during the pre-spawn and the fish are starting to make their way upriver or when stripers are heading back down to the lake after their spawning run is over (post-spawn). It is at times like these when fishing a secondary point

This picture depicts an angler fishing a point downhill (casting up shallow and retrieving their fly back in deeper water). *Photo Credit: Tyson England.*

can be one of your best tactics. The other great thing about secondary points is that since they get overlooked by many anglers, this type of structure gets way less pressured. In striped bass fishing, areas that are less pressured usually become go-to spots for those willing to put in the time to figure where and how to fish this specific type of structure.

If you are new to any reservoir and need to start blind casting in order to figure out the feeding pattern, it's probably a good idea to start fishing points. Even if the fish are not stacked up on the points, the likelihood of finding a lone fish is always best on this type of structure. This is especially true during low light periods on nearly all reservoirs. Nearly every freshwater striped bass angler I have talked to thoroughly fishes points no matter what part of the country their reservoir is located.

How to Fish a Hump

If you hear that fish are congregating on the humps that are twenty to twenty-five feet deep, you really need to take note. During this pattern the fish can rarely be caught anywhere else on most reservoirs. This is a very specific pattern that striped bass will follow year in and year out. Humps are areas of land that rise up out of the deep to form shallow-water mounds of sorts. This pattern usually takes shape during the late spring and again in early fall. As the striped bass are transitioning from shallow water to deep water or vice versa is when this becomes the go-to pattern. The best part of fishing a hump is that all it takes is locating as many as possible and then finding the ones that are holding the fish. The key to this pattern is to make sure you are fishing around the entire hump. Some humps can be small in size while others can stretch out for hundreds of feet in circumference. There is no telling where the fish will be, and the likelihood is that when the fish get onto the hump pattern, they are usually doing so in groups (both small and large). If you do not fish the entire hump thoroughly, you might be missing the key holding area. Always try to find a hump that has brush attached to it, as forage will use that for cover and the striped bass will be circling it. Sometimes you might find a little surface activity of stripers chasing bait directly over or close to the hump. When fishing a hump, you can fish to stripers at all levels of the water column. You might try throwing a top-water fly first, followed by a slow-sinking intermediate or even a fast-sinking line. Try to mark as many of the humps as you can find on your reservoir by using a GPS so you can return to them again and again. Some electronics will take all the guesswork out of locating your reservoir's humps, while others will show them once you have researched them and

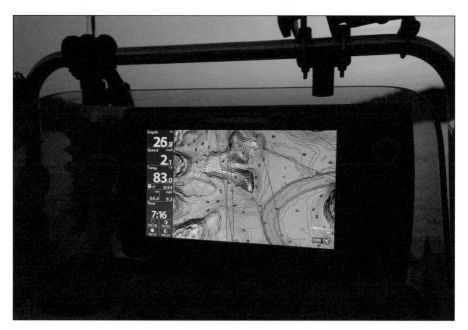

Both early and late in the striper season, anglers should blind cast around reservoir humps that are twenty- to twenty-five-feet deep and surrounded by deep water. *Photo Credit: Josh England.*

found them on your own using a topo map or by studying the readings on your GPS. Either way, it is important to be able to find and fish this type of structure over and over, as this pattern can last many weeks on most reservoirs around the country. This pattern will repeat itself every year, making it doubly important to try to figure out which humps consistently fish well. Humps that are located close to or just off the river channel will consistently be some of the most productive humps to fish.

Conventional anglers who fish to freshwater striped bass always have their best success with two lures when fishing humps. These are a weightless Zoom Fluke fished just under the surface and a slow-sinking Sebile Magic Swimmer. Fly anglers can imitate both lures by tossing a Game Changer fly when this pattern is taking shape. Just decide whether you want to throw it on a slow-sinking or fast-sinking line. You may need to change up the retrieve some to elicit a strike from ole lineside. There are times when burning the fly in as fast as possible will elicit a reactionary strike, while there are other times when a start and stop herky jerky retrieve will work best. You just need to experiment on your reservoir and see what the fish respond to. Of all the different types of structure there is to fish on a reservoir, hump fishing may be the most consistent, but also the hardest of all structures to locate. Anglers need to spend the time finding these honey holes

Some humps will be marked by the Corp of Engineers, if they manage that reservoir. Anytime you see a reef marker out in open water, it is likely that you have found a hump. *Photo Credit: Josh England.*

so you are ready for some consistent fishing when this pattern fires up. The best part about fishing the humps pattern is that most of the guesswork on where to find stripers is taken out of the equation.

How to Fish a Saddle or Blow-Through

Of all the different types of structure you can find on a reservoir, saddles and blow-throughs are easily the most sought-after of all structure to fish. While both types of structures may appear to be like one another, they are in fact inherently different. Their similarities are that both types of structures are usually associated with being attached to an island. It may be that a piece of land and an island are adjoined creating either a blow-through or a saddle. Or it might be two islands that are adjoined by both as well. What differentiates a blow-through and a saddle is the depth of water they are found in. A blow-through usually means you have found a high spot of water that is shallow on either side of the high spot. As an example, if you find two islands next to one another with an underwater spit of land connecting them, and the water on either side of the underwater spit of land is shallow (under five feet), you have found a blow-through. What makes a blow-through unique is

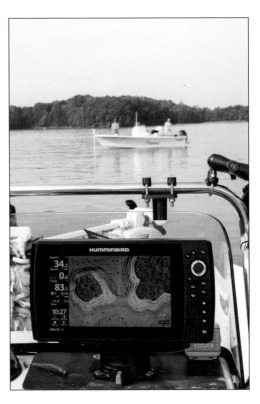

Saddles and blow-throughs are underwater high spots that are usually connected to the shoreline and an island. Find and fish both of these reservoir structures, as they can be extremely productive spots. *Photo Credit: Josh England.*

that there is usually current that will run through it. This current is a fish attractor, as the striped bass can find easy meals as forage tends to try and hide in structure like this. We find that blow-throughs fish extremely well during spring. Some blow-throughs may be out on or near the main lake while others may be found inside a creek or a cove. Those located out on the main lake are likely to fish more

This blow-through is easily seen from the drone photo. It is an underwater high spot that connects a piece of land to an island and stripers love to ambush forage in this type of structure. *Photo Credit: Tyson England.*

consistently. If your reservoir has a dam attached to it, then blow-throughs that are closer to the dam will fish better, as they will get the benefit of more current due to the dam generation. When fishing a blow-through, I would recommend throwing an intermediate fly line with any sub-surface fly you have confidence in. Another good option is to throw a floating line early in the morning or late in the day with a top-water fly. Blow-throughs are some of my favorite structures for finding fish.

Saddles are like blow-throughs in that the areas where they are found can look a lot like the areas where blow-throughs are found. The difference is that saddles are found in deeper water. If we were to use that same example of two islands being adjoined by an underwater spit of land, the depth of water on the both sides of that underwater spit of land will be at least ten feet deep for blow-throughs. A saddle may be fifteen feet deep and the water on both sides of the saddle may drop to thirty feet. The high spot that attaches the two islands together is termed a saddle. I fish saddles religiously on my reservoir and I fish that impoundment at all times of the year. It is easily the most important structure that I fish for striped bass with regularity and consistency in fish catching. You need to pay attention to your fishfinder when you run your boat between an island and a close piece of land, so you can see if there is a saddle attached to it. It will certainly show up on your GPS if you pay attention when you run through it. Or you can look at the reservoirs topo map to try and locate saddles. My Humminbird fishfinder is set to show me every saddle and blow-through on my lake. By setting up contour

Striped bass tend to hang around saddles. Steve Walburn caught this striped bass blind casting a saddle. *Photo Credit: Jim Klug.*

highlighting on my Humminbird unit, I can have every blow-through and saddle highlighted. However, you must purchase Humminbird's proprietary Lake Master chart in order to have that option. It takes all the guesswork out of finding some of the most important and best fishing structure. When fishing a saddle, I usually opt for a fast-sinking line and work my fly by casting across the saddle and retrieving it back over the high spot. Once again, saddles are great places to work top-water flies on floating lines in the early fall and late spring, especially early and late in the day. I really like tossing a Pole Dancer fly and watching it walk the dog over the high spot. (When a fly or a lure stays on the surface when retrieved and moves left-right-left-right, that action imparted by the fly or lure is said to be walking the dog.) I have had some of the most explosive takes I have ever seen when fished over a saddle. Saddles are so effective due to the amount of current that runs through them. When I am planning my strategy of where to fish on any given day, a saddle many times is the very first piece of structure that I run to fish. I want to get on this structure and fish it before another boat fishes it ahead of me.

How to Fish A Seawall or Breakwater

Seawalls are structures that serve the purpose of protecting marinas. If there is a large marina on a busy lake, you'll often see wooden structures that have been put up to break the wakes of passing boats. These walls stop the waves from coming into the marina and help protect the boats that are docked there. Without seawalls, the boats would be rocking back and forth and could be damaged, especially if they aren't properly tied down. Seawalls, also called breakwaters, are fantastic pieces of structure that attract forage seeking refuge from predators. Because of this, striped bass can be found feeding on or around them at different times of the year. What anglers need to know is that seawalls produce best in the springtime, especially when the surface water temperature gets up to around 70°F. This is usually the time when the forage will start to spawn, often around seawalls. Forage fish such as threadfin shad and blueback herring will lay their eggs, which often stick to the seawall. Striped bass are savvy enough to know this, and you can watch them run the seawall and crash the forage on the surface. On my lake we see this happen more frequently with our blueback herring forage. While the stripers can be found anywhere along a seawall, the ends of the wall seem to consistently produce the most action. You might also look for any bend in the wall, as the fish seem to like those areas as well. My lake has many big marinas and we always spend time looking at seawalls starting around the end of April and continuing through May. Pay special attention to the walls on or around the new and full moons, as these lunar phenomina often get the spawn going.

Seawalls are commonly found by marinas and can be some of the most productive structure to fly fish on a reservoir. This is especially true when threadfin shad or blueback herring are spawning. *Photo Credit: Josh England.*

I always toss a fast-sinking line when I am fishing a seawall. I might try a popper too, but my go-to outfit is a fast-sinking line and a sub-surface fly like a Clouser or baitfish pattern. You might even consider tossing a Game Changer, as that is another money-in-the-bank fly pattern. Some seawalls are only fishable on the outside because boats are tied up on the inside. However, there are also some free-standing seawalls where there are no boats on the inside. These seawalls are there to prevent the wakes of other boats from getting back toward where the docks are located. In this case anglers should fish both the outside and the inside of the seawall. One tidbit of note when fishing seawalls is to remember that when tossing a fast-sinking line, you may run into some cables that were put in to help secure the seawall. Believe it or not, they will appear on your fishfinder and will

Tyson England releasing a striped bass he caught while targeting a seawall. *Photo Credit: Josh England.*

look like fish (with a heavy arch). They are *not* fish markings, and over the years I have lost more than a few flies to them. You know the old saying, "no pain, no gain."

If you start fishing seawalls, one final tip is to come back in the dark to look for underwater dock lights. Marinas, seawalls, and dock lights usually run together. I have found more dock lights on seawalls and big marinas than any other place. On my lake there are a few seawalls where there are three underwater dock lights all within fifty yards of one another. I can promise you that if the fish are gathering on an underwater dock light at night, then they will be cruising around that entire structure come first light.

How to Fish a Pocket

There is a pattern that we see on nearly all reservoirs at different times of the season, especially when the striped bass are moving up and onto pockets. Pockets are indentations on the shoreline. You can find them on both the main lake as well as in coves. Saltwater anglers describe pockets as bowls. When two points are close to one another, the land that adjoins them is called a bowl, especially if it is

Structure fishing can be especially productive when the stripers are shallow and hanging around pockets. *Photo Credit: Josh England.*

circular in shape. When describing that kind of feature on a lake, most anglers call it a pocket. Simply put, pocket fishing for striped bass can be fantastic once the fish have taken up residence there. Pocket fishing can happen in fall, winter, and spring, with different pockets producing at different times. On my lake, pockets located on the main lake are the ones we target in October and November. Usually you will find an island out on the main lake. If there is a pocket structure on that island, that pocket is definitely worth fishing, especially in fall. If you find a well-defined pocket as you are riding along the shoreline of the main lake, try fishing that as well. Be aware that these pockets fish best during lower light conditions. This is probably because you are in shallower water. Fish will go into the pockets searching for forage and can be suckers for a properly tossed sub-surface fly. Pockets are obvious when you see them, though many anglers overlook them when trying to figure out where the stripers are hiding.

In the winter, pockets can be one of your home-run structures to blind cast to. Once the water temperatures on your reservoir drop to about 50°F or lower, the stripers are usually found heading up to the north part of the lake as they look for forage seeking the warmer water. Forage will always look to find even one degree of temperature that is warmer during the colder months. Pockets found inside of coves offer shallower water and thus will warm up a little more quickly when the afternoon sun hits that part of the lake. That is why I like to throw flies into the pockets that are located inside of a cove at sunset. The lower light combined with the slightly warmer water temperature can change a day from being a day of lemons to a day of lemonade. I like fishing shallow pockets with an intermediate line and fishing the deeper pockets using a fast-sinking line. It is hard to beat a Somethin Else fly in the winter when pocket fishing. That is easily my go-to fly pattern, with a small Clouser a close second. When you are looking for fish that are surface feeding up onto the banks in the dead of winter, it's also a good idea to keep your eye on the pockets for the first hour or two after first light. I cannot tell you how many times I have seen a small group of stripers corral and ball up a bunch of threadfin shad into a pocket early in the morning.

Finally, once we get back into the warmer springtime weather, you can expect your reservoir's patterns to overlap some. You might find fish on the points as well as in some of the pockets back out on the main lake. What usually happens in fall happens in reverse during spring. In spring, the fish are moving south and are out on the main lake's points, humps, and pockets, as opposed to being back in the creeks and coves. While in the fall the fish are on the main lake's points, humps, and pockets and heading into the coves as the surface water temperatures start to fal, they do the opposite in spring. Savvy anglers will not overlook any structure, and once they see a pattern forming by catching a few fish out of the same type of

This striper was caught and released in the early spring when the fish were starting to seek out forage in the backs of pockets as the water started to warm up faster than on the main lake. *Photo Credit: Josh England.*

structure, they know where to target fish for the next few weeks. This is what we call the truest sense of patterning the striped bass.

How to Fish A Fly in A Reservoir (Retrieve)

One of the most important aspects in getting a gamefish to eat your fly is how you present and manipulate it. In angling terms, we call this feeding the fish. There are times you can cast your fly out and quickly get a hit, and other times when the fish will simply not bite. There can be many reasons why the latter can occur. Are you matching the hatch? Is the water clarity preventing the fish from seeing your offering? Are you retrieving the fly too fast? Too slow? Does the fly you are using have enough inherent movement to elicit a strike? These are just some of the many reasons why a fish might refuse your offering. Knowledgeable anglers constantly change flies as the conditions dictate what they should throw.

Let's assume you are dialing in to exactly what the fish are feeding on and conditions are not out of the ordinary. In other words the water is not too dirty, and the fish are either showing up on the surface or are making spaghetti-like marks on your electronics. We know the fish are there! There are many types of

It is important to keep your rod tip low to the water when starting your retrieve for striped bass. This allows you to stay in contact with your fly line and allow for a good hook set when the bite does eventually come. *Photo Credit: Josh England.*

retrieves that work well when targeting striped bass in fresh water. Let's start by discussing the retrieve when tossing a top-water fly. It has been my experience that a constant, steady movement is what will elicit a strike. So, if you are fishing a Pole Dancer fly, it is best to constantly walk the dog with your retrieve. No pauses or lapses in the retrieve is needed. You want to continuously work the fly back toward you, always making sure the fly is moving left, right, left, right (walking the dog). The same can be said when fishing a Crease Fly or Gurgler. I like a steady, constant retrieve. If a fish makes a pass on your fly and you miss the strike, continue your retrieve, and chances are that fish may strike again. In contrast, pausing the fly after a strike will almost always result in no more strikes by that striper. It may be that when you pause, the fish gets a better look at your fly and sees that it is not truly the forage it is seeking. You can retrieve too fast as well. Sometimes a fast retrieve will not look as realistic as a steady, moderate one. A fast retrieve may work great on false albacore, but for freshwater stripers you want a moderate and steady retrieve when fishing on top.

When fishing a subsurface fly, the retrieve is *everything*! It does not matter whether you are fishing a slow-sinking intermediate line or a fast-sinking line. The single best retrieve when fishing subsurface is a few short quick strips followed by a pause of two to three seconds and then back to a few short quick strips again. It is always best to vary your retrieve by starting with three short

Georgia fly angler Keith Ohrstrom releasing a fat striped bass from Lake Sidney Lanier after using the short strip and pause retrieve. *Photo Credit: Josh England.*

quick strips followed by a pause and then two short quick strips followed by a pause and then three or even four short quick strips again. This start-and-stop technique will allow your fly to look like an injured baitfish. Striped bass are suckers for that kind of retrieve. I am not saying that a steady retrieve will not get you a bite, but a strip-and-pause retrieve *will* outfish all others. This is especially true when the fish are feeding just under the surface. You may see splashes of the fish feeding on small threadfin shad just under the surface, and those anglers who have the patience to pause, sometimes up to five seconds before their next set of short quick strips, will often be rewarded. I run into folks on my lake who simply cannot hook up when the fish are breaking the surface during a subsurface blitz. I know that if they are properly matching the hatch with their fly, then the reason they are not hooking up is either because they're using a steady retrieve or one that's too fast. It is very easy to get excited when you are caught up in a striped bass blitz. Cooler heads always prevail when this occurs, however. Take a deep breath and slow down! This may be the most important piece of advice I can give you in this entire book.

Another retrieve technique worth mentioning is one that we use when fishing a keel-weighted fly. A keel-weighted fly is one that has the weight on the rear. I could write an entire book on flies and their design, but suffice it to say that how and where you weight your fly can determine how you can manipulate its action. By making a few hard strips followed by a brief pause and then a few more hard strips, you will have your keel-weighted fly jackknifing, which creates a darting effect on your retrieve. So instead of having a fly going up and down, you are making it go side to side. This can only be achieved by the way you design and retrieve your fly. Dave Sellers, who is an avid freshwater striped bass angler in northern California, designed such a fly with his SST pattern. SST stands for Sellers Striper Teaser and, when using a hard strip/stop retrieve, you will get this fly darting from side to side. His goal was to create a fly that moved in the water like a conventional angler's Zoom Fluke soft plastic bait. There are many ways to keel weight a fly to get that darting action, but Sellers was the first one to come up with that technique.

Lastly, a steady retrieve can sometimes be a striped bass angler's best friend. In my experience, either a Wiggle Minnow or Game Changer fly is best for this. For some reason there are times when a strip-and-pause technique will not buy you a strike when fishing these two flies, but when the retrieve is changed to a steady, constant retrieve, the fish will often hit it hard. Anglers need to pay attention to what is going on around them and always be thinking when the fish are there but do not appear to be interested in their offerings. The first thing to do is think about your retrieve. Stay in the moment and be strategic.

Short, quick strips followed by pauses are what normally work when targeting striped bass in fresh water. *Photo Credit: Jim Klug.*

How to Hook a Fish (Strip Strike)

When feeding a fly to a striped bass, it is important to remember how to set the hook. Think of nearly any saltwater gamefish and use the same techniques you would use if you were fishing for redfish, snook, bonefish, or false albacore. Setting the hook on gamefish has been discussed for over fifty years, and very little has changed. What is most important is that the angler strip strike once he or she feels the take from a striper. To discuss in its simplest terms, there are basically two ways to set a hook on a fish that has just inhaled your fly. The way most of us learned is to just raise the rod and the fly should embed itself in the fish's jaw. We call this technique "trout setting" the fish. Trout setting is as old as the earliest days of fly fishing and can be very effective when you are fishing with an extremely light tippet. This is how nearly all fly anglers learned how to set the hook on trout. Anything harder than a slight lift can break your tippet, resulting in a lost fish. Trout setting does not work well for saltwater gamefish, however. In salt water, anglers are accustomed to fishing with heavier tippet, and it is important to secure that fly into the fish's jaw with a sharp tug. The technique used to hook set a saltwater fish that ate your fly is to use your stripping hand and give a short, firm pull once you feel the strike. Then raising the rod up will allow you to feel the connection to the fish and allow you to reel up any loose line in the water, on the deck

Learning how to strip strike versus setting the hook, as in trout fishing, will account for more stripers caught. *Photo Credit: Henry Cowen.*

of the boat, or in the stripping basket. On larger gamefish, it is important to get the line onto the reel and fight the fish on the rod without having to hand strip the fish back. The chances of losing a hooked fish are less likely if you can get the loose line back onto the reel. Larger fish should be fought on the reel using your reel's preset drag system as opposed to using your two fingers on your rod hand to act as your drag system. Let the fish determine whether it should be fought on the reel or be retrieved by hand. I see more fish become unbuttoned in the beginning of a fight due to the improper transfer of loose line onto the reel. A proper strip-strike hook set, in which you never give the fish any slack line, will help prevent it from coming loose. Once the fish is hooked and you are fighting it on the reel, remember not to high stick the rod. Not only can you break your rod from high sticking, but holding the rod up high gives you less leverage to tire it out the fish. The rod should not be higher than a 60-degree angle when fighting a fish.

Once the fish is brought to the boat or to the wading angler, a strip-and-slip technique is called for. This technique was shown to me many years ago by California fly-fishing striped bass pioneer Dan Blanton. I believe this technique was developed in northern California by striped bass anglers who pioneered some of the best tactics and flies that are still used today by striped bass anglers across the country. As the fish gets within landing range, if you were fighting the fish on

Once hooked, striped bass will put a bend in the rod like few other fish can in fresh water. *Photo Credit: Josh England.*

the reel you pinch the line against the cork grip of your fly rod using two fingers and, with your stripping hand, pull off three or four feet of line. Next, draw the rod up or to the side and then slip the slack line that you drew off the reel, which will allow the leader to come to you. You can now grab the leader and lower your rod so as not to break your rod tip. More rod tips are broken during the landing of a good-sized gamefish than at any other time. It is a good idea for fly anglers to learn how to use this technique.

Chapter 6

Tactics Used to Locate Striped Bass in Rivers

SEASONAL PATTERNS USED TO FIND RIVER STRIPERS

When seasonal patterns are discussed in freshwater striped bass fishing, it is mainly in regard to how and where the fish are moving throughout the river

Fishing rivers during the early spring spawning run is always a good bet for fly anglers to hook some good-sized fish. *Photo Credit: David Cannon.*

system based on the four seasons. This is mainly a water temperature discussion, as that is clearly the determining factor in striped bass movement. We do know a few things in regard to these seasonal river movements. For example, not all fish live in the river year-round. For those rivers that do hold bass year-round, monitoring bass seasonal movements is somewhat easier, as we know the fish enter the rivers in spring and leave by summer's end. For these fish it is a matter of looking for them when the spawning run is fully in force and then again during what we call post spawn through the entire summer. For the springtime spawning run, it is wise to look for fish gathering up near the most turbulent water around spillways and shoals. This is where they will gather in large numbers to release and fertilize their eggs. This is only going to occur in the springtime, and the stripers spawn only one time per year regardless of weather patterns. For post-spawn periods, as the season progresses into the heat of summer, the fish will spread out throughout the entire river system. One thing is for certain: Once the spawning run is over, the fish will go on a major binge, and this becomes the most opportunistic time for anglers looking to catch river stripers. After having made a long journey up the rivers and into the mouths of the tributaries, the stripers are in search of food.

Finding summertime stripers in rivers is a little easier than finding them in reservoirs. Savvy anglers should fish the slightly deeper water and find the seams where stripers tend to look for food. *Photo Credit: Henry Cowen.*

They no longer have reproduction on their minds. As they are heading back down to the lower part of the river system, anglers should look to areas such as bends in the river, flats, creek mouths, pockets away from shoals, and deep holes. The fact is that the stripers can be found nearly anywhere in their journey downriver after the spawn. The water tends to still be a tad chilly at this time, and I have found that flats with lots of fallen timber can be great areas to fish. The shallower flats tend to warm up as the afternoon sun help raise the water temperature just enough so that the forage will gather there.

Once the summer arrives and the waters get warmer, the stripers can be patterned farther upriver where the cooler and more oxygenated water will be. Forage will be spread throughout the river system and stripers can start focusing more on crayfish instead of baitfish like gizzard shad. This is when most anglers will need to either wade fish or float the river in a raft or, at the very least, have a jet drive on their boat. I would spend most of my time fishing areas around spillways and shoals at this time of year. For those anglers fishing rivers without many shoals, now is the time to fish the deeper holes with sinking lines. Summertime in many striped bass rivers is about the only time where the fishing is not entirely about finding the food that stripers are feeding on. It's also about locating water where they will be comfortable, and that means finding areas with lower water temperatures and areas with more oxygen. If your river has underwater springs feeding it, these are also good places to look for stripers during the summer.

Fall, winter, and the first part of spring will see striper anglers mainly looking at the lower part of the river to find fish. This is especially true if you have a reservoir attached to the river system. The headwaters are simply too cold to hold the forage the stripers are looking for. If you are fishing in a river system year-round, with no reservoir attached, then the fish will spread out. In winter, look for the warmest water you can find. If you have a power plant attached to your river system, you can be assured the fish will winter over in that area in great numbers. For year-round river anglers, the late fall and especially wintertime can be some of the most difficult times to locate fish. But if you find the warmer water of a certain tributary or any area that can be one or two degrees warmer than the rest of the river, you will likely hit a homerun. This is how seasonal patterns can affect a river and how stripers use the seasons to best survive.

HOW WEATHER PATTERNS AFFECT RIVER STRIPERS

When you're fishing to striped bass in reservoirs and even in salt water, weather patterns can play havoc with how the fishing will be. High- and low-pressure systems can have the fish feeding as if it were their last meal, or it can be as if they are swimming with their mouths shut tight. You must have a strategy centered on where the fish might be based on the weather pattern that day. This is not so much the case with river stripers, as they seem to be less affected by weather patterns.

Striped bass that reside in rivers either some or all of the year like consistent weather patterns in their environment. Here is a perfect example: Reservoir stripers that feed on threadfin shad love to eat well on overcast days with a falling barometer. Once we get bluebird skies and high pressure, the fish will feed but not as aggressively. On the other hand, fish in the river seem to feed best on sunny days with consistent high pressure. It is on days like that when the fish seem to feed mid-morning and throughout most of the day. We know the reservoir fish generally feed best during low light conditions. This can be true for river fish as well, but in general, river stripers prefer consistent weather patterns. River fish just do not seem to be as low-light sensitive as those living in reservoirs. No one is certain why this is, though it is believed to be because river stripers may feed all night, and that once the low light starts to appear in morning they are simply done eating or are feeding much less aggressively. I will say that if you want to catch a striped bass on a topwater fly, then low-light periods are positively your best bet. While you may not see many river striped bass crashing on the surface to eat forage, you will see this happen on occasion at first and last light. Once the

Rob Smith of The Fish Hawk fly shop tangles with an Etowah River striper during a sunny day in Georgia. *Photo Credit: Henry Cowen.*

sun gets over the treetops and the weather pattern shows a sunny day with high pressure, the fish will fire up and usually the feed will get better as the day goes on. That is why anglers fishing rivers do not have to feel rushed to get out of bed for the first light bite. Striped bass anglers fishing the river can sleep in on most days. The only cause for getting up early is if the river you are fishing gets pressure from many anglers and you simply want to claim your spot before someone else gets there first and fishes it.

Another nice thing about river fishing for stripers is that a windy weather pattern will not have the same effect on a river as it might on a big reservoir. Sometimes a windy day on a reservoir can make for some tough fishing, especially if you are looking for surface feeding fish. However, on a river you are generally more sheltered from the wind, and this allows even the most intermediate of casters to still have a shot at catching a few fish. A windy weather pattern on the river can push the forage around some, cool the water temperature, and dirty up the water, but for the most part, anglers can fish through those conditions. This is not as easily done on a reservoir.

Finally, the last weather pattern worth mentioning is rain. It's my opinion that rain on a reservoir is rarely good for fishing. A steady drizzle is okay and never shuts the fishing down, but a steady downpour will shut down the fishing

River stripers require that anglers use stout tackle due to the faster currents. The fish will simply fight harder. Guide Rob Smith uses a 9- or 10-weight rod when he fishes the rivers of Georgia and Tennessee. *Photo Credit: Henry Cowen.*

in a moment's notice. Most river striper anglers do not seem to feel that rain will affect their fishing until the river muddies up. It certainly may be an inconvenience to the angler, but the fish could not care less. At the end of the day, what anglers need to know is that while weather patterns do affect striped bass, they do not affect them as much on a river. Again, I urge all anglers to keep a good record book of their successes and failures so that you can begin to better pattern these great gamefish.

WATER FLOW AND HOW IT AFFECTS FINDING RIVER STRIPERS

When we discuss the term "water flow" in river fishing, what we are really referring to is the height of the river. In most situations anglers fishing rivers for stripers are also looking at the same data in the river that trout anglers are looking at. We talk water flow in terms of CFS (cubic feet per second) and what that number is at the time we are thinking of going fishing. CFS information is usually available to anglers in nearly all rivers by going to the National Water Information System, which can be found at www.waterdata.usgs.gov website. Simply plug in your state and the area you wish to fish, and gather the latest information on

When striper fishing a river, most anglers prefer to fish when the water level is going down versus going up. Notice how the waterline on the cement wall shows that this river's water level is dropping. *Photo Credit: Josh England.*

water flow. Water flow will vary by new water coming into the river system (from rain) or from a release from a dam upstream. Striped bass can be very sensitive to water flow, and will adjust their feeding pattern based on high or low flows. It is important to keep good records of when fishing was incredible versus when it was particularly tough, paying close attention to the height of the river that day. This is all what water flow is all about.

Water flow affects striped bass fishing in many ways. The height of the river will dictate when the stripers will feed. It will also dictate where the stripers can be found feeding. Finally, it will also determine what kind of water clarity the river will have, as that will also affect how the fish feed.

Striped bass are travelers and can make long treks both up and down a river system. Water flow determines much of this travel throughout the year. It will also determine travel patterns for stripers that are just temporarily in a river, for a spawning run, or for the summertime. Most anglers who fish for striped bass in a river will look to fish the deep holes. This is a good strategy, although when the CFS is high, looking for fish in a deep hole may not be your best choice. When you are fishing when the river's CFS is high, it's also important to note whether you are fishing during a time of a rising water level or a falling water level, on the downside of the high water. Having spoken to many a river rat, I've found that most anglers prefer to fish during a more constant, steady flow as opposed to during rising and lowering river heights.

Rob Smith has fished striper rivers here in the Southeast for over thirty years. He is one of the true experts on striper fishing rivers in Georgia, Alabama, and Tennessee. When not out guiding for stripers in the summertime, he can be found educating folks to the sport of fly fishing at The Fish Hawk fly shop. Rob positively loves fishing for stripers in lower water instead of higher water. He prefers consistent water flows but is not hesitant to venture out and fish to the stripers even when conditions are not ideal. The key, he says, is to have a strategy based on the conditions that exist the day you are on the river. I have found that given the choice of rising versus falling water, it is always better to fish falling water. The fish seem to be more on the feed during such periods. Another reason I like falling water is that high water usually means poorer water clarity. This is especially true when the river is rising. However, as the river begins to fall, the water clarity will eventually get better and thus your fishing should improve. On occasion, the water clarity will not change when the water level is rising. In these instances, it is okay to fish the river, although you will need to figure out where the fish might be feeding. This is a time to look at spillways and shoals, as the shallow shoals can get really hot for striped bass fishing on rising water.

A falling water level can be the trigger that gets the fish to start feeding. Todd Arnold caught this fat striper out of his kayak. *Photo Credit: Todd Arnold.*

When the water level on the river is low, the condition most striped bass anglers will have to deal with is clear water. Clear water simply means that the fish will be able to get a good look at the fly being presented. This will lead to more follows and fewer eats if you do not figure out how to feed the fish. This is when moving the fly a little quicker can help elicit a strike. The fish will not have as much time to examine a fast-moving fly and will have to make a quick choice to eat or not to eat. We call these types of strikes "reactive bites." When you are fishing a lower water flow, it is best to concentrate your efforts in both slower, deep water or just off the flats in the troughs.

Anglers will find challenges under all conditions when striped bass fishing in rivers. That is why having a strategy and monitoring all past fishing trips can help determine what the best strategy to employ will be. One thing we know for sure is that striped bass fishing, whether in a river or a reservoir, is a thinking man's/woman's game. You should not just go out and wet a line without having some sort of strategy to tip the scales to your side.

HOW WATER TEMPERATURES AFFECT STRIPED BASS AND THEIR FORAGE

During the spring spawning run, both the air and water temperatures can still be quite chilly on striper rivers. Dress appropriately when fishing during this period. *Photo Credit: David Cannon.*

Striped bass and the forage they feed on are both affected by water temperature. This is especially true in river systems. Almost all rivers will see significant striped bass runs up the tributaries during the spawning period. This usually occurs when water temperatures in the reservoirs are pushing into the fifties. Once those temperatures rise into the high fifties, the stripers make their run up and are more easily found by anglers. Of course, not all stripers live in reservoirs. Some stripers live in rivers year-round. In this case, the fish will make runs farther up into the headwaters and do their business there before heading back down into the lower sections of the river. According to long-time striped bass angler Bill Butts, who targets these fish in the south-central region of the United States, it is difficult to pattern the spawning runs of striped bass that live their entire lives in a river system. We do know that these river stripers head north for their yearly spawning runs when the water temperatures rise into the high fifties. We also know that during winter, these same fish will look to find the warmest waters in the river system and will hold there until the waters begin to warm up in spring.

During the warmest months of the year, many striped bass find comfort living their entire summer in rivers. This is because the reservoirs simply become too hot for their survival. When this happens, they will then look for the cooler oxygenated waters that rivers offer. It is during this summer period that anglers should concentrate their efforts looking for stripers in moving water. Just keep in mind that the striped bass will take refuge throughout the entire river system in summer. The fish will spread out and can be found in many sections of a river rather than in one concentrated area, as one would expect during the spring spawning run. The temperature of the river throughout the summer months will also determine where you might find these stripers. Most fish will be cruising the river system looking for forage. If we have a particularly dry, hot summer, the fish will take shelter in deeper holes as well as at shoals and spillways. These areas offer the striped bass the coolest water available. The forage will likely be in the same area. Most forage (especially gizzard shad) are water temperature sensitive too. Should we happen to have a cool and wet summer, then the fish will spread out even more in the rivers and finding fish will be a little more difficult. When this occurs, anglers need to consider looking for the fish up against the shoreline and on flats as well as deep holes and pockets that are just off the shoals.

One of the easiest places to find feeding stripers is below a dam. The cool, highly oxygenated water seems to be a holding pen for both forage and gamefish. *Photo Credit: David Cannon.*

Understanding how temperature affects striped bass in rivers and how to apply that information will certainly give you an upper hand in finding and catching these wonderful gamefish. Water temperature and feeding habits are all intertwined in the striper game. You must put the entire puzzle together if you want to be successful.

How Water Clarity Affects Striped Bass in Rivers

While water clarity in reservoirs has been discussed in another chapter, water clarity in rivers is an even bigger deal for anglers wanting to target striped bass on the fly rod. The reason for this is that most times, water clarity in a river has a direct relationship with the height of the water. This relationship will help determine where you should be targeting the fish.

One would think that super clear water makes the fishing better since the stripers can see your offering that much easier. That is true. But what anglers need to know is that this can be a major disadvantage. Fish that hunt in crystal-clear water can take a longer look at your imitation and refuse to strike at it. Conversely, fish that hunt for food in dirty water will not see your imitation as easily and will have to decide whether to strike the fly or not the minute it comes by their face. In a perfect world it is probably best to fish water that is somewhat stained, not too clear and not too dirty.

Water can get dirty from either a release from a dam or from rainwater entering the system. The clarity of water also reflects how much water is in the river at that time. If the river is dirty, the likelihood is that the river is high. If the river is clear, the likelihood is that the river is low. This should help you determine where to look for the striped bass. When conditions of clarity are extremely dirty and the water is high, fishing for striped bass in rivers may be a lost cause. However, if you must go during these conditions, then it is best to fish a dark colored fly. Something in black or blurple (black/purple) would be your best choice when the water is on the dirty side. Another tactic is to make sure you are throwing flies that are bulkier in design. A bulky fly will push more water and, although stripers cannot see the offering as easily in dirty water, they can hear it coming. It is also a good idea to fish a fly with a rattle designed into the fly. Any additional sound will act as an attractant and help stripers find your fly. When fishing dirty water, it is also best to fish your fly more slowly than you normally would. If the river is chocolate brown, which can happen after a heavy rainfall, give the river a day or two to settle back to normal flows and better water clarity.

Stained water can mask your fly offering better than clear water. It is best to fish a more bulky fly that pushes more water when fishing in a stained river. *Photo Credit: Josh England.*

When a river is low and more than likely clear, throw fly imitations that best match the forage. This is also the time to consider tossing a fly that is chartreuse in color. Chartreuse is best fished in clear water rather than dirty water. Simply, fish see chartreuse best in clear water and do not see it as well in stained or especially dirty water. Color helps present a fly's silhouette to the fish, and knowing what colors work based on a rivers particular water clarity can make the difference between a day of catching versus a day of fishing. When the water is clear, fish your fly a little more quickly. You do not want to give the striped bass a good look at your fly, but rather have them be forced to make a reactionary decision to either strike your offering or pass on it. When a river is clear, you will notice fish that follow your fly right back to the boat or to your feet without hitting it. This is common in clear water. As an angler you will have to try to "feed them," as we say. This can be accomplished by fishing flies that have more movement in their design. Another tactic to use in a clear river is to downsize your offering. Fish do not get offended by seeing a smaller imitation and can be fed a little easier. Downsize your leader and tippet accordingly. This can all make a difference when trying to feed fish in super clear water.

What is most important is that you learn how to fish all the conditions a river may offer at various times of the year. Striper fishing takes a bit of strategy when

Stained water can be a definite advantage for the fly angler. However, if the river turns muddy, it's best to wait a few days for the clarity to get better. *Photo Credit: Josh England.*

conditions are ever changing. Anglers who are strategic and plan their trip according to these changing conditions will catch more fish.

HOW TO LOCATE FORAGE IN A RIVER

When fishing for freshwater striped bass in a river, one of the absolute keys to success is being able to locate the forage fish. Finding out where a striped bass's next meal is hanging out will result in more hookups and consequentially bring more fish to hand. There are many types of forage found in river systems throughout the US that hold striped bass. The most common of the forage species is the gizzard shad. River gizzards can vary in size and are the same species found in reservoirs. They can be as small as three to five inches in length and as large as a foot or longer! Gizzards seem to be predominant in nearly all river systems across the country except northern California, where stripers seem to feed mostly on crawfish and other forage fish including, according to fly innovator and striped bass angler Charlie Bisharat, trout, squaw fish, American shad, bream, suckers, and whatever else is available. There may be other forage species indigenous to parts of the country that stripers will feed on. Threadfin shad can be found in some southern river systems. Skipjack herring can be found and are predominant in rivers throughout Alabama and Tennessee. However, this striped bass candy is

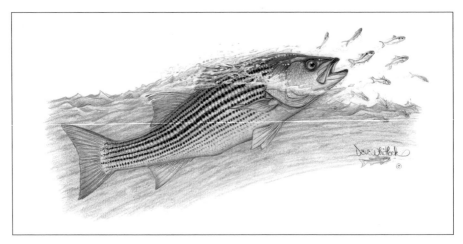

Occasionally you can find striped bass busting gizzards on the surface in a river. Most of the time it will happen during the lower light periods of the day. *Photo Credit: Dave Whitlock.*

not found in Georgia. This is what makes striped bass such opportunistic feeders. They can adapt to their environment. They can be found feeding on nearly any undersized fish or crustacean found in the waters where they reside. However, for most rivers across the country their main diet will be made up of gizzard shad and crayfish. For anglers, knowing where to locate these baits is a key to success.

A falling water level along with the structure from a bridge is always a good bet when trying to find the forage. *Photo Credit: Josh England.*

The key to finding a striped bass's forage is to figure out their travel patterns. If American shad make a spring run up a certain river, it is likely that the stripers will be close behind them when they make that run. Knowing when that shad run occurs is the key to finding the stripers. Most of the time a yearly pattern will begin due to a specific rise in water temperature and will combine with a specific moon phase. Anglers need to take note of these yearly patterns so that they can try to fish to the striped bass when they occur. When striped bass are feeding on either crayfish or gizzards, there is not so much of a pattern occurring; rather, the forage is in the river system, so that is where the stripers go. Some of the obvious places to find forage in a river are entrances to creeks, shoals, flats, deep holes, and blowdowns (trees that have fallen), with emphasis on newly blown down vegetation. This is the type of structure the forage use to hide from predators. The key to finding bait is to basically look everywhere. Striper rivers in most cases are easier both for finding fish and catching them. Rivers that have a striped bass habitat are

Ryan Kennedy caught this large striper fishing a deep hole where both the stripers and the forage were congregated. *Photo Credit: Ryan Kennedy.*

just smaller in size compared to most reservoirs. When looking at a river, an angler can break it down no matter how big it is. It is similar to breaking down a trout river. When you look at a reservoir, it almost all looks the same, in that it appears large, open, and wide. So, without offending anyone who fishes for freshwater striped bass, I will say this only once: It is easier to figure out and catch striped bass on a river than on a reservoir. Yet when it comes to being successful on either a river or a reservoir, finding the forage is the key.

Chapter 7

Tactics Used to Catch Striped Bass in Rivers

How to Fish a Deep Hole in a River

When fishing specific structure in a river, it is important to know how to fish it as well as where to place the fly. Fishing a deep hole in a river offers the angler a few variables. For example, it is critical to know how far the hole stretches in the river—not only its length but its width as well. If the hole runs up to and near the bank, it is likely the fish may hug the bank. In this case, anglers need to throw their fly and work it as close to the bank as possible. It is also important to properly work the deep hole with the fly. That may mean using a fast-sinking line if the hole is at least five feet deep throughout. If it is under five feet, the fish may still stack up in that hole, but anglers might be able to get away with a slow-sinking intermediate line. Either way, it is probably best to make sure that you cast across the hole and count down some before retrieving. It is not likely that the striped bass will be cruising near the surface in a deep hole. The current at the bottom of the deep hole has got the lightest current for the stripers to deal with. That is why so many fish, be they striped bass or trout, like to sit in the bottom of the deeper holes. They burn less energy there, which is what all fish try to do. Casting down and across while allowing the fly to sink will let you work the outer reaches of the hole best. It is almost like swinging a fly for trout. The difference is you want to start working that fly back with a more erratic retrieve, to make the striper think your offering is struggling in the current.

The only time I fish upriver when working a deep hole is if the hole starts right at the tailout of a shoal or if the hole is super deep. If you are fishing a hole that might be ten feet deep or more, then it may be best to cast upriver with a

Longtime freshwater striper fly angler and expert Bill Butts with an Arkansas River striper he pulled out of a deep hole. *Photo Credit: Bill Butts.*

fast-sinking line and then work the fly back to you. In this instance you may need to work the fly back a little more quickly, as the current will be pushing the line down and toward you. Another reason to fish the fly more quickly upriver is to avoid getting hung up on the bottom. It is not the most desirable way to fish a deep hole, but sometimes it may be your only choice.

Another strategy to employ when fishing a deep hole is anchoring up and thoroughly working your fly around the entire hole (both lengthwise and width-wise). If you are fishing a faster river and you get into a deep hole, you may have no choice but to anchor up and work your way downriver. It is also advisable to anchor up above the deep hole if it is big and wide. Then you can fish straight across and even down and across as you probe for stripers. Another tactic might be to use your drag chain when the river is not running too fast. The use of a drag chain gives anglers an opportunity to slow their drift and work the entire hole. You should also consider using your electric trolling motor when fishing a deep hole. An electric motor allows you to move upriver or downriver or to fish left or right more easily. I prefer to point the nose of my boat upriver and fish the hole with the stern facing downriver. If you are rowing your boat, anchoring up is probably your best choice.

Your river boat should have electronics to help you locate the deep holes where stripers may be gathering. Finding rock walls along the river could mean you have found a deep hole. *Photo Credit: Josh England.*

No matter how you choose to fish a deep hole, the one thing you want to try to avoid is having a bow in your line after making the cast. It is important to always try to create movement on the fly. The fly must always be active and moving in this situation. Therefore, a Game Changer fly may be your best choice when fishing a deep hole, as it is always imparting action. Should you find you are getting a bow in your line (like when swinging a fly), you will see that your fly is looking lifeless with little action on it as it comes straight through the river current.

Once you find a deep hole in the river, mark it on your fish finder. This ensures you will be able to find and fish it again in the future. Deep holes are one of the most important pieces of structure to learn how to fish when you're on a river.

How to Fish a Creek in a River

Some of the best structure to find when fishing in a river is a creek mouth. Creeks offer forage a place to hide, as the current in the creek is never as strong as it is in the river itself. Striped bass and other gamefish know this, which is why it always pays to fish a creek mouth if you come upon one. What is interesting is that the fish (especially stripers) generally will hold in two or three places in a creek

The mouth of a creek in a river is almost always a high target area for finding striped bass. *Photo Credit: Josh England.*

mouth. The two most obvious places to fish are the points on either side of the creek mouth. If I were a betting man, I would put my money on the upper river side of the creek mouth. This is where bass are almost always found. The first hundred feet into the creek mouth is also worth a few casts. They could be on either side of the entrance into the creek or even in the middle of the creek. You just need to fish it thoroughly, since stripers tend to move some and not lay up as trout would. Fishing all the way up into the creek is certainly worth looking at, but I have not found that to be the most productive water unless it is a long and deep creek. If that were the case, I would fish the entire creek. There is, however, one place where striped bass are known to gather up near a creek mouth, and that area is just before you get in to the creek itself. It may be a stretch of two hundred feet before the creek mouth. When you fish here, you want to make sure your fly is hitting the bank. The fish are usually patrolling up and down the river just above the creek. If I have experienced this once, I have experienced it many times over on many different stretches of different rivers. If there happens to be fallen wood laying along the bank, then that is even better! Anglers will have to use their best judgment as to what fly to throw based on the water flow, water clarity, and how deep the water is. Most of the time I would toss an intermediate line almost onto the bank and work my way slowly down to the creek mouth. If you find your cast is falling ten to twenty feet short of the bank, then move closer into the bank, as

If you find a creek mouth that also happens to have a freshwater source flowing into the river, then you have found a honey hole. *Photo Credit: Josh England.*

you want that fly to almost land on the bank and drag it into the river. These fish will literally be hugging the bank. If I hook a fish, then I rest that area and hit it again on the way back if possible. Many times, when fishing a known spot where stripers can gather in numbers, hooking one fish can spook the school, but in time they will often move back up into that area. Anglers need to show a little patience and rest the hole. This is a very typical strategy when fishing a river. Creek mouths are prized by striped bass river guides and savvy anglers alike. This is an area that can never be overlooked or underfished. If fishing a river that receives more pressure than one would like, getting to that creek mouth and fishing it before anyone else does may be a strategy that you might need to employ.

How To Fish a Bend in the River, or Distinct Point

Trying to find structure in a river where either forage of striped bass tends to congregate is not as obvious as one would like. When you're fishing for stripers in salt water, the most productive structure to fish is obvious. Pilings, rockpiles, lighthouses, sandbars, bridges, rips, and jetties are just some of the more obvious areas to find fish. When you're fishing a reservoir, some of the same structures exist except it may not apply to forage or stripers. Reservoir striped bass do not always

Many times, a bend in the river will hold striped bass, as it appears to be a staging area, especially during the spring spawning run. *Credit: Josh England.*

use that structure to find their next meal. Yet anglers will be able to clearly locate and fish that structure and take notes as to where their successes might lie. In a river, structure is not always as easy to see or find, although some places are more obvious. One of those places to fish are distinct points or points on bends in the river. These are areas a striped bass may stop and rest or even stop to feed while working their way up or down river. It might be only one single fish or possibly a school of fish that finds this structure.

Distinct points are easy to locate when you're looking either up or down river. The key is to approach the point quietly and make sure you fish the entire point. That means fishing across the front of it as well as fishing above and below it. If there is any sort of wood on the point and in the water, then that point becomes even more attractive to the striped bass. It is important to eventually throw your fly up onto the bank when fishing a distinct point. However, do not start by moving in close enough to throw the bank. You might spook any fish that were sitting out on the point. Start on the deep end and work your boat in shallow. This ensures that no stripers will feel you coming and spook off. There is no telling which side of the river point the fish will sit. Striped bass are extremely opportunistic in rivers and they tend to move around more than you would expect. Unless the point is sitting in a deep hole, your best bet is to use a slow-sinking intermediate fly line. Your fly choice, fly color, as well as your retrieve will all depend on what the river conditions are that day.

If you couple a bend in the river along with a shoal, you will have likely found a rich environment for stripers. *Credit: Josh England.*

Sometimes, finding a distinct point in a river may not happen, and in that case you should try to find and fish a bend in the river. Striped bass always seem to find a bend in the river. Fish such spots thoroughly. That means fishing slowly and fishing right up and onto the bank. Striped bass like to travel close to the bank, as they are known as shoreline travelers in a river system. Start fishing a bend in the river at least a couple of hundred feet before the river bend to a couple of hundred feet after it. If the bend is full of wood in the water, then it is likely that the striped bass will find the forage hiding around the wood. Many times, a bend in the river may also be around a deep hole. The deep hole might be on the side of the river where the bend is, or it might be across and on the opposite side of the bend. Use your electronics to find that deep hole around the bend, as it might be full of striped bass. Pay attention to all the topography surrounding a bend in the river. Finding structure like this may not be obvious, yet this type of area may turn out to be one of your prized honey holes to fly fish. If you are fortunate to have a winding river that holds striped bass, then you automatically have a lot of water to cover in order to find success. When this is the case it is important to use your electronics to mark the bends in the river that seem to consistently produce good fishing. Now you will never have to go back to memory to know which bend in the river was the honey hole since your fish finder will have permanently marked it for you. While you may not use your electronics nearly as much on a river as you would on a reservoir, they can still be an important piece of equipment to have when striper fishing a river.

How to Fish a Shoal

Not only are shoals great places to search for stripers, but they allow wading anglers the opportunity to hook into one. *Photo Credit: David Cannon.*

Locating striped bass in shoals is possibly the best way to fish a river system. Shoals are defined as natural submerged ridges, banks, or bars that consist of or are covered by sand or other unconsolidated material and which rise from the riverbed to near the surface. In other words, shoals are places where the river is shallow. Shoals in rivers are usually highly oxygenated, cooler water, which is one reason why striped bass love to hang around them. A shoal can be small or stretch far and wide across a river. They are considered prized structure by river striped bass anglers. It may be that stripers love that cooler, more oxygenated water. It also may be that the fish can more easily find an easy meal in a shoal's more turbulent water. Either way, bass anglers should always target shoals.

Fishing a shoal is not as difficult as one might think. Since shoals are usually shallow, anglers afoot should always consider fishing these structures. Anglers fishing out of a boat need to look at a shoal to find the holes and pockets where stripers will most likely be. A hole or pocket located in or around a shoal can be as small as five or six feet in circumference and able to hold a striper. Pockets located in or around a shoal offer striped bass a place where the water is not as turbulent, so they do not need to expend as much energy. That makes pockets prime places for striped bass to either rest and be comfortable or hide while waiting to ambush forage. Some shoals may have many pockets and holes located around them, and anglers should not overlook any area that appears to offer some refuge from the more turbulent shallow water. Basically, opportunities abound when you're trying to locate striped bass in shoals. This is the one time a floating or intermediate fly line can be used in the river. Although I almost always opt for a slow-sinking intermediate fly line on shoals, in this case a floating line may be an advantage due to fewer encounters with hooking the bottom, as well as your being able to mend line when working the fly in the shallow water.

If I had to zero in on one specific area of a shoal to fish, it would be the tail-out section of the shoal. This is where the water will get a little deeper, as this is where the shoal ends. Stripers like to get right up and into the white water. This means that anglers in a boat can maneuver up from the bottom of the shoal and throw right into the tail out. If there is some slower water in between the tail out of the shoal, like a pocket, then you want to work that pocket thoroughly. Fishing the seams is also another good tactic. A seam is where the faster water meets the

Shoals can be tricky to navigate both on foot and in a boat, but the risk is well worth the reward. *Photo Credit: Todd Arnold.*

slower water. Chattahoochee River striper pro and guide Rob Smith of The Fish Hawk fly shop loves fishing shoals. I have been out on the river and watched Smith race over to this type of structure and claim his position for his guided customers when there are multiple boats fishing the river. If that does not lay claim to how important that type of structure is, then nothing will. It is always best to throw across the shoal, although sometimes having to work a fly upriver may be the only way to work certain water. If the shoal is wadeable, then fishing across or even down and across becomes the best angle to take. If the hole or deeper run in a shoal is the water you are targeting, then you might even consider dead drifting or high sticking your fly at the striped bass. While it may be a tad harder to feel the bite, sometimes it is just tough enough to properly work a fly when the angle presented is not allowing the fly to look natural in the water. Trout anglers are usually experts at that kind of technique.

I have spoken with river anglers who only target shoals when striper fishing. They will move up and down the river and fish this type of structure, bypassing all other types of structure in the process. Most of these folks say that shoals are a primary area to fish anytime striped bass are found in rivers, and is especially productive during the fish's spring spawning.

Using Blowdowns to Help Find River Stripers

Most of the time when we discuss the different types of structure available to help locate striped bass, there is usually a commonality to both reservoirs and rivers. High spots in rivers are known as shoals and the striped bass can be found there. High spots in reservoirs are called humps, saddles, or blow-throughs, and striped bass can be found there. The same could be said for points, bends, and creek mouths. Whether found on a river or in a reservoir, that type of structure is important in locating striped bass. However, not all structure works on both reservoirs and rivers evenly. For example, if there is one type of structure that is extremely important on rivers but not very important on reservoirs, it is blowdowns. Blowdowns are basically trees that have fallen into the river and create structure along a bank. Some rivers are lined with blowdowns throughout while others have some fallen wood every now and then. Striped bass love to hang around blowdowns on rivers, especially freshly fallen blowdowns. The reason striped bass can be found around freshly fallen blowdowns is because of the lack of silt build-up on the trees that have recently fallen. You will find that fallen trees that have been in the river for some time will have more silt build-up on their lower ends. Blowdowns in deeper water are more likely to hold stripers than those

Fresh or newly downed blowdowns are favored by most striped bass anglers fishing a river. *Photo Credit: Josh England.*

in shallower water or where more silt has shallowed the water. Forage species will use blowdowns to seek cover, which is one of the reasons why striped bass can be found near fallen wood.

When fishing a river and specifically targeting fish using blowdowns, it is important to remember to throw right up and onto the bank. The striped bass can be hiding in a few areas around fallen wood. They can be on the upriver side of the wood, the downriver side of the wood, or even sitting up and into the wood. For anglers targeting striped bass in blowdowns, the money shot is usually the downriver side of the fallen wood. The downside of a blowdown helps reduce the current for fish looking to ambush prey. If you happen to be fishing fallen wood that is in mostly shallow water, then throwing to the upriver side can yield positive results. This is especially true if the blowdown appears old. Most anglers overlook the shallow upriver lies when targeting fish in older fallen wood, and I am here to tell you that it pays to fish it all thoroughly.

Most of the time anglers should stick to using a slow-sinking intermediate line when fishing blowdowns. However, if the blowdowns are alongside a deep hole, then fishing a faster sinking line can be an advantage. Many times, when I am fishing the downriver side of a blowdown, I will throw back upstream of the wood and work my fly a little faster. This is the same tactic that brown trout

When fishing a blowdown, try to put your fly right into the wood. That is one of freshwater striped bass fly fishing pioneer Dave Whitlock's favorite areas to target on a river. *Photo Credit: Josh England.*

anglers use when they are targeting big browns on streamers. Depending on the flow of the river, it may be necessary to employ a hand-over-hand retrieve when fishing upriver in order to keep movement on your fly.

The only issue anglers need to remember when fishing blowdowns is that the striped bass, once hooked, will use the wood to their advantage. If you happen to hook a good fish, it is likely that striper will try to run back up and into the wood and break you off. Anglers should be aware of this gamefish tactic and prepare ahead of time by fishing 20-pound-test tippet and using a faster action rod, which will allow you to muscle the fish out into the river, away from the wood. It is for this reason that I recommend a 9-weight rod when river fishing striped bass and targeting blowdowns.

Fly Positioning and Retrieving the Fly

Fishing a river is different from fishing a reservoir. This is especially true when discussing the placement and retrieval of the fly. In reservoirs, you could almost always use the same retrieve whether blind casting a point, a hump, or even when fishing to surface feeding striped bass. However, when you are fishing a river, the conditions and the structure dictate what type of retrieve is needed as well as where the fly should be presented.

Just as in reservoir fishing, striped bass in rivers are fooled more easily when anglers employ a series of short retrieves followed by a pause. *Photo Credit: Josh England.*

When fishing white water or shoals, you will need to fish faster. This is all due the fact that there is more current around shoals and any white water. For fly placement, the further up and into the white water you place the fly, the better. Once your fly lands in the white water, a fast retrieve will be required in order to get any movement onto the fly as the current tries to bring the fly back toward you. This is all assuming you are throwing upriver. If you can throw across and into the white water, then you will still have to use a fast retrieve except you will have an easier time coming into contact with your fly rather than having the current sweep it back to you. Consider using a hand-over-hand retrieve in this situation. There are other situations whereby a fast hand-over-hand retrieve would be your desired retrieve. Whenever you are throwing a fly upriver, even in non-white water, you might need to move the fly fast in order to impart action to the fly. That might be the only way you can get a bite. Another time a fast retrieve will be required is when you are fishing clear water. You simply cannot give striped bass an opportunity to get a good look at your offering. A fast retrieve will elicit an instinctive reaction for a bass to attack the fly, and that is when a hand-over-hand fast retrieve can be effective.

When fishing in slower water or when fishing in water that is stained, it is important to work the fly a little more slowly or naturally. This will allow the fly to look more realistic in the water with regards to movement. In this situation it is best to fish a fly with short quick strips, followed by a pause. Striped bass will almost always strike on the pause. If a series of short quick strips and a pause does not elicit a strike, then the angler needs to make a series of longer strips followed by a pause. The important factor in the retrieve of a fly in a river is to continually change it up until you have figured out what seems to trigger strikes by striped bass. There always seems to be a definite strategy needed when trying to figure out what the fish want each day. Anglers who are constantly changing their retrieve are the ones who will be rewarded more often. Once a successful retrieve is found, stick with it until it stops working. Then, go back to experimenting on the retrieve until you find what begins to work and continue to repeat it. Fish may change their habit based on water clarity, water height, water flow, weather conditions, and moon phases. Continually experimenting with a different retrieve is what separates those who fish from those who catch fish.

Placement of the fly can be extremely important when striper fishing in a river. Most of the time anglers need to throw up and onto the bank. If you are close but not on the bank, you may miss feeding a striped bass. Whether that is because the striped bass are sitting right up on the bank or because the forage is

Sometimes you have no choice but to work your fly by casting directly upriver. In this case, a faster retrieve is necessary in order to keep your fly moving and to keep you connected to your fly line should a strike occur. *Photo Credit: Jeff Durniak.*

up on the bank makes no difference. If you are fishing the bank, then get your fly up and onto the bank and not ten feet off it. Ten feet off the bank is not on the bank. You need to almost hit the dry land of the riverbank and, if need be, pull your fly into the river when starting your retrieve. If you are throwing into blowdowns on a river, then you need to nearly hit the blowdown. Yes, you will certainly lose some flies fishing this way, but that is where the stripers need to see the fly. Whether they hit it immediately or follow the fly out of the structure, that is where you must place your fly. Ask a saltwater snook angler how many flies he or she has lost throwing flies into the mangroves. This is risk/reward fishing. No pain, no gain. The bottom line is that distance from the shoreline matters in river striped bass fishing. Accuracy will play a part in whether you are rewarded with an eat. If you are not confident with your casting accuracy, then you simply need to go out and practice. Over time, your confidence will grow, and tossing a fly into a pocket, brush, or any tight quarters will seem natural.

HOOKING A FISH (STRIP STRIKE)

When the strike of a striped bass finally happens, it is important to make the proper hook set. Setting the hook on a river is no different than setting the hook on a reservoir or in salt water. A strip strike is the ideal technique used for setting

A strip strike is essential to stay connected to the fish when that strike finally does come. Here, Mark Keller fights a Chattahoochee River striped bass. *Photo Credit: Josh England.*

the hook. It's accomplished by keeping the rod at a low angle when retrieving the fly and then giving a short, firm pull with the retrieval hand (not the hand holding the fly rod) to set the hook. Once you have set the hook, a slight raise of the rod should allow you to both fight the fish as well as clear any line off the deck of the boat or from your stripping basket in order to fight the fish on the reel. Strip striking is a technique that has been around for years and little has changed. However, anglers accustomed to fishing for trout and either nymphing or dry fly fishing are more accustomed to simply lifting the rod up in order to set the hook. This technique is known as a trout set and it will not work well with striped bass. You are fishing a bigger fly with a larger hook and it is important that the hook set penetrate the jaw of the striper. Trout setting leads to many lost fish when fishing for larger gamefish. There are times when a strip strike will not work well, however. This usually is the case when you're fishing for striped bass and casting upriver. The current coming downriver toward you will put slack line into your retrieve. If you feel a bite in this situation, you may have to sweep the rod hard to your side and downriver in order to make a good connection. Another tactic when fishing a fly upriver is to use a hand-over-hand retrieve. A hand-over-hand retrieve will help you stay in contact with your fly line and have a better chance of feeling any strike from a striped bass. When a strike does occur, either make a short strip strike or make a sweeping angle left or right to hook the fish. This is a

Georgia guide Garner Reid bending some graphite on an Etowah River striper with Connor Jones working the oars. *Photo Credit: David Cannon.*

technique often used by saltwater anglers fishing for false albacore and other species that require a faster retrieve.

While either of these techniques will work to set the hook, I have noticed over the years that most of my customers have little experience with the strip strike and often fall back to the trout set. This almost always leads to either lost fish or a complete miss altogether. Trout setting a fish with a streamer usually pulls the fly away from the fish intending to eat it. To catch striped bass consistently, it really does pay to master the strip strike.

How Fishing Pressure Affects a River

Fishing pressure on any body of water can change a fishery from what once may have been considered elite to overfished and not worth the effort. We see this type of thing in all bodies of water, salt or fresh. Fisheries can only take so much pressure before the recreational angler starts to see the negative changes taking place.

Today we know for fact that the entire East Coast saltwater striped bass fishery is in danger, as the coastal population of striped bass is nowhere near what it once was. This is the second time in my lifetime that I have experienced this. Back in the early 1980s, I lived through a total striped bass moratorium, whereby no one was allowed to kill striped bass until the fish had a chance to repopulate

When the word gets out that the stripers are putting on the feed bag, you never know what you are going to find when you arrive at the ramp. *Photo Credit: Josh England.*

themselves. Here we are thirty years later, and we may be experiencing that same situation all over again.

I moved down to Georgia and started fishing Lake Sidney Lanier back in the late 1990s. There were few striped bass anglers fishing the lake back then. Over the past twenty-plus years the striped bass fishery has exploded, and today we see no fewer than twenty boats out fishing for striped bass everyday. While I was always fly fishing for them on Lanier, there was only one other angler fly fishing for stripers on my lake back then. Today we have close to one hundred boats that are dedicated to catching stripers on the fly rod. That is what I call progress. It is also creating more fishing pressure on this fishery, and you can tell the fishing has gotten harder and harder over the years. We still have as many fish in the lake as we used to, but we just have way more anglers sharing the resource.

When it comes to fishing pressure, a river can be the most affected by it. Rivers are so much smaller than most reservoirs or saltwater environments that they simply cannot take as much pressure as some other types of water. Not only are rivers smaller, but they are also shallower. Both fishing pressure and recreational boating pressure can move fish out of an area and over time make that recreational fishery more complicated and more difficult to catch fish. Therefore, of all the bodies of water fished, most river anglers are more tight-lipped about their fishery than that of all others. I am not saying anglers cannot boast about

It is always important to give anglers enough room when fishing a river. Remember, low holing is a no-no. *Photo Credit: Josh England.*

their catches on any given fishery, but social media and the like can do a lot of damage once the word gets out about a certain fishery. Heavy fishing pressure can often make the fish skittish and harder to hook. Remember, it's not always new fish in a certain section of the river. Fish may summer over and live a certain amount of time in a certain section of the river. The more they are harassed, the harder they are to fool. Anglers fishing in a more heavily pressured river may need to strategize more and fish flies or colors the fish may not have ever seen before. They may also have to lighten up their tippet or use longer leaders to fool more pressured striped bass.

One of the biggest concerns fishermen will face on a river receiving more pressure is that of angler courtesy. As more and more folks fish a river and pressure starts building, we see that certain areas get fished harder on that river. There is a term called low holing, and this is something we see on rivers that have a lot of pressure. Low holing occurs when an angler in a boat is floating downriver and fishing a certain area. Along comes another angler who goes in front of the boat that is floating and thus is getting the first shot as both boats fish their way downriver. Anglers need to know to give a boat that is already fishing a good amount of space before stopping to fish that same side of the river. It would be best practice to fish the opposite side. If you simply must fish the same side, then give the first boat at least a half mile leeway before starting your float. It is also important to make sure when you pass that first boat, you slow down and idle past. That is just good fishing etiquette. Lack of etiquette can lead to ill will and hurt feelings or sometimes worse. I have witnessed some messy situations due to lack of etiquette.

This is the reality of many striped bass rivers across the country as this fishery is becoming more popular. Freshwater striped bass fishing has exploded in popularity over the last few years. Having a saltwater gamefish to fish for when you are many miles away from salt water leads to more and more fishing pressure, as many anglers want to get a chance at a hard-fighting gamefish. Everyone needs to learn to live with one another on the river (and on all bodies of water for that matter). At the end of the day, a high amount of fishing pressure can lead to extremely high blood pressure for all anglers and having the proper fishing etiquette can be the only choice if we are to all share this resource.

Chapter 8

Equipment for Striped Bass

STRIPED BASS TACKLE: RODS, REELS, LINES, LEADERS

When it comes to tackle for stripers in rivers and lakes, it is basically an easy setup. Rods from 7 to 10 weights are the norm. If I were to zero in on the perfect rod setup for rivers, it would be a 9-weight. I also prefer a slightly faster action 9-weight to handle the short weighted head of an intermediate fly line. For lakes you could go with an 8- or a 9-weight, but I prefer the 8-weight as most of the fish will average five to ten pounds on my reservoir. There are lakes throughout the country that seem to have an abundance of smaller fish in the two- to five-pound category, however, and for those impoundments I would consider a 7-weight rod. I will say it is always best to have a couple of outfits rigged and ready for fishing no matter where you fish. Most of the time you will be fishing either an intermediate slow-sinking line or an integrated shooting-head fast-sinking line. There are occasions when a floating line might be called for, but we will discuss that when we get into more detail on line choices. For now, if I were going to pick a rod or two, my top choices would be a nine-foot-long fast-action rod to handle the intermediate and floating line set ups and a medium-fast-action rod to handle the fast-sinking line set ups.

There are a lot of great rods out there today, so I am not going to get into too many specifics with regards to rods. It is a very subjective choice to be made by each angler. I will tell you that while I fish high-end rods from some of the premier fly-rod companies, I also fish some of the more economical rods being made overseas, and they too are just tremendous fishing tools. Rod manufacturers seem to be closing the gap on value-priced rods and their performance compared to premium-priced rods. My clients get to fish them all, and I have had

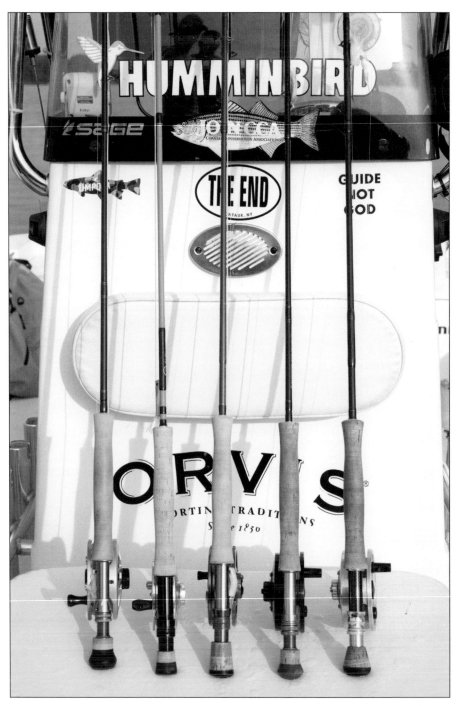

Anglers looking to purchase a fly rod for freshwater striped bass can feel comfortable with rods ranging in weight from 7 to 10. An 8- or 9-weight rod would be a perfect choice. *Photo Credit: Josh England.*

no complaints about the tackle I keep rigged in the boat. When I get a chance to take a busman's holiday, I personally fish the original Orvis Helios, which is a fast-action nine-foot rod that is just a delight for tossing floating and intermediate lines. Conversely, when tossing a fast-sinking line, I still use a TFO Professional Series rod. Here are two completely different set ups that are priced in two separate ranges. Makers like Scott, Sage, Orvis, T&T, G Loomis, Winston, St Croix, TFO, Echo, and Redington all make rods that will fit an angler's needs. There are many other smaller, lesser-known rod brands that I have cast that will work just as well. With rod manufacturers getting more and more technical with their high-modulus graphite blanks, taper designs, and improved components, it is my opinion that the most important part of the equipment equation is the line we purchase. More on that later.

Whether you choose a one-piece or multipiece rod should be based on convenience more than anything else. Lately there has been a slight resurgence in one-piece rods. I have fished them extensively and I can tell you they are the bomb! I love how they feel and throw a fly line. However, one-piece rods are not easy to store, so this is where each angler needs to determine what works best for him or her. Another type of rod that has been talked about lately is what the industry calls "short sticks." These are fly rods in the 7-to 11-weight range that have an overall length of between seven and a half to just under eight feet. These rods have some advantages to them. Short sticks allow you to make a quick accurate cast with less false casting. They also allow the angler to put maximum pressure on a hooked fish that goes deep. Anglers fishing in a narrow creek might prefer these rods, as might anglers fishing out of a kayak. It is just easier to land a fish using a short stick than a longer one. However, the disadvantages to these rods far outweighs the advantages. Anglers tossing short sticks have less control of a hooked fish that tries to gunwale you. In other words, if you are fighting a fish on the port bow of the boat and the fish surges under the boat to the starboard side, it is much harder to reach down under the boat with a shorter fly rod. If you must quickly duck around the electric trolling motor to get control of that surging fish, it is way more difficult to do so with a short stick. The same can be said if that same fish runs to the stern from the bow and crosses under the boat. Using a short stick makes adjusting the hooked fish behind the big motor to the other side a much more difficult task which could result in a lost fish or even a busted rod. When casting a short stick, a minimum number of false casts are required to make a nice cast out to the fish. Two false casts and the rod is loaded and ready to go. Once they go beyond two false casts, most anglers tend to drop their cast behind them with these shorter rods, and the cast has been lost. This is not a good thing when fish are on the surface feeding and you need to be fishing with a sense of urgency. For these reasons alone, I just prefer a nine-foot fly rod.

When it comes to fly reels, anglers have a plethora of choices to choose from. Fly-reel manufacturers have been enjoying a boom in the making of reels that are lighter, have better drag systems, and can even pick up fly lines more quickly with one full rotation of the handle. For striped bass, most anglers need only look at a reel that has a good drag system and can hold a minimum of 150 to two hundred yards of backing. There are basically two different types of drag systems: disc or spring and pawl. There is no reason to fish anything other than a disc drag system as it gives the angler more stopping power when battling a hard-fighting fish. Spring and pawl fly reels are best suited for trout or pond fishing for small fish. Not all trout are best fished using a spring and pawl drag system, but for simplicity's sake we will leave it at that. A disc drag's start-up should be smooth to protect light tippets and maintain consistent pressure throughout the fight. Disc drags also offer a wide range of resistance adjustments to help you meet the conditions at hand. A disc drag is a type of system that uses compressed washers made of various materials to create friction against the spool in order to apply tension on the line. While there are many different types of drag systems out there, most manufacturers use a full draw bar made of a cork drag or possibly some other synthetic drag system made of nylon, Teflon, Delrin, Rulon, carbon fiber,

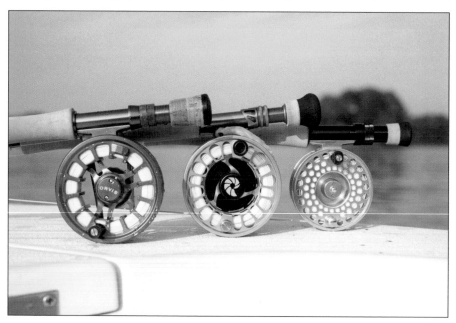

Fly reels should have a good drag for these powerful fish, and be capable of holding a minimum of 150 yards of backing. *Photo Credit: Josh England.*

or some other polymer or plastic for a washer. While all these systems work well, using cork in a full draw bar drag system seems to be the most popular way to go. It requires a little more maintenance (lubrication) than other drag systems that use synthetic materials. Cork drags are usually found in most high-end full-draw bar reels nowadays. That is because most cork drag systems have the best stopping power and can be set to a more precise stopping setting. Some disc drag systems are sealed to protect the inner workings of the system. That is an important feature for saltwater fishermen, but probably not so much for freshwater anglers. While a non-cork drag system will work perfectly for stripers, its major upside is the lack of maintenance needed. Most less expensive reels will have what is known as clip on drag system using either a Rulon or carbon fiber drag. They will work perfectly fine too. Overall, disc drags continue to meet the needs of anglers after hard-fighting fish like striped bass.

Another option anglers have when choosing a reel is whether to buy a large arbor spool or not. A reel designed with a large arbor spool will have one major advantage over a more traditional mid-arbor spool, and that is that the large arbor will pick up more line with one revolution over a mid-arbor spool. That will allow you to fight a fish more quickly and bring it to the net for release, plus it make you less tired when battling a hard-fighting striped bass. Reel manufacturers are now designing fly reels with large arbor spools that can hold sufficient backing and keep the overall weight of the reel down.

One great improvement made by some reel manufacturers is having the clutch used to change the retrieve from right handed to left placed in the spool versus on the reel's housing (where most manufacturers place them). This option allows for folks to keep a few extra spools around and just pop in either a left-handed or right-handed retrieve. It saves a boat load of time every night when I'm in full guide mode and constantly changing set ups for clients who retrieve left or right handed. Two companies that have done this to some of their reels are TFO and Orvis. For anglers buying reels to use only themselves, this is not as important a feature, as their reels will always be set up to retrieve the way they are most comfortable.

After buying your reel, you will next need to add backing to fill the spool before adding the fly line. Most backings are made of either Dacron or braided polyester, with Dacron probably being your best choice. The braided polyester backings are used when you're trying to fill the reel with more capacity. The downside of braided polyester backings is that they can do some damage to your fingers (burning) if you are fighting a hot fish that is pulling the line off in a hurry. I would suggest you use 20-pound-test Dacron backing fill your reel. Once the backing is added, secure a large Bimini twist loop to the backing. Not only is a

Fly fishing for freshwater stripers is more of an intermediate skill set fishery. Anglers will be required to make at least forty-foot casts with minimum false casting. *Photo Credit: Josh England.*

Bimini twist loop strong, but it will allow you to change fly lines whenever needed by using a loop to loop connection. This is the way saltwater striper rigs have been set up for years. Since all quality fly lines are sold with a loop on both ends, it only makes sense to set up your backing to accommodate that loop on the line.

Now we shall discuss which fly line to select. Of all the improvements made over the past twenty years in fly tackle, fly lines seem to have come the farthest. Fly-line manufacturers use a few different materials when deciding what the core of their fly line is to be made of. The materials they use help determine the performance of that line based on the conditions at hand. Hot, humid weather versus cold weather tends to be the biggest factor when determining what the core of the fly line should be, with monofilament or a multi-filament braid preferred. The coating used will also determine how the line will cast. Once again, it is the environmental conditions that best determine what the combination of core and coating should be. It's best to base your line choice by the water temperature and climate you'll be fishing.

Fly line selection is simple for freshwater stripers. If you get serious about the fishery, you are going to need three types of cold-water lines: floating, slow-sinking intermediate, and fast-sinking. The two lines that are money in the bank are slow-sinking intermediate and fast-sinking line. The reason for this is simple.

Having an assortment of lines at your disposal is best practice if fishing from a boat. This way you are prepared for fishing all levels of the water column. *Photo Credit: Josh England.*

Unless you are fishing super shallow water (under three feet) or tossing poppers, the likelihood is that the slow-sinking intermediate will be your workhorse line. This holds true in both lakes and rivers. A floating line is great if you are sight fishing in super shallow water and do not want to spook any fish, as stripers get awfully spooky in thin water. There are times when a popper or slider will do the trick, and that is when a floating line is called for. The only other time I would consider tossing a slow-sinking intermediate is in the early fall when the fish are feeding just below the surface and you are looking for your fly to fall at an extremely slow sink rate. Stripers absolutely love to eat a fly on the freefall. Sometimes even a slow-sinking intermediate line will pull a fly down too quickly when the fish are feeding in the first eighteen inches below the surface. I would guess that 95 percent of your striper fishing will be done without the use of a floating line.

A fast-sinking line is what it is, a line that will have a sink rate of between six to eight inches per second. When fishing lakes in the winter, there are many days we find the fish over the channel or in the mouth of a cove hovering around fifteen to twenty-five feet below the surface in big schools. They may be a tad shallower or slightly deeper. Either way, a fast-sinking line will allow you to use the countdown method to get to these fish. We will discuss the countdown method in more detail in another chapter, when we discuss feeding the fish. There are many types of fast-sinking lines available. Some are full sinking while others incorporate a slow-sinking running line integrated into a fast-sinking head. These heads can range in length from ten to thirty feet long. I prefer these integrated fast-sinking lines and would select a line that has a head that is at least twenty-five feet long. These types of lines are being made by nearly all the fly line companies, including Teeny, Orvis, RIO, Scientific Angler, Airflo, Cortland, and Royal Wulff. The thin diameter of the running line of these types of fast-sinking integrated heads allows the line to sink down to levels where fish spend most of their lives; well below the surface! This has been my go-to line when it comes to winter striper fishing on lakes. There are folks who swear by full fast-sinking lines, and I'm sure they have their place in many fisheries, but my experience tells me it is easier to pick up and cast an integrated fast-sinking line than a full sinking line. The only major difference is that a fast full-sinking line will not have the belly that is created by an integrated fast-sinking line due to the level sink rate of a full fast-sinker. Scientific Angler is now making what they call a triple density line, which is basically an integrated line that take most of that created belly away by layering a progressively faster sinking line to the running and integrating it into the fast-sinking head. In general, a type six fast-sinking line is what is called for in this category of lines. Another choice would be to toss a 300- or 350-grain fast-sinking density

A good assortment of lines includes a floating, slow-sinking intermediate, as well as a fast-sinking line on the boat on most days. *Photo Credit: Josh England.*

compensated line. Some guys are still tossing the old T11 and T14 shooting-head lines for super-fast-sinking capability. Any or all these lines will do the job and get your fly to the fish below.

A slow-sinking intermediate fly line is easily the most popular of all the striper lines. These lines sink an average of between one and a half to two inches per second. Most anglers fishing rivers for freshwater stripers use this type of line. There are occasions where some river anglers might opt for a type three sinking line. This is a line that sinks more quickly than a slow-sinking intermediate but much slower than a fast-sinking integrated line. To me it is a specialty line and not one that anglers need consider when starting to fish for stripers. Intermediate lines have a casting quality that will remind you of a floating line. However, their properties in the water will clearly outperform those of a floating line. When fishing to stripers that appear to be breaking the surface, your first choice should be to toss an intermediate fly line. That is because it will get subsurface a little more quickly than a floating line. Another great property of intermediate lines is that many are now made with a clear tip. This was designed to allow for more stealth when fishing either shallow or near the surface. There are basically two types of intermediate line that anglers need to understand. There are full intermediate fly lines, where the entire one-hundred-foot line will sink slowly, and there are integrated intermediate fly lines where the first seventy feet off the rear

Anglers can choose to create their own leader setups or buy pre-rigged knotless tapered leaders. *Photo Credit: Josh England.*

of the line is floating, and the last thirty feet is a slow-sinking head. We call these types of lines F/I (floating/intermediate). While both a full intermediate and an F/I type line will work, I prefer the F/I line as it allows me to pick the line up off the water more quickly when I am casting to stripers that are moving quickly and surface feeding. Surface-feeding stripers can change direction on a moment's notice, and the properties of these F/I lines are much more user friendly when an errant cast was made and needs to be picked up and launched out again with a sense of urgency.

Leader set up for freshwater striped bass is nearly the same as that of saltwater stripers. The only difference is that when you're fishing a lake and the fish are over dead trees, a stronger tippet may be required. Let's look at the recommended leader set ups for all the various lines to be used. When fishing a floating line, the best leader set up will be that of a tapered nine-foot-long leader with a tippet of 16- to 20-pound-test monofilament. I do not fish fluorocarbon leader when tossing a floating line, as fluorocarbon tends to sink slightly, as opposed to monofilament. For an intermediate set up, I would recommend a seven- to nine-foot-long leader that has a tippet of 16- to 20-pound-test. In this case, however, I would use a fluorocarbon versus a monofilament leader. This is where having a little more stealth built into your leader can help. You can purchase either of these leaders from companies that produce knotless tapered leaders, including

Having the proper leader setup can help anglers get the most distance when making long casts to fast-moving fish. *Photo Credit: Josh England.*

RIO, Scientific Angler, Umpqua, and Orvis. Or you can twist up your own tapered leader by blood knotting 40-, 30-, and 20-pound-test together. Lastly, when it comes to fishing a fast-sinking line, the easiest setup is to simply fish a short, five- to six-foot straight piece of 15- or 20-pound-test fluorocarbon. No need for a tapered leader for this setup, as we don't need the fly turnover and land outstretched for an immediate retrieve. On this setup, we need the line to sink below the surface to levels, sometimes as deep as twenty-five feet. A short fluorocarbon leader will achieve a faster sink rate than a longer leader will. Many anglers have their own recipe for the best leader setup, but these few listed above have never failed me yet.

Knots Needed for Fresh Water Stripers

There are many types of knots anglers need to know in order to correctly set up their tackle for striped bass. For the sake of simplicity, we will cover the most practical knots used for attaching the fly line to the backing of your reel, the knots used for leader assembly, and finally the knots used for attaching your fly to the tippet of your leader. There are many more knots to use for any of previously discussed needed uses, but I will give you the ones that I have used for nearly thirty years and that have worked for me. Once you have mastered these few knots, you are ready to go out and toss flies at freshwater striped bass.

Let's start by discussing the knot used to attach the back of the fly line to the Dacron backing. Remember, most fly lines come with a welded loop on both the front and back ends. This means that we can assemble our backing using a loop to loop connection. Some folks will suggest that creating a loop using a large triple surgeons knot to the end of the Dacron backing will suffice. Truth be told, it probably will. However, if you want an even stronger connection that will never fail, it's best to use a Bimini twist loop onto the end of the backing. Make sure your Bimini twist loop is at least eight inches in length so it will fit over the entire fly line. Coat the knotted area with some Krazy Glue or Loon UV Knot Sense and you'll have a surefire connection that will give you years of service. Now all you need to do is loop to loop the backing over the fly line and wind it onto the reel.

When making your own leader, there are several different knots that can be used to assemble different sizes of either monofilament or fluorocarbon. Most guides and fly shop folks will recommend either a triple surgeon's knot or a blood knot. I am a believer in the blood knot system for these types of connections. The only time I ever opt for a triple surgeon's knot to connect leader material together is if I am in a rush and need to tie a knot quickly. This is usually the case when I see fish blitzing the surface and I need a change in the tippet section to the section

The use of a loop knot will allow you to get the most movement on your fly. A loop knot tied to your fly allows for more freedom of movement. *Photo Credit: Henry Cowen.*

below it. A triple surgeon's knot is much faster to tie and secure. During all other situations, a blood knot is my knot of choice.

Lastly, there are many knots you can use to secure the fly to the tippet section of your leader. There is no one answer as to which knot is the best, although most experienced striped bass anglers opt for a loop attachment to their fly. A loop knot will give the fly the most freedom of movement, thus breathing more lifelike action into the fly pattern. This may not seem to be important, but when the fish are feeding selectively a loop knot can be essential in helping to elicit a strike. My favorite of the loop knots is either a Uni-loop (a.k.a. Duncan loop) or a Kreh loop (a.k.a. non-slip loop knot). Both of these loop knots are strong and should not fail the angler. A Palomar knot is another excellent choice when you need a loop knot. Anglers need to understand that when they use a loop knot to attach their fly to their tippet, they sacrifice strength, as many straight loop-less knots have higher degrees of breaking strength. Because of this, many anglers use a knot like an improved clinch knot, which has no loop. It's all a matter of choice and what the angler wants to accomplish. If I were fishing a big Tennessee lake or river fish during the spawning run, I'd probably opt to fish a straight non-loop knot for fear of possibly losing a fish of a lifetime. The same holds true if I were fishing in a lot of brush or trees, as there is less chance of knot failure if your hooked fish takes you into the wood. If you want to dabble further into the knot debate, look no further and buy a copy of *Practical Fishing Knots*, by Lefty Kreh and Mark Sosin. While written many years ago, many still consider it be the bible of fishing knots.

FLIES FOR FRESHWATER STRIPED BASS

Probably the most subjective subject to discuss when pursuing any fish is what flies to use. Flies are such a personal subject when we start discussing any fishery. This is certainly true for freshwater striped bass. There are so many streamer-type patterns that will work, and it all depends on what features of the fly the angler thinks are most important when trying to fool a striped bass. For the most part we can look at successful saltwater striped bass patterns and use them. However, some of the best freshwater striper patterns were specifically designed with this fishery in mind. While many fly patterns are variations of a fly designed by its originator, it is important to give credit where credit is due. Just because someone changed a color, increased or reduced the size, or traded out one material for another, it is important to know where the foundation of that fly came from. Let's face it, there is only one Bob Popovics, Dave Whitlock, Blane Chocklett, Bob Clouser or Charlie Basharat. These guys have designed and originated some of the greatest streamer-type patterns of all time. With that being said, and while there are probably hundreds of fly patterns that will entice freshwater striped bass nearly anywhere in the country, it makes sense to home in on the best flies that seem to work in nearly all fisheries (rivers and lakes). I am going to offer up a baker's dozen fly selection that can be fished as pictured or tweaked by the angler to fit the circumstances at hand. The key is to match the hatch best in your fishery. It may be that you will size up or down a pattern that we mention or change the color slightly to best interpret your local forage species. If your water is more tannic, you may decide to bulk up the fly in order to push more water to get the fishes' attention. If you are fishing clear water, you may decide to add some additional flash or even design the pattern to be a tad sparser in order to best elicit a strike from ole lineside. The thirteen flies we will choose will offer the angler the opportunity to fish the entire water column of surface, slightly sub surface, or deep. Pair these flies with the right fly line and there is not a striped bass on the planet that would not want to eat one of these patterns. The selected flies are proven and are tried and true winners across the country.

I have spoken with freshwater striped bass guides and anglers from California to Oklahoma and Virginia to Missouri as well as many places in between and it's refreshing to know that nearly everyone has the same confidence in many of these patterns (or similar ones). While certain fisheries have their go-to patterns, one thing is absolute in all areas across the country, and that is that having confidence in the fly pattern being fished is half the battle. Most guides or anglers probably fish two or three patterns nearly all the time. All they do is change color or tweak the size depending on the season or the fishery they chose to fish that day. Anglers on the West Coast like Dan Blanton, Steve Santucci, and Mike Costello all have their favorite patterns in their favorite colors, but yet they all agree that they could get by with a Flash Tail Jig Hook Clouser, Spot On Baitfish, or Whistler pattern for sub-surface fishing and a Gurgler or Pole Dancer for top-water fishing. Ask someone on another lake or river system a thousand miles away and half to three quarters of the flies mentioned will overlap into their fishery as well. Let's look at what many in-the-know folks believe are the must-have patterns for freshwater striped bass.

Top-water fishing is certainly the most exciting way to catch just about any fish. It's especially fun when it comes to freshwater striped bass. Having the visual of a large gamefish smash a fly on the surface can make an angler go weak in the knees. You can fish top water in rivers as well as in lakes. Striped bass will not eat off the top any time of the year, however. It is all about water temperature and how much light is left that will determine whether you can coax one into eating off the top. Anglers tossing top-water flies will need to throw a floating line along with a nylon leader. There is no need for fluorocarbon when tossing a top-water

The Joe Blados Crease Fly is one of the best top-water patterns ever designed. While considered a noisemaker, the Crease Fly's best attribute is its shape which, when sitting on top of the water at rest, can still elicit a strike. *Photo Credit: Josh England.*

fly. While there are a host of great top-water flies to choose from, the three best for fishing freshwater stripers are Joe Blados's Crease Fly, Jack Gartside's Gurgler, and Charlie Bisharat's Pole Dancer.

The crease fly is an all-encompassing top-water fly that can be manipulated to swim some and pop some depending on how you retrieve it. Made with foam and bucktail, the crease fly can be as deadly when it comes to rest on the surface as it is when being retrieved. At rest, the Crease Fly, due to its minnow-like shape, will roll slightly on its side and give off a baitfish look. Even when at rest, the bucktail will undulate a bit and look like an injured baitfish, which striped bass simply cannot refuse. There have been many interpretations created over the years after Blados initially designed his Crease Fly. Some folks like to add a rattle inside the foam body while others such as fly tier Ron Dong have created a nearly indestructible version. Either way, the Crease Fly gets my nod as one of the best top-water baits a flyfisherman can throw. Crease Flies may be the best selling of all top-water flies sold commercially.

Jack Gartside's Gurgler may be the most well-known of all the top-water flies anglers use when trying to coax a strike from a striped bass. The gurgler is made with foam and bucktail, although many tiers have created versions of this fly by substituting an array of different materials. The Gurgler works best in slightly less

Jack Gartside was one of the great fly tiers of modern fly fishing. While popular and effective flies come and go over the years, his Gurgler is certainly a fly that anglers will use to call fish up to the surface for years to come. *Photo Credit: Josh England.*

turbulent water and can call a fish up that is lurking below. Like the Crease Fly, a Gurgler can entice a striped bass to explode on it whether moving or at rest. What makes a Gurgler a little more diversified than your typical crease fly is that a Gurgler can be tied not only to imitate small- to medium-sized forage fish, but can also be tied to represent large forage. By changing the materials used, a tier can twist up gurglers to reach eight to ten inches in length and still be relatively easy to throw with an 8- or 9-weight fly rod. Both a Gurgler and a Crease Fly, while considered top-water popping-type patterns, are not what I would call big noisemakers. If making a lot of noise is what you are trying to achieve, you might consider a Bob's Banger-style popper or Flymen Fishing Company's Double Barrel- or Howitzer-style popper. While these are great poppers, I am not convinced a loud noisemaking pattern is as necessary in a freshwater lake as it is in salt water. One could argue that a noisemaker is a good idea when fishing in a river with good flow to it. Gurglers are commercially tied and can be bought at fly shops throughout the country

Probably my favorite top-water fly to toss is Charlie Bisharat's Pole Dancer. Bisharat, who we dubbed the mad scientist in fly design, is a brilliant tier who creates patterns with outside-the-box thinking. His Pole Dancer fly is what conventional anglers would call a Zara Spook–type bait. Its action walks the dog. A pole dancer when retrieved will go left then right and continue to zig, zag, and dart on the surface with minimal effort needed by the angler to create this action. While I have caught hundreds and hundreds of striped bass over the years on a surface fly, I have never seen a more violent surface strike than when a striped bass explodes on a Pole Dancer. They do not want to simply eat it; they want to crush it! The Pole Dancer fly is commercially tied in lengths up to nearly nine inches long in its 5/0 version and could be tied longer using a flash tail.

When it comes to ten subsurface streamer fly patterns that anglers need to know about, it is important to understand that we might be fishing these flies in different parts of the water column. Sometimes the bait and the feeding stripers are up super high in the water column (within two feet of the surface), while other times the bait and the stripers might be down twenty-five feet. While a fast-sinking fly line can get you down to deep feeding fish, there are times an intermediate or a floating line is needed to keep your fly just under the surface. Some of these flies we are about to discuss can be tied smaller or larger to best match the forage you are targeting.

To give you the ten best subsurface flies, remember that some were designed large off the vise so they can imitate a larger forage species, while one or two were designed to imitate young-of-the-year threadfin. When a striper is gorging on threadfin shad in the one- to two-inch size, the fish seem nearly impossible to fool

Fly tier Charlie Bisharat is known in fly-fishing's inner circles as the mad scientist. His Pole Dancer was unique in that it was the first top-water fly to create a walk-the-dog movement on the surface. If a striped bass goes to eat this fly, anglers will see the most violent strike they have ever witnessed. *Photo Credit: Josh England.*

Striped bass just cannot help themselves when they see a Pole Dancer being retrieved on the surface, dancing left, right, left, right. It is one of fly fishing's most exciting scenes the moment the fish crushes the fly. *Photo Credit: Henry Cowen.*

on the fly. That is when movement and matching the hatch are critical in order to be successful. These ten subsurface fly patterns can vary to fit what you think will fool the fish into eating your offering. They are: Chocklett's Game Changer, Boyer's Wiggle Minnow, Popovic's Beast, King's Kinky Muddler, Blanton's Flash Tail Whistler, Clouser's Deep Minnow, Bisharat's Spot On Baitfish, Whitlock's Sheep Shad, Paul Van Reenen's (Just Add H2O) Polar Fiber Minnow, and Cowen's Somethin' Else. All these patterns have their time and place when they are most effective. Carrying these streamer patterns as part of your freshwater striped bass assortment is sure to have you put a bend in your rod on nearly any and every river or lake in the country.

Let's start with the fly patterns that are usually fished higher in the water column. Blane Chocklett's Game Changer is a revolutionary, all-encompassing streamer pattern that folks will talk about thirty years from now as one of the most consistent fish catchers. While this fly can be fished to all depths of the water column, a Game Changer fishes especially well when paired with an intermediate fly line. This fly's movement due to the fish spines incorporated into its body is what makes this pattern a homerun. You can tie this fly to imitate threadfin

Blane Chocklett's Game Changer is a revolutionary subsurface pattern. While this fly will catch fish in any fishy environment, it is particularly effective when tied to imitate gizzard shad. As this book went to the press, Chocklett was already working on a juvenile threadfin shad pattern that incorporates micro fish spines. He created these spines in order to get the fly to the two-inch size required to catch stripers eating tiny threadfin. *Photo Credit: Josh England.*

My buddies were fishing a particularly good point for twenty minutes without getting a bite. I rolled in as they were leaving the point and on the second cast, using a Game Changer, this striper showed himself. Both anglers in the other boat went out and bought game changers the next day! *Photo Credit and lesson learned by Josh England.*

Author, guide, and fly tier extraordinaire Blane Chocklett shows off a Virginia striper that fell for his newly created Game Changer. *Photo Credit: Shane Maybush.*

shad three inches in length to gizzard shad that push ten inches. When a constant retrieve is employed, this fly looks as if it is alive in the water. I liken it to a conventional anglers' Sebile Magic Swimmer (one of the most deadly and effective striped bass baits ever designed). Chocklett and his fly designs clearly make him one of the rising young superstars in the industry today.

Many, many years ago Bruce Olson, Umpqua Feather Merchant's fly specialist, first introduced me to a wonderful fly pattern: Todd Boyer's Wiggle Minnow. I remember Bruce asking me, "Henry, how'd you like to try the most fun fly you'll ever fish?" Obviously intrigued, I asked him to send me a care package. One week later a couple of boxes of Wiggle Minnows showed up at my front door, and I have been fishing them ever since. What makes a Wiggle Minnow so effective is the front taper that allows this fly to move left/right continuously, as a plastic-lipped swimbait or jerkbait would. Made almost completely with foam, the wiggle minnow is a pattern you can fish in all water columns. To me it's most fun to fish it with either an intermediate or floating fly line. A good alternative to a wiggle minnow and new to most shops' fly bins is Kevin Arculeo's BC Baitfish, which is a cross between a Wiggle Minnow and a Game Changer.

Todd Boyer's Wiggle Minnow may be the most fun fly a fly angler will ever fish. Once retrieved, its wiggling action will have you thinking you are fishing a conventional anglers jerk bait. I have had my best results fishing it with a steady hand-over-hand retrieve. *Credit: Josh England.*

What self-respecting striped bass wouldn't consider eating Bob Popovic's Beast Fleye? Many of his fleyes revolutionized saltwater streamer fishing and gave countless numbers of fly tiers a base to begin their tying careers. I liken Popovic's tying tree to that of the way the National Football League looks at coaching trees. New York Giants head coach Bill Parcells has inspired more great NFL coaches then one can imagine. Parcells's coaching gave way to the likes of Bill Belichick, Nick Saban, Tom Coughlin, Sean Payton, and many others who have influenced professional football. Popovics is that kind of once-in-a-lifetime fly-tying coach. Many of his patterns have led to the success of catching gamefish across many different fisheries, but for freshwater striped bass his Beast Fleye is poetry in motion when imitating a large gizzard shad. The same could be said for those fisheries that have American or skipjack shad. The key to this pattern is the use of natural materials (bucktail), which allows this fly to keep its weight down and allows anglers to toss larger flies using lighter rods. I'd suggest using a 9- or 10-weight rod if you are going to toss a beast fly of at least nine inches in length. The beauty of the beast is that when the fly comes to rest, the longer lengths of bucktail make it look alive and breathe even while not moving. When Popovics took his Hollow Fleye and added an extension, the beast was born. Its hollow style is revolutionary, and many a fly has been designed around this pattern's style. It has inspired tiers

From the vise of the greatest fly tier in fly fishing's modern era, Bob Popovic's Beast Fleye allows anglers to imitate a large forage species without sacrificing castability. Made from natural bucktail, this fly comes alive when you start your retrieve. *Photo Credit: Josh England.*

around the world to create baitfish flies that elicit more strikes. An alternative to a beast fly would be a Cowen's Magnum Baitfish, which allows for a large pattern to be tossed on a lighter fly rod.

Jonny King's Kinky Muddler is a fly that is worth noting. Made from both natural and synthetic materials, this fly is best used when trying to imitate forage fish in the mid-sized range, from four to seven inches in length. The Kinky Muddler—while fast becoming the go-to fly for anglers wanting to land a roosterfish—has also been a go-to fly pattern for freshwater striped bass fishermen. This is a great fly that, due to its bulked-up head, pushes a lot of water and can really make a difference when fishing either a river with a fair amount of current or lakes that may be more stained in color. I have been fishing many of King's fly patterns over the years and he is truly one of the young masters in the sport. A good alternative to a Kinky Muddler would be a Tabory Snake Fly, whose deer-hair head pushes a lot of water, or a Bisharat's Airhead, which is popular in the south-central part of the country.

Dan Blanton is one of fly-fishing's iconic anglers. He helped give rise to the popularity of striped bass fishing with a fly rod on the West Coast. While Blanton has been fishing for both fresh- and saltwater stripers for more than sixty years, his

Jonny King's Kinky Muddler is yet another fly from the bench of one of today's most innovative tiers. The Kinky Muddler is already known as a roosterfish slayer in salt water. When you need a fly that pushes a lot of water, the Kinky Muddler should be your first choice when striper fishing. *Photo Credit: Josh England.*

Dan Blanton's Whistler has been used successfully on West Coast stripers for over forty years. It is a go-to pattern that is in everyone's fly box. According to outdoor TV show host and celebrity O'Neil Williams, "Stripers don't know where they live." That statement is true, as a Whistler will catch striped bass anywhere in the country. *Photo Credit: Josh England.*

West coast freshwater striped bass fly fishing pioneer Dan Blanton shows off a recently caught striper from his home waters of San Luis Reservoir. Everything grows big in California! *Photo Credit: Dan Blanton.*

fly patterns continue to fool striped bass in lakes, rivers, and oceans. One of my favorites is the Blanton Flash Tail Whistler. The Whistler style of flies was created back in the 1970s and continues to reinvent itself as new materials and hooks arise in the tying industry. A Flash-Tail Whistler will take striped bass eating all types of forage species except possibly the young-of-the-year (under two and a half inches in length). Any baitfish in the range of three inches on up to nine inches can be imitated with a whistler-style fly. This fly will move and breathe nicely in the water and can be tied in an array of colors to imitate nearly all prey living in your watershed. There are a host of freshwater gamefish, from peacock bass to northern pike, that anglers should consider tossing a Flash-Tail Whistler at as their first choice. A good alternative to Blanton's Whistler would be the venerable Lefty's Deceiver.

You cannot go to any fishery in either salt or fresh water without taking some of Bob Clouser's Deep Minnow patterns with you. As American Express used to say about their credit card, don't leave home without it! Arguably this is the single-most important streamer pattern ever designed. Striped bass love Clouser Minnows, and for good reason. They can imitate nearly any kind of baitfish. The only time a Clouser Minnow might not be as effective is when the forage the stripers are eating is super small or large. Clousers may be most anglers' first choice when it comes to selecting a pattern to tie on. They are sold commercially and are in every fly shop that has their lights turned on. Tied with bucktail, a Clouser will breathe and move so naturally in the water that stripers simply cannot resist hammering it. This fly can be fished in an array of colors to match the hatch, but it is hard to beat either all white, chartreuse over white, olive over white, or gray over white. Lefty Kreh once told me it is the most important streamer pattern ever developed and has probably taken more species of fish than any other. A Clouser Minnow is basically a flyfisherman's bucktail jig. Variations of it have been designed and fished effectively for nearly thirty years. One of the better Clouser-style inspirations worth fishing and mentioning is Blanton's Jig Hook Flash Tail Clouser. Blanton helped popularize the use of sixty-degree bend jig hooks and when tied with an extended tail of flash, the fly is simply deadly. It's a West Coast favorite. The Coyote, tied with a zonker strip, is another Clouser-type fly that incorporates a spinner blade on the front to imitate a Roadrunner-style conventional jig.

You cannot go fishing for freshwater stripers and not have a baitfish-style fly in your fly box. Probably the most popular baitfish-style pattern most anglers have heard about or seen is an Enrico Puglisi baitfish. Baitfish patterns are tied wide bodied, so they imitate any number of forage species. However, while many baitfish-style patterns have been designed over the years, my clear number one

What can you say about Bob Clouser's Deep Minnow (referred to as a Clouser Minnow) that has not already been said before? It is easily the most relevant sub-surface fly ever designed and is a must-have pattern in any striped bass angler's fly box. *Photo Credit: Josh England.*

If you could only fish one fly for the rest of your life for striped bass, your choice would have to be a Clouser Minnow. This fly has probably accounted for more caught stripers than all others put together. *Photo Credit: Josh England.*

Once again from the vise of West Coast striper angler Charlie Bisharat comes a fly that is not well-known but should be. Bisharat's Spot-On Baitfish is a striper slayer. If you need to fish a subsurface baitfish pattern, then look no further than this one. This is one of those flies a guide will keep under his or her cap to have an advantage. *Photo Credit: Josh England.*

go-to of these is Charlie Bisharat's Spot On Baitfish. The mad scientist is not only a top-water-fly designing genius, but he can hold his own with a great sub-surface pattern too. I think the most important feature of a great baitfish pattern is that it must have the ability to sink into the strike zone quickly. Most baitfish patterns do not, and that is fine if you're fishing the very top of the water column or fishing in shallow water. Bisharat's Spot On Baitfish was designed with dumbbell eyes, so it sinks quickly into the feeding zone. The issue I have with many baitfish patterns is they are tied weightless and it takes time for the fly to become waterlogged and sink into the fishes' feeding zone. Tied on a sixty-degree bend jig hook, this fly breathes and moves in the water as well as any baitfish pattern I have ever seen.

The angler who helped pioneer and popularize fly fishing for freshwater stripers is easily one of the industry's iconic figures, Dave Whitlock. Dave is not only an avid angler of this species but a heck of an artist too! He also created some of the best fly patterns a striped bass ever saw come across its nose. Whitlock is well-known for many freshwater fly patterns, whether it's for any of the temperate bass species, trout, or carp. His facial rendering would be on the Mount Rushmore of fly fishing. Whitlock's Sheep Shad series was designed many years ago but is still fooling fish in fresh water today. While newer patterns come out all

When Dave Whitlock designed his Sheep Shad series of flies, fly fishing for freshwater striped bass was in its infancy. Fast-forward to today and this fly is still catching striped bass that are eating threadfin and gizzard shad. It is a must-have fly that needs to be in every angler's fly box. *Photo Credit: Josh England.*

the time, along with their new synthetic materials, the Sheep Shad (weighted or unweighted) deserves a place in every angler's fly box. His flies were designed to take fish out of the south-central region of the country but have proven effective wherever stripers swim.

Back in the nineties I was introduced to a South African fly fisherman named Paul Van Reenen, who was selling some cool synthetic fly-tying materials. His company, Success Flies, had found a niche with tiers across the country. One of the patterns he brought to market was called the Polar Fiber Minnow. Made from Polar Fiber, this supple synthetic material was tied hi-tie-style. The Polar Fiber Minnow became all the rage. In the water the fly rarely fouled (due to its epoxy head) but it breathed and moved like few other flies tied with synthetic materials. Its durability was fantastic compared to that of flies tied with natural fibers, and its fishing-catching ability was off the charts for both freshwater and saltwater gamefish. Fast-forward to today; Success Flies was sold off and the folks from Just Add H2O are now producing both the fantastic synthetic materials as well as the Polar Fiber Minnow. Easy to tie, the Polar Fiber Minnow is one of my go-to patterns here on Lake Lanier. While the commercially tied versions are from just under three inches to up to nearly five inches, and can represent both a threadfin

The Polar Fiber Minnow is a fly that was designed in South Africa. This baitfish pattern moves and breathes like few others. It is one of my favorite patterns to tie super small and throw to stripers that are gorging on young-of-the-year threadfin shad. *Photo Credit: Josh England.*

or gizzard shad, the one- and one-half-inch Polar Fiber Minnow that I tie myself is an absolute striper slayer when the fish are feeding on young-of-the-year threadfin shad. A good alternative to this pattern is Jonny King's Hoo Fly.

The last must-have fly pattern is called a Somethin' Else. I came up with this pattern as a cure for catching striped bass when they are eating young-of-the-year threadfin shad. It took many tries and a host of different materials to figure out this pattern. However, it all came together back around 2004 when we were continuously seeing groups of stripers gorging and rolling on their sides, eating one- to two-inch-long threadfin shad just below the surface. You would think getting tight to a fish would be a no-brainer when you saw the number of fish blitzing just under the surface. It appeared to be a top-water feed, but it wasn't. There were rings, splashes, and busts, but the fish were eating slightly under the surface and would not accept a top-water fly. The bust was a tail kick by the striped bass to get back deeper again. The fish would simply roll on their sides, take in a mouthful of young shad, then give a kick with their tail to go down and circle back up again. They were nearly impossible to hook until the Somethin' Else pattern came to be. A Somethin' Else fly is nothing more than a Clouser Minnow tied super small using Polar Fiber material with a hot pink Fluoro Fiber throat behind the

Cowen's Somethin' Else fly at first looks like nothing more than a Clouser Minnow tied with Polar Fiber material. What makes this the most effective freshwater striped bass fly when fish are eating juvenile threadfin shad is a combination of the hot pink Fluoro Fiber throat along with the breathability of the Polar Fiber. It is simply a guide fly that will outfish all others. *Photo Credit: Josh England.*

Stripers can be extremely finicky when feeding on small bait. A Somethin' Else is my go-to fly when I encounter this situation. *Photo Credit: Josh England.*

eye. Freshwater stripers will eat most flies on the pause when a fly is free falling. The Polar Fiber allows you to match the hatch by size and still give off a lot of breathability (movement), which a typical bucktail-tied two-inch Clouser will not do. Bucktail needs some length in order to breathe when retrieved or when at rest. Allow a Somethin' Else to free fall by making a couple of strips followed by a two- to three-second pause, and hold on! The hot pink Fluoro Fiber works so well because it allows the stripers to pick out the fly from the thousands of threadfin swimming around and huddled up. The hot pink Fluoro Fiber is also the *only* color and material that changes hue depending on how the light hits it. I believe fish see this color change and it gets their attention. If fish are feeding on itty bitty threadfin and you do not have this fly in your box, chances are it will be a long day.

Chapter 9

Boats and Related Equipment

TYPES OF BOATS (JET VS PROP)

In order to fish for striped bass successfully, you are going to need to get somewhat political. An angler is going to have to decide whether to row or wade. Having the use of a powered watercraft greatly increases your chances of being successful as it allows you to fish more water. Anytime an angler increases the amount of water available to fish, the likelihood of success increases exponentially. There are many

Sixteen- to eighteen-foot-long aluminum boats are a popular choice on most striped bass reservoirs. *Photo Credit: Josh England.*

different types of watercraft available for anglers to use to catch striped bass, and quite frankly, they all have their places depending on the water being fished. Let's look at which boats are best suited for which water.

When fishing an impoundment, there are a few choices that can give you the best opportunity to get into the fish. My first choice is a center-console, bay-type boat. A good hull for lakes anywhere in the country is a modified-V hull center console. These boats offer open areas on which two casters can be comfortable fishing together, one out of the bow and the other at the stern. These modified-V center consoles are known as "bay boats," as they are used primarily by inshore saltwater anglers, and transition extremely well to freshwater lakes. Boats from sixteen up to twenty-three feet in length are ideal.

Once you have figured ot what length suits your needs, then your budget comes into play. The size of the motor along with the quality of the boat you choose will determine what price point you are looking at. Suffice it to say that when you're looking at a new rig, the cost can range from one thousand to three thousand dollars a foot. What I love about bay boats is their overall stability in the water. They are generally seven to eight- and a half-foot wide (beam length), and that is what gives anglers the comfort and stability to fish from. Another feature when choosing a bay boat is to try to get something with both a forward deck and a rear deck. This way you can stand over the cockpit or inside of the boat and free yourself of any possible snags of your fly line. Some bay boats can obtain a top end speed of over 50 mph and take you from one spot to another in a very short period. This allows you to fish a wide range of water. Anytime you can move around and search more water, the likelihood of finding the fish increases greatly. Lastly, bay boats are quite seaworthy due to their modified-V hull design. Fishing on a lake to many may seem like a quiet and tranquil undertaking. However, anglers who fish some of the bigger impoundments know better. While not having big water like you might see on the ocean, my lake (Sidney Lanier) can at times get waves that are close together and can top out at over three feet in height. Even though it is not dangerous, it can make for a rough ride going from one place to another. That is the reason why bay boats are the preferred choice by most freshwater striped bass anglers. While there are many great boat manufacturers to choose from, one boat builder designs its boats specifically with the flyfisherman in mind. Jones Brothers Marine out of Morehead City, North Carolina builds a high-quality center console bay boat that was designed from the ground up with input from the fly-fishing community. Bay boats are also easy to trailer, so keeping one in the water isn't always necessary.

Other popular boats we see on area lakes are bass boats and walk throughs. Bass boats with all their NASCAR-style glitter can be sound choices for striped bass anglers. They have open floor plans, which allow for very comfortable fishing platforms. Bass boats are light, which makes them super-fast on the water. I have been in bass boats that can reach speeds as fast as 70 mph. They come in sizes ranging from sixteen to twenty-two feet. They do have a few drawbacks, however, the most significant being that they have no place to safely store a nine-foot fully rigged fly rod. Such rods have to be broken down and stored inside a hatch. Bass boats also do not ride as smoothly as center consoles do in rough water. However, for lake fishing, they are good choices, as they have a ton of compartments for storage of tackle. The biggest advantage to a bass boat is that, due to their lightness in weight, they can chase surface-feeding fish with the electric trolling motor down better than any other boat. Their aerodynamic design allows these boats to glide through the water with ease. Walk-through boats are set up similarly to bass boats, but their big advantage is that they have that big windshield from the captain's helm across to the passenger seat. You get protection while running from spot to spot but still get the open bow and back cockpit areas to fish from.

Pontoon and deck-type boats have their place on striper lakes as well. They are perfect rigs for the family man who wants to truly have a dual-purpose boat, one that allows him to chase stripers as well as have a pleasure craft for the family. Nowadays, both pontoon and deck-boat manufacturers are making models that have fishing packages designed into them. That means having an open deck up front to allow for an electric trolling motor as well as ample room for an angler to cast from. While the old-style pontoon boat is still being made with two aluminum pontoons, boat manufacturers are now making tri-toons that have three pontoons in the water. This allows the owner to attach a larger and faster outboard motor to the back end of the rig. Tri-toons can obtain speeds of upwards of 50 mph. While not ideal fishing platforms, pontoons and deck boats are still reasonable choices if the family has some say in what boat to own.

On the lake scene, we have been seeing more flats boats lately. They are the perfect option for freshwater striped bass anglers, as they are designed for fly-fishermen. Their open platform and clean decks make them ideal fishing boats for lakes. Here in the South, the reason we are seeing so many flats boats is that many of their owners can drive to the coast and get a fix on fishing for redfish, tarpon, and trout. However, in recent years they have learned that there is a freshwater species of fish close to home that can give them a saltwater fix without having to drive many miles to fish. There are two downsides to owning a flats boat for freshwater stripers, however, and one is a biggie. No matter how you cut it, flats boats tend to be wet in their ride. When the lake is fairly calm, this is never an issue. If the weather and wind blow up, then riding five miles to get back to the ramp in

Micro skiffs like this sixteen-footer from Towee Boats are very popular choices for fishing striped bass on lakes and rivers throughout the country. *Photo Credit: Josh England.*

a flats boat can be a wet and wild ride. The bigger concern on fishing a flats boat is that in the dead of winter, when the fish are feeding and the weather is cold and gnarly, flats boats offer little to no protection for anglers taking a ride to the fishing grounds. If you fish out of a flats boat for winter stripers, you'd better dress like you were going snowmobiling!

Jonboats and smaller boats under seventeen feet, which I call micro-skiffs, are a great way for anglers to get into the freshwater striper game at a reasonable cost. Micro-skiffs allow anglers to put on small engines—say from 6 to 20 hp. These boats allow anglers to chase fish and have enough room so you can mount an electric trolling motor, but do not have the range that boats with larger engines do. I can tell you that there is no way to have more fun than to hook into a fat double-digit-sized freshwater striper and fight it on a fly rod while getting pulled around in a micro-skiff. While I guide out of a twenty-two-foot-long Ranger bay boat with a 225-hp engine, I also occasionally take my river boat—a sixteen-foot Towee Calusa micro skiff—to fish the lake. When I do that, it makes me wonder why I want to guide out of the big center console when I'm having so much fun fishing out of the Towee. Any micro skiff will work just fine on area lakes. You just must be mindful of the weather, as not to get caught far out from your put in (ramp) and have bad weather roll in. The advantage to owning and fishing out of a micro skiff is twofold: First, they are the stealthiest of all boats you can fish out

Jonboats will work on both reservoirs and rivers that have striped bass in them. Just remember that on big reservoirs you will have to monitor the weather as well as boat traffic, as these boats cannot handle the rough water as well as bigger boats. Here, angler Keith Ohrstrom gets a little netting help from daughter Kimberly. *Photo Credit: Josh England.*

of. When approaching freshwater striped bass that are on the surface, it is important to be quiet as you get into casting range; second, micro skiffs can be a perfect river boat too. You rarely could fish any of the other previously listed watercraft on a striped bass river. Most rivers are either too shallow or too rock-strewn to use anything but a boat meant to handle such conditions.

Canoes and kayaks are the last type of watercraft that anglers might consider using to fish a reservoir. While these small unpowered watercraft are easily the stealthiest of all boats, they are also limited in that you cannot fish a lot of new water with them. You will just have to pick an area and concentrate on it, while all the other previously mentioned power boats give you the option of picking up and leaving to explore other waters in your lake. I see more and more anglers fly fishing for striped bass out of kayaks in both salt and fresh water. They are affordable, easy to store, and get the angler farther offshore than, say, a pair of waders.

Finally, I am going to mention one more watercraft that I have started seeing fishing for striped bass over the past few years. I am not a fan of this type of watercraft, as there is no way to approach the fish with stealth as they simply cannot accommodate an electric trolling motor. I am talking about the scourge of all

Kayaks are a good choice of watercraft when fishing a river, as shown by Georgia angler Todd Arnold. They will fish on a reservoir as well, but you need to be cautious due to the boat traffic. *Photo Credit: Todd Arnold.*

fishing boats, the jet ski. Most folks you see on jet skis are oblivious to fishermen and often get too close to our personal fishing space. This is due mostly to ignorance and not understanding what we require in order to catch fish rather than just being plain old rude. I am even starting to see jet ski advertisements showing jet skis being sold with a fishing package. This would clearly be my last choice in choosing a boat to fish a lake.

When looking for a watercraft to fish a river, we are usually looking at a completely different set of circumstances. Many rivers have obstructions that will cause damage to the lower units of most boats. So, it is important to make sure your watercraft can safely and properly fish the river you are thinking of trying. Let me start by saying having a jet motor is clearly the best way to fish most rivers. Nearly all the outboard motor manufacturers now sell engines that can be purchased with a jet foot rather than a prop. While not all rivers require the use of a jet foot, many across the country do. If you plan to fish a river that may require going through some rocky areas and you have a prop engine, you may want to investigate affixing a prop saver or prop guard onto the lower unit of your outboard. These can be installed and taken off in a matter of minutes.

If you are in the market for a river boat for freshwater stripers, you have a number of options, including aluminum jonboats, drift boats, or even micro skiffs . Anglers not under power might even consider using a raft to fish a striped bass river. All you'll need to remember is to get a shuttle system going so you can get back to your car at the end of the day. Finally, anglers can also use canoes and kayaks to target striped bass in rivers. I see many fly-fishing anglers every year fishing out of these types of boats on my local river (Chattahoochee River) and having a lot of success. For those anglers who cannot afford a watercraft or have no place to store one, there are two other options to fish to river stripers. The first is to use a float tube (as with rafts, you'll need some sort of shuttle arrangement). A fellow angler and I would park one vehicle at the takeout, take the shuttle up to the put in, and then float the river, stopping and fishing at certain shoals and deep holes by standing on a rock and tossing flies to the fish. We have had some success doing this and it has allowed us to fish a larger stretch of the river. If you cannot get your hands on a float tube, then there is always the wading option. Again, it is not the optimal way to do it, but it can be effective.

This seventeen-foot G3 aluminum side console was the winning boat in the 2018 Southern Striped Bass Open, which is a fly-fishing-only tournament. Jimmy Harris and the gang from Unicoi Outfitters took first place in this aptly named boat, *Blind Squirrel*. *Photo Credit: Josh England.*

RIVER BOATS AND SETTING THEM UP PROPERLY

When fly fishing for striped bass in a river, it is important to make sure your boat is properly equipped to meet the challenges a river may offer. While some rivers are made up of sandy bottoms, others are full of rocks and shoals. While both types of bottoms will hold their share of freshwater stripers, anglers need to take note that the boat they are using can handle certain river makeups. A rocky river can wreak havoc on a boat that is shallow drafting but has a propped engine, while a sandy river allows anglers to consider using a shallow draft boat with a propped engine. It is important to learn about a river before heading out to fish it. The river systems in Georgia that I fish have both sandy and rocky bottoms. There are some sections that I can fish with my Towee micro skiff with its propped engine, but there are also sections of the Chattahoochee River that are full of shoals and rocks that would kill my propped engine. When fishing such rivers, a prop guard or prop saver is a must. For rivers that are full of shoals, it is advised to fish a boat that has a jet prop versus a propellered engine. A jet prop allows you run through the some very skinny water as well as the rockiest of rivers without damaging your engine. The key to running a jet prop in a rocky river is to not slow down when you get super shallow. A jet prop, when on plane, will

Most river boats are equipped with jet props so they can scoot over shallow obstructions in a river. The key to setting up a jet prop is to keep the weight out of the stern of the boat for a shallower draft. *Photo Credit: Josh England.*

run shallower than running at slower speeds. This is not something that anglers will feel comfortable doing the first few times. However, over time you will find it easier to run on plane through some very hairy looking water. Learning where to run the boat comes with experience. In other words, while you always want to run your boat through the rivers channel, there are times where the channel becomes shallow or has shoals, and you have to pick your spots as you run through these structure-strewn areas. Once you run these spots a few times, you'll find it gets easier. Just remember that a bottom can change from year to year based on the amount of flow it receives due to storms or water releases from dams above. The key to managing a shoal in a jet boat is to slow down as you approach the shoal and look at where you think you can run through it. Also remember it is much easier running your boat upriver and reading the water than it is running downriver and reading the water, as it is easier to identify the seams that will allow you to pick your running lanes.

Once you have mastered running your boat in a river, you will be known as a true river rat, and figuring out where to fish for striped bass will be your next challenge. When fishing a river, many folks prefer to fish their boat in reverse or backwards (bow facing upriver). The reason for this is that it is easier to control the boat and maneuver in nearly any direction when the bow is facing upriver. One more thing to know about jet props and running a river—lighter is better when choosing a boat. A boat that is lighter will run higher and shallower. Weight is a detriment to most jet-boat anglers. It is important to try to keep the weight out of the stern of the boat, as that will let you jump the boat up onto plane quickly when in shallow water. When rigging a jet boat, it is always best to be a minimalist.

When setting up a boat to fish in rivers, there are a few must-haves in order to be successful when targeting freshwater striped bass. For example, it is important to make sure you have an anchor on board. Anchors will allow you to stop the boat and thoroughly fish a section of the river without having the current take you away. Plus, anchors can be important for safety reasons. If your engine happens to conk out and you are nearing a shoal, an anchor can stop you from drifting away until you can figure out what is wrong with the engine. The type of anchor one uses in a river is different from the type one would use in a reservoir. Anchors used in rivers can be of three kinds: it can be a block of lead shaped like half a diamond (which we see in most driftboats), it can be mushroom-style, or it can have three or four prongs. When fishing a rocky river, the chances of an anchor getting caught on the bottom and not coming free can happen more frequently than we would like. Therefore, your more typical grapnel- or Danforth-type anchors are not used when running your boat in a river.

This sixteen-foot Hog Island Skiff is a roto-molded plastic boat that has become very popular with striped bass anglers fishing rivers. *Photo Credit: Ryan Kennedy.*

Another piece of equipment worth having when fishing rivers is a drag chain. A drag chain is exactly what it sounds like. It is made up of a fifty- to seventy-five-foot-long rope along with a bunch or chains that are shackled together to form enough weight so that it will help slow your drift when lowered over the side. Current and flow will affect the way your fly moves through the water as well as how it tracks through certain areas. A drag chain will allow you to better position yourself in order to fish the water more thoroughly and slowly.

Anglers should also have either a set of oars for rowing through and fishing certain areas, or an electric trolling motor. You will need one or the other. While both will work just fine, many guides prefer rowing in a striper river, as it is stealthier and allows for the best boat positioning. However, if you are fishing out on your own, then rowing can become a disadvantage and an electric trolling motor is more desirable, at it allows you to both position the boat and fish at the same time.

Another neat gadget anglers can put on their river boat is a power pole or a Talon. Attached to the transom, a power pole allows you to temporarily affix your boat to a sandy bottom and hold the boat in place so you can fish an area without moving. It is like anchoring without having to manually lower and raise the anchor. A simple push of a switch and the power pole can be lowered down and stop a boat's movement in water that's between eight and twelve feet deep, depending on which model you buy.

Most river striper guides here in the South prefer to set up their boats so they can row their clients, the idea being that they can be stealthy and keep their boat in a better position when targeting stripers in shallow water. *Photo Credit: David Cannon.*

EQUIPMENT NEEDED ON A BOAT

No matter what kind of watercraft you are fishing out of, there are certain must-have items that you need to be successful. Some of these items include: electric trolling motor, fish finder, mapping technology (GPS), stripping bucket, binoculars, and sunglasses. Some of these items have been discussed earlier, but we need to discuss them more thoroughly.

The single-most important accessory you need to have on your boat is an electric trolling motor. It is important for both rivers and lakes. Freshwater striped bass can be very spooky at times, especially when feeding on the surface or in shallow water. The only stealthy way an angler can successfully get within casting range is to employ an electric trolling motor. These motors can be mounted in one of three places on your boat: the bow, the stern, or on the lower unit of your outboard. Most anglers opt for the bow-mount trolling motor, as having a motor on the bow allows your boat to be most responsive when you're moving around. This is especially true when you are chasing surface-feeding fish which can appear and disappear in a matter of seconds. One minute the fish are feeding on the surface in front of you and the next minute they have gone down. Then, a few minutes later, they reappear off your three o'clock and begin to feed on the surface again. Having a bow-mounted electric trolling motor allows you to constantly adjust your position so you can best set yourself up for a shot at these surface-feeding fish. If you are going to invest in an electric trolling motor, buy the most powerful engine within your budget. Today, companies that manufacture electric trolling motors have 12-volt systems (one battery), 24-volt systems (two batteries), and 36-volt systems (three batteries). When deciding which system is best for your setup, keep in mind that more batteries mean more weight in your boat. How powerful a trolling motor is will be based on a number defined in "thrusts." There are thrusts starting at 36 (least powerful) and range up to 112 (most powerful). The number of thrusts will determine how many batteries you will need to power your trolling motor (one, two, or three). The number of batteries you employ will also determine the length of time you have to use your trolling motor. More batteries equal more available trolling motor time. Trolling motors can range in price from a couple of hundred dollars to upwards of nearly three thousand dollars. Motors are getting really high tech these days, with lots of features that can aid in your fish catching as well as make your day on the water simpler. Probably the single-most important new feature you can get on a trolling motor is "spot lock." Spot lock allows your trolling motor to pick up your GPS coordinate and keep you anchored to that spot once you enable that feature. On days when you are fishing to a piece

of underwater structure and the wind picks up, spot lock can make the difference between fishing and catching. There are a host of other significant high
tech features that trolling motors offer, and I encourage you to do your homework to decide what you positively need to have versus pie-in-the-sky features
that are nice but not particularly necessary. The two most prominent companies
manufacturing electric trolling motors are Minnkota and Motor Guide. Both
have been doing so for many years and both manufacturers are excellent. I have
owned both over the last twenty-plus years, but personally am a big Minnkota
fan and have been running their engines for most of those years. One reason
I have chosen Minnkota is that their parent company is Johnson Outdoors,
which also owns Humminbird fish finders. Now, through Bluetooth, you can
link your fish finder up to your trolling motor and have them working in sync
together. The last bit of information we need to touch on with electric trolling
motors is the way we operate them. They can be operated via a hand control,
foot pedal control, or wireless remote control. Many guides prefer the wireless
remote, as it keeps their hands free so they can help their customers and still
run the motor. While a great feature, I must admit that a wireless remote is the
least responsive of all options. A hand control is the most responsive, with the
wired foot pedal next. I have worked them all and must admit that a foot pedal
is all I ever use. A foot pedal, while it takes a little getting used to, allows anglers

A properly equipped striper boat has an electric trolling motor, electronics, and a landing
net to help bring fish to hand. *Photo Credit: Josh England.*

to continually fish by not taking their hands off their fly rod. This positively leads to more productive shots at surface-feeding fish. Using a hand or wireless control means you are constantly taking your hand off your fly rod to adjust and position yourself.

The next must-have item for lake fishing is a fishfinder. Many companies make good fishfinders today, including Humminbird, Lowrance, Furino, Simrad, and Garmin, among others. For anglers fishing out of smaller boats, it makes the most sense to get a combo unit. A combo unit employs both a fishfinder and a GPS (mapping system) in one unit. These combo units can be purchased in a variety of sizes. They vary by screen size. They can be as small as a five-inch screen or as large as a twelve-inch screen (as of this writing). If you buy a combo unit with a larger screen, you can split the screen so that part can be showing sonar (finding fish) and part can be showing GPS (in order to put you on a specific spot). Let me be open and tell you that I am a big Humminbird fan. (Full disclosure: Yes, I am on their ambassador program!) However, I chose Humminbird for one reason only: their Lakemaster charting. Humminbird Lakemaster charts are proprietary to Humminbird only. They make charts to cover lakes throughout the United States. The detail on these charts are second to none, in my opinion. They also have a feature called "contour highlighting," which allows users to dial in every hump on the lake they are fishing. This is a gamechanger as far as I am concerned. Anglers who are river fishing can make their own chart that tells them how to run the river they are fishing by marking the path both up and downriver with a Humminbird unit. A sonar fishfinder is not necessary on most rivers where stripers are being caught. It has its place every now and then, but on a lake it's a must have.

A stripping bucket or basket is another important piece of equipment worth having in the boat. You want to be able to manage your line without it being blown all over the boat or having to reel in every time you move from one spot to another. A stripping basket allows you to have your outfit ready to cast, and at times you may find that you barely have enough time to make a quick cast at surface-feeding fish. Remember, when fishing to surface feeds, anglers need to fish with a sense of urgency. If you cannot afford to buy or are not handy enough to make your own stripping bucket, you can always opt for a stripping basket that you wear around your waist. Saltwater anglers have been wearing these for years. They allow fishermen to avoid dealing with their fly line tangling on something inside the boat (like a cleat, the trolling motor, or their foot). Whether fishing a lake or a river, employing a stripping bucket or stripping basket will at some point mean fewer lost fish or more hookups.

Another good piece of equipment to keep in your boat is a stripping bucket. This is the best way to manage your fly line, as shown by Georgia anglers Keith and Erik Ohrstrom. *Photo Credit: Josh England.*

Binoculars are another must-have item, especially when fishing a lake. Striper lakes are often large, and it is simply too hard to see fish busting the surface or birds diving from great distances. Having a good set of binoculars has put me on fish more times than I care to remember. For fishing, it is best to get a pair of binoculars that has a magnification of 42 or 50. This will allow you to see far off in the distance. They are primarily used for three things: sighting surface-feeding fish, sighting diving birds, or locating other boats which might be on the fish.

The final piece of equipment I would not be caught without is a pair of sunglasses. Sunglasses allow you to see what is going on around you on the lake or river and take the glare out of your viewing. That could be the difference when seeing a heron on the bank or fish busting the surface. From a safety standpoint, it also protects you from flies being tossed through the boat by other anglers who are totally focussed on the fish and not paying attention to where they are casting. I unfortunately have witnessed this firsthand too many times. If flies are being waved through a boat, then a pair of sunglasses should always be worn. All it takes is one incident and you will be a believer in wearing sunglasses.

Managing your fly line with the use of a stripping bucket is especially handy on those days when it all comes together and a short-lived top-water feed happens. *Credit: Josh England.*

WADE FISHING AND EQUIPMENT NEEDED

Whether striper fishing a river or an impoundment, there are certain things an angler should remember to carry with him or her. Wading is a totally different game and easily more challenging than fishing out of a boat. There is an old saying that I still believe is true, one that says catching one fish while wading is worth five out of the boat. If you like a challenge and want the satisfaction that you have truly accomplished something in the fly-fishing world, then go catch a freshwater striped bass or hybrid while wearing waders (or wet wade). Most folks who fly fish with their feet planted on hard ground know they are in for a challenge. However, there are a few things that anglers should consider having with them if they plan on trying to catch a striped demon from the shore or the banks of a river.

One of the most important items a shore-bound angler should have is a stripping basket. Stripping baskets are worn around the waist and allow you to wade and manage your fly line. Anglers have been employing stripping baskets while wading for over thirty years. You can make one yourself or purchase one from your local fly shop. If they do not sell them, then look online and I am sure there are a number from which you can choose. I have used the Orvis durable stripping basket for years and it has held up well. I have gotten so used to wading for fish

Row vs wade? That is always the question when striper fishing a river. Here photographer David Cannon hooks into one of Unicoi Outfitters' pets while wading on their private water in Helen, Georgia. *Photo Credit: Jeff Durniak.*

Having a landing net available when wading makes landing these big fish easier. It's even easier when you have a guide at your disposal. *Photo Credit: Jeff Durniak.*

When wade fishing a river, it is always a good idea to have a stripping basket with you. It will help you manage your fly line, and when you finally hook a fish, you can simply spin it to your backside once your line is back on the reel while fighting your striped bass. Note this angler's pack across his back. A small pack can allow for extra tippet, leader, flies, and pliers. *Photo Credit: Henry Cowen.*

with a stripping basket that I now take one with me nearly everywhere I fish. I'll take it when wading a beach in Florida for snook or even when I am hosting a weeklong trip to the tropics for bonefish. The last thing you want is to have a fish lost due to line around feet, getting tangled in some brush or vegetation, or just wrapping around your legs. Having a stripping basket also allows you to make quick unobstructed casts without worrying where your line is. It is easily the most important piece of equipment a wading angler should have with them.

Another piece of equipment any wading angler should have with them is sunglasses. Sunglasses not only protect your eyes when fly casting, but can be extremely helpful in allowing you to see through the water. Sunglasses help reduce glare and the likelihood of stepping into a hole or on an unseen rock or limb.

Waders are yet another piece of equipment an angler should consider. Some folks prefer wet wading, and if that is the case, then make sure you are at least wearing a pair of wading boots. Wading boots can help you walk through a river with more confidence and ease due to their rugged grip soles. If you want to avoid

Todd Arnold with a three-year-old striper caught while wading in an undisclosed Georgia river. Just as in salt water, one fish caught from the shore is worth the same as five from the boat. *Photo Credit: Todd Arnold.*

the discomfort of having sand go down your shoes, a good set of wading boots along with a set of gravel guards should be employed. Most striper rivers will have fairly cold water, so unless you are fishing the dead of summer, wearing a light pair of waders as opposed to wet wading is probably a good idea.

Wearing a vest has become passé these days. Most anglers wading afoot are carrying either a waist pack, chest pack, or sling pack to hold all their flies and accessories needed for an outing. Make sure you have extra leaders, tippet, pliers, and the like before you venture to your favorite fishing hole.

I love catching fish while wading. I cut my teeth on striped bass back up in New York City and Connecticut while wearing waders. Anytime I get an opportunity to catch striped bass and not be in a boat, I take full advantage of the opportunity.

STRIPED BASS
CATCH & RELEASE

SUGGESTIONS TO HELP BOOST SURVIVAL RATES

DO

DO cradle the fish, with one hand under the belly and one under its shoulder.

DO resuscitate the bass by pulling it through the the the water by the lower lip. Stripers have no teeth. Never move it backwards. Only forward or figure eight.

DO get the fish back quickly! Try to Limit air exposure to 15 seconds.

DO use barbless hooks for quick release.

DO use circle hooks when baitfishing.

DO release the fish without taking it out of the water if possible.

DO leave deep hooks inside fish. Cut leader off close... it is better than digging.

DON'T

DON'T lift fish by the mouth. This can cause serious internal injury.

DON'T release without first resuscitating.

DON'T kick a fish. You will damage internal organs.

DON'T drop the fish. Dropping causes serious injury.

DON'T touch the red gill rakers. They are the equivalent of human lungs.

DON'T gaff a fish you want to release.

DON'T lift fish by the tail.

DON'T drag the fish across dry sand.

HANDLE ALL FISH WITH CARE & RESPECT

Proper holding technique   Striped Bass   Resuscitate before releasing

IMAGES: BOB POPOVICS & TOM LYNCH

supported by:

This catch and release poster shows anglers the proper care and handling of striped bass. It is every angler's responsibility to help protect the resource. *Photo Credit: Bob Popovics and Tom Lynch.*

About the Author

Author Henry Cowen and his four- legged babies Starlet (black) and Sweet Pea (caramel). *Photo Credit: Tina Cowen.*

Henry Cowen grew up in Brooklyn, New York, where he learned to fish for striped bass at an early age. He is an Umpqua Feather Merchants fly designer as well as a writer for many nationally renowned fly-fishing magazines, including *American Angler, Fly Tyer, Fly Fishing in Salt Waters, Saltwater Fly Fishing* and *Angler* magazines. He started guiding for freshwater stripers around 2000 and has been at it ever since. Henry and his wife, Tina, reside in Atlanta, Georgia, with their two dogs, Starlet and Sweet Pea.

About the Photographer

I met Josh England nearly fifteen years ago when a young, energetic angler asked me if I could take him on a guided trip to catch his first striped bass on a fly rod. Since that day, no one would have ever guessed that this division one college football linebacker turned primo freshwater striped bass angler would develop into one of the industry's great outdoor photographers specializing in a fly-fishing lifestyle.

Josh's pictures have been featured in publications such as *The Fly Fish Journal*, *American Angler*, *Eastern Fly Fishing*, *The Dun Magazine*, *Angler's Journal*, *Fly Tyer*, and *The Drake*. His photos capture the moment in a very artistic and creative way. While many of his photos are of fishing in salt water,

Photographer Josh England. *Photo Credit: Josh England.*

warm water, and cold water, Josh has shown an affinity for freshwater striped bass.

Photography was a hobby for him that started back when he was in high school. While a fisherman his entire life, Josh took up fly fishing around 2000 and landed his first fly-caught striper with me back in 2005. For a fulltime paying gig, Josh runs a division of a company called Signature Floors & Design located in Cumming, Georgia. He and his wife, Courtney, have two children: his son and fishing partner Tyson and his daughter Leighton. You can view more of Josh England's works at www.joshenglandphotos.com.